The Author and six of nine siblings. School picture 1955

Tara's Halls

Tara's Halls

Growing Up in Hard Times in
Ireland: An Inspiring Memoir

Tom Gallagher

ISBN 13: 9781516910779
ISBN 10: 151691077X
Library of Congress Control Number: 2015913407
CreateSpace Independent Publishing Platform
North Charleston, South Carolina

This book is dedicated to my brothers, Jimmy and Eamon, and my sisters, Maureen, Patricia, Kathleen, Eveline, Anne, and Christina.
And in memoriam, to dear Angela, who left us in 1980.

Oft in the stilly night,
Ere slumber's chain has bound me,
Fond memories brings the light
Of other days around me,
The smiles, the tears,
Of boyhood's years,
The words of love then spoken;
The eyes that shone,
Now dimm'd and gone,
The cheerful hearts now broken!
Thus, in the stilly night,
Ere slumber's chain hath bound me,
Sad memory brings the light
Of other days around me.

Thomas Moore
Irish poet, 1779–1852

And to my old friend, back when the earth was young, Tony Moran, of Lisloughna, Charlestown, Co. Mayo, RIP.

Acknowledgments

MY FOUR CHILDREN, Michael, Elizabeth, Tara, and Erin, grew up as I did, mostly without their father. This is my greatest regret. I am grateful that the bonds of love and affection between us were never broken, despite the time and distances that separated us. Some distances remain but only in geography, and so do the bonds of love and friendship and blood, unbreakable as ever. For this I am blessed.

I am also the proud grandfather of Tristan, Fionnuala, Erris, Caoimhe, Oonagh, and Teagan.

I love you all and pray for your happiness, for this is the ultimate measure of success in life. May each of you find happiness, may happiness find you, and may you stay wedded always.

And Jun, my wife, my love, my best friend. For being there. For sharing with me the joys and trials of life. I thank you from my heart.

And my editor, Sue Ralston, for your encouragement and thoughtful commentary and, finally, the outstanding team at CreateSpace publishing and AME marketing. Thank you all for a job well done.

CHAPTER 1

❧

And the men who once came home with the Winter spawning salmon...from the factories and the steel mills and the coal mines and the building sites of England...to fertilize their lands and their women...now come no more.

WITH SENTIMENTS TO this effect, the author and journalist John Healy, from County Mayo, my home county, once described the harsh, seemingly unending cycle of life for the rural poor in the West of Ireland. Farms too small or land too poor to support families often meant that fathers worked in England for much or most of the year, sending home the weekly remittance to help make ends meet. Thus it was in my family.

I was born the third son and sixth child on a small farm in a small village in the hard winter of 1947. To find the village of Madogue, you would take the byroad near the "Half-Way Bush" from the main Dublin-Ballina road. No signs would greet you or show you the way, but a few hundred yards off the Main Road, you would be in the village, a village of hills and hollows, of small farms and modest to humble farmhouses scattered over a brown-green landscape. The Half-Way Bush was, in fact, an old blackthorn tree planted ages ago, we were told, to mark the halfway point between the towns of Swinford and Charlestown.

Eventually, there would be ten of us in our family, three boys and seven girls. A century earlier, in the grip of the Great Hunger, Ireland endured "Black '47," probably the single most devastating year in Irish history. In contrast, 1947 might have been described as "White '47," for God blessed my arrival with more snow than had ever been seen in Ireland before or since. This same weather pattern dumped mountains of snow all across North America and Europe. Blizzard conditions throughout Ireland brought everything to a standstill. Even the local Jubilee nurse, the heroic Nurse Brown, who doubled as a midwife and who would happily walk across the blistering Sahara in bare feet to birth another soul, could not make it to our little house to see that I was accorded a reasonably dignified entree into the world of subsistence farming. We managed without her—but with the welcome help of a neighbor, Ellie Kate McIntyre, a few fields away. To be fair, it must be said that I don't remember any of this, but so I'm told.

Our house—originally thatched, but now with a new galvanized roof—in Madogue (or MullenMadogue as it was called in ancient times) was a fairly modest dwelling, with a full-sized bedroom at one end, a large kitchen in the middle, and a small bedroom at the other end, and sans anything but a door and a small window near the ceiling. Most of us were born early in the year, spaced out at a nice, leisurely one per annum or thereabouts. Where there was a miss, there was as likely a miscarriage, and once a stillbirth that almost took my mother's life. Most of us were conceived in the spring when my father would come home from England for a few short weeks to do the spring's work, putting down the tillage, cutting the year's supply of turf, and making the next baby. This method of family planning worked well for many families around us, in their small houses on other small farms. When we started school, we had classmates who were not only our own age, but often were only a few days or weeks older or younger than ourselves, and even sometimes shared the same birthday. Often, families matched boy for boy and girl for girl, so no matter where in the family you were, you had your counterpart in another family—or several families—a few fields away or in the next village. It was almost as though God ordained it this way, so that no one would be alone, or be the odd one out.

Indeed, if someone had a birthday in June or July or August, there had better be a good accounting for it. There was only one Immaculate Conception, and that was the Blessed Virgin Mary, thank you, who gave the world the Baby Jesus, who came into the world to save mankind from eternal damnation—or at least to save Christians, or maybe just Catholics. Or perhaps a well-to-do father who made his money in America and was able to come home, and who didn't have to go to England to earn the few extra pounds. Or maybe a farmer with a few more acres of arable land or a few less mouths to feed, who was able to stay home year round, or maybe a cute fellow with "pull" who was able to secure his weekly dole every Thursday regardless of the size of his farm or the number of cows and pigs he had. And truly blessed was he who had done his bit in the War of Independence and whose reward from a grateful and mostly dominant Fianna Fail government was a nice IRA pension to ease the pain of having been "on the run" from British forces during "the Troubles." Fianna Fail took care of its own with jobs and pensions, and few of these veterans boarded the emigrant ship to America or crossed the pond to the eternal enemy, John Bull.

There were, of course, other reasons why men went to England—and why some never returned: escape from debilitating poverty; escape from the responsibility of wife and children for whom they could not or did not want to care; escape to freedom from the norms of a narrow, conformist, and parochial social order and all-intrusive Catholicism; freedom to find a new and better life; and the opportunity for anonymity or oblivion without shame. Some carried a confused and unspeakable love-hate feeling for home and country, often never to be reconciled. They might not speak well of Mother Eireann, but they would not tolerate any foreigner speaking ill of her. You could see the chip on the shoulder a mile off, just waiting to be knocked off—but try if you dare. They found solace with kindred spirits who were equally alienated from the Old Country, or they found it with the ever-forgiving and beloved Arthur Guinness and John Jameson, or they found it through forced amnesia of all that was before, or they didn't find it.

While Healy lamented in his minor classic, *The Death of an Irish Town*, that these generations of men who returned each year to do their fertilizing now "come no more," my father, Eddie Gallagher—or Ned Grantum as he was known to many—did come home faithfully each year of my childhood. He cut the year's supply of turf, plowed the fields and sowed the spuds and oats, put out the top-dress on promising meadows—and did his other duties, for which I'm not ungrateful. But grateful or not, even by Irish standards our family was large, and sometimes I would wish that it could have been a more manageable four or five. Two or three would have been selfish, suggesting interference with the laws of God and nature and, therefore, probably a mortal sin. Five seemed just about right—three boys and two girls or three girls and two boys. Either way would have been entirely acceptable to me. Obviously, I had to be one of the five. Otherwise what was the point?

While we were a large family, I was comforted by the fact that there were families even bigger, eleven or twelve. Sometimes these numbers broke the camel's back when bare subsistence crossed the line into malnutrition and hunger. Then it was the unhappy responsibility of the local welfare man to remedy the situation. Our welfare man was a local, big farmer but by all accounts a good and decent man who acted only when it was absolutely necessary. The remedy was usually a sudden, unannounced visit to the home by county welfare officials, accompanied by a couple of gardie to make it official and not unduly alarm neighbors who may think that a mass kidnapping was underway. Children, as many as could be found, would be rounded up and taken to the County Home. Here they would be fed and clothed and schooled by the state at a level not much above subsistence, and where they might stay for months or years until economic circumstances at home improved.

Sometimes the nuns would lend a helping hand, taking hungry and ragged children in as charity cases, housing them in their convents, and caring for their bodies, minds, and souls—especially their souls. They might be let back out one or two at a time, and suddenly we would see them in school again. We would be happy to talk with them and renew friendships, but we were fearful of asking them where they had been—and they wouldn't tell us. After a few months or a year, they were just as likely to disappear again, and we would know that they had been taken back to that unmentionable place.

I was terrified that this might happen to us because when I looked at them they were the same as us. My brothers and sisters had ill-fitting and well-worn hand-me-down clothes and leaking Wellingtons too. Like them, we looked a bit "rough." Often I would have a bad dream where I would be running in terror through the fields, being chased by dark, human-like shapes without recognizable features. I would keep falling for no reason and then wake up at the moment of capture, soaked in sweat. Sometimes my dream would not let me escape, and I would be pulled in helpless terror from my hiding place in the bog by these dark, faceless creatures and dragged up the *boreen* to a black van on the Main Road. I would be trying to scream, but no sound would come out. Inside the van I would see other children, sitting on benches, crying. The dreams rarely changed and, always, the black van was there through the mist.

My mother was the youngest of eleven, but her people, the Morans on her father's side and the McHughs on her mother's side, were an industrious, hard-working lot. My maternal grandfather, Pat Moran, although a "blow-in" from up the country, possessed the highly prized twin blessings that defined the best of Irish manhood: he was a horse of a worker and he was easy on the drink. My father was one of only two children, at first blush cause for a raised eyebrow at least. The reason, though, was that his mother, Maggie Conway of Cully, County Sligo, was thirty-three years old on her wedding day, practically an old maid in those times, and well past her prime child-bearing years. "Sure, washn't she a lucky woman to have any childher at all," said a neighbor, "an' then to have two fine sons at that." Maggie Gallagher, née Conway, might not have entirely agreed with her good fortune.

Moving from a comfortable home and farm on good flat land in Cully to nine hilly and swampy acres in Madogue was a sobering experience. If the hills could have been bulldozed into the hollows, there might have been something to work with. These few acres, closing at one end in a *V* near the Madogue River, were squeezed between two much larger

5

farms: the Peytons' on one side and the McIntyres' on the other. Our little farm marked part of the boundary between the villages of Corthoon and Madogue—for the McIntyres were a prominent Corthoon family and the Peytons were a prominent Madogue family. From the bottom of the *V* to the river, the McIntyres and Peytons shared a common fence, bringing Corthoon and Madogue together in a wet and swampy union. At the other end, save for a boreen out to Madogue Road, they also shared a common fence, putting the Gallagher place in a rather peculiar position, kind of like a little principality surrounded by kingdoms, with a narrow opening to the sea. From time to time through the years, both kingdoms would express interest in acquiring our little principality, and we would express interest in selling it, but it never happened. The task of bulldozing hills into hollows was a daunting one.

The farm in Madogue did have an outstanding feature that caused my imagination to run wild with anticipation. There was an ancient ring fort on the land. You could tell by looking at it that it wasn't a natural feature, that it was made by man long, long ago. Our fort was a round mound of earth about eight feet high and thirty yards in diameter. Dad had told us that from the top of any fort in Ireland you could see eight others—they were built in clusters of nine in an area of a few square miles. I loved the challenge of spotting the other eight and usually could. In school we were told that these forts dated back more than two thousand years, before the Celts came to Ireland. They were used by these early Irish people as places of refuge in times of attack by invaders or unfriendly neighbors, or maybe some marauding tribe of cattle thieves. Before our ancestors discovered the magic of the drink, their favorite pastime was stealing each other's cattle. The forts were hollow inside, and people and animals could hide until the danger passed or until some wild-eyed, hairy ancestors accidentally tasted some fermented apples and swore off cattle-stealing forevermore.

As a child I was convinced that somewhere deep down in the insides of our fort there was treasure galore—chests full of gold and silver—and that all we had to do was find the secret passageway. I wanted to be the one to find the opening and the treasure that I knew was hidden inside. I would be the hero bringing out gold and silver goblets, and chains and bracelets made of pure gold. Maybe even Malachy's collar of gold was in there.

Let Erin remember the days of old
When Malachy wore the collar of gold.

With all of this priceless wealth, we wouldn't be poor anymore, all thanks to me. We could have anything we wanted. We would be addressed respectfully, by our proper name, pronounced properly—no nicknames. We would be famous, we'd be in all the newspapers, and people would look at us with great envy. Of course, I knew that they wouldn't really be happy for us. They'd want us to share our wealth—and we would too, but selectively. I already knew who would benefit from our generosity and who wouldn't. My challenge was to find the opening. Dad had said that he and his brother, Uncle Tom, had found the opening when they were young lads but that the place was so vast and dark inside, with caves and tunnels everywhere, that they gotten lost and barely made it out. They went back in again, this time with a lantern and unwinding a spool of twine as they went. The twine was tied to a bush on the outside. Dad said that they walked until the twine ran out…and then they heard the banshee wail and their hearts stopped. They knew that the banshee wail warned of death. Dad said that it was probably guarding the treasure, and he and Uncle Tom could go no further, and anyway they had no more twine.

They told their father of their adventure, and he went completely white with fright. He told them that they were two very lucky boys and that if they had challenged the banshee, that would have been the end of them. The next day their father closed up the entrance and made them swear on their bended knees that they would never, ever do such a foolish and dangerous thing again. So there was no point in asking Dad to show me where the secret entrance was. I would just have to find it; deal with the banshee, probably by facing her down with a crucifix (if it worked on Dracula, it should work on an old, toothless banshee); and bring out the treasure and end all our troubles.

Every chance I got I dug holes into the side of the fort. I even dug down from the top, figuring that it might be easier to go in through the roof. No matter how much or in which direction I dug, the result was always the same: more hard-packed earth and no entrance. I was frustrated but ever hopeful. I imagined what it was going to be like when I finally punched through the last few inches of soil and stared into black emptiness. I could feel the rush of cold, stale air as it made its escape. The thought of this magical moment was almost too much for me. Cold shivers ran up and down my spine, and I was covered in goose bumps. Boy! What a day that would be. I knew, of course, that I wouldn't be prepared to go in right away. I would conceal the entrance with whins and brooms and grass while I pondered the banshee.

I would have to be fully prepared. The banshee may have died. It had been ages since Dad and Uncle Tom heard her heart-stopping wail. I was heartened at this thought. I was almost sure I would have the courage to get around a skeleton. Then I thought, maybe banshees don't even leave skeletons, and there will be nothing between me and the treasure at all. Then it occurred to me that if dead banshees didn't leave skeletons, they probably don't die, so I was back to pondering what I would do about the banshee. I knew that I would pray a lot before I went in, entire rosaries by myself. I would have to be in a state of grace. This meant going to Confession on a Saturday to rid my soul of sins and then receiving Holy Communion the next morning. I would have to enter the fort on that Sunday after Mass, while I was still in a state of grace. I would have a crucifix in case I needed it.

Maybe I wouldn't need it. Maybe the banshee would listen to my sad story of misfortune and see that I was only trying to help my family. I could see it in my mind's eye. I'd have a torch in my left hand, a crucifix in my right hand, and twine tied around my middle, leading all the way out to the entrance. After the banshee stopped wailing and saw that I was still there, she'd ask me why I'd dared challenge her warning, and I would explain our terrible circumstances and why the treasure was our only hope. Understanding our awful plight, she would say: "You are a very brave lad. You have proven yourself worthy. Take all this wonderful treasure with my blessing. Now I am free from my dark and lonely vigil, free from this place where I've been for more than two thousand years. I am free; I am free."

In my boyhood I would return many times to the fort to look for the secret passageway and contemplate my encounter with the banshee. I never found it, but I did come across a few other banshees who were living above ground in broad daylight.

I did not like the nickname "Grantum" that my family had, even knowing that it was commonplace for families to be given nicknames. Nicknames served a purpose in Ireland, where there was a bewildering repetition of surnames, even in places no bigger than a fairy glen. I always thought it strange and funny that in a single village of maybe forty families with a dozen having the same last name, they'd all claim to be unrelated. You probably didn't have to look too far back to see where the bloodlines connected. Nicknames were, of course, helpful in properly identifying the family in question when people were talking about each other, Ireland's second-favorite pastime. So one family of Durkins would be the "Mericans," another the "Murtys," another the "Sinkers." Different Gallagher families would be the "Darkies," the "Seans," the "Grantums." The Mericans had sons and daughters who went to America and returned as Yanks. They would have been called the "Yanks," but another family already had that nickname, and another had title to "Yankees." Some nicknames were hard to fathom and went back so far that no one seemed to know where they came from. Others nicknames like the "Grabbers" and the "Braggers" weren't and could only be used when those families were not participants in the conversation and were nowhere in sight. Nicknames were also useful in facilitating introductions:

> "An' who might you be now—you're not from 'round here, are you?"
> "Well, I used to be. The name is Gallagher. I was born in Madogue and raised in Culmore."
> "Arrah, sure them places are fulla Gollahers. Which wan are you?"
> "My father was Ned Grantum."
> "Ah, Eddeen Grantum. I knew him well. By God! He could play the flute, he could—'an use his fists too."
> "Are you a Yank then?"

The origin of Grantum could be traced to the town of Grantham in England. In the late nineteenth and early twentieth centuries, my grandfather, Jim Gallagher, used to work in that town in the late fall and winter of each year. He was the only one in our area who used to go to that particular town—hence our family nickname, modified to fit the Irish tongue, which had some difficulty with "th." Still, we, the young Gallaghers, growing up in the 1950s and 1960s, disliked it intensely. To us it was a label, a not-so-subtle way of saying, "Now don't be putting on any airs and graces. We know who you are: you're a Grantum."

On the other hand, we were also called "Moran," my mother's maiden name. This, too, was a fairly common practice, especially when children were growing up on the mother's farm, as we were. In short, the farm was "the Moran farm," hence, we were the Morans. Likewise, while my mother was a Moran, she and her siblings, when growing up, were often called McHugh because, prior to Pat Moran marrying into the place by wedding Mariah McHugh, my maternal grandmother and Pat McHugh's only daughter, the place was known as "the McHugh farm." In time the neighbors accepted the blow-in from Castleroyan, and the farm in Culmore became the Morans. Still, to us, the Gallaghers, growing up in

Culmore, the name Moran was equally unwelcome. So I grew up with a rich, if not entirely appreciated, selection of names: Tommy Gallagher, Tommy Gollaher, Tommy Grantum, and Tommy Moran—and to the occasional dimwit who couldn't manage any of these, I was Tommy Gollar. Jaysus!

CHAPTER 2

WHEN MY FATHER came home from England in the spring, it was a big event, and I looked forward to the day of his arrival with great anticipation. I wasn't quite sure why I looked forward to it so much, for there were so many of us for him to greet and pay attention to. While he was home, it was always a race against time to get all of the necessary work done before he had to leave again, so it was very rare and very special when I was able to talk with him. Perhaps it was just the excitement of having a man in the house—my own dad.

My father worked in Birmingham in the English Midlands, on building sites and in breweries, and later in a bakery. Whatever money he made, he would send most home in cash, in a blue, reinforced, registered envelope, and keep what was left for himself, from which he would pay for his lodgings on Haughton Road, buy his weekly necessities and, hopefully, have a little left over for his beloved and unconditional friends, Arthur Guinness and John Jameson. So many, many times, in all kinds of weather, I signed that little receipt in acknowledgment of receiving the registered blue money envelope from Jim McNicholas, our postman.

For the journey home, Dad would take the train from New Street Station in Birmingham to Holyhead in Wales, where a boat would take him across the Irish Sea to Dun Laoghaire, near Dublin. Arriving in the "Ould Sod" in the early morning, he would ride a CIE bus 150 miles from East to West, down long, winding roads, through the big, rich fields of Kildare, Westmeath, and Longford, and through the smaller, poorer fields of Roscommon and into the wilds of Mayo, where the stony, boggy, piss-poor fields weren't worth a fiddler's fart. The bus would pull into Charlestown at about 6:00 p.m. and stop in the same spot it always stopped, near the center of town and exactly halfway between the two best-known and most popular pubs: The Ideal Bar, nicknamed Tom Jerry's, on the left corner by the bridge; and Jim Phillips's Imperial Hotel on the right corner by the same bridge. Dad didn't have far to walk—about twenty yards in either direction. And without fail he always walked one way or the other. He did not stay on the bus for the last three and a half miles out to the farming village of Culmore. Without a few pints to fortify him, he just couldn't do it.

My mother would always bring one of us to town with her to meet him. Usually, it was one of the older children, but I had the special honor once, and it was memorable. I was ten years old. Mom rode the bicycle into town with me sitting on the carrier behind the saddle. We waited on the sidewalk by Jim Phillips's hotel, pub, and grocery shop for the bus to arrive. When I saw it coming down Barrack Street, my heart began to pound. Mom was nervous, walking around in circles, checking her reflection in Phillips's shop window. The bus stopped and people got off. We waited and then he got off. Even though I had seen him only a year earlier, I didn't have a good memory of his face—and there were few family pictures in our house—but I knew it was him because I could see Mom tense up.

He looked like a film star: tall and elegantly dressed in a blue suit, white shirt, a colorful bow tie, shiny tan shoes, and a gray hat, slightly tilted to one side. To me, he was incredibly handsome, a combination of Errol Flynn and Jeff Chandler, whose pictures I had, along with those of Gabby Hayes and Virginia Mayo and Grace Kelly and others that I'd been collecting from toffee bars. We got our penny toffee bars at Tom Horkan's shop at the other end of our village. One kind came with a picture of a famous film star, usually American, while another kind had a picture of a car—mostly big, flashy American cars. The toffees were okay but a bit hard on my teeth. It was the pictures I really wanted. They were called transfers because you could dip them in water and then transfer the picture onto a sheet of paper. I had whole pages of them.

Now, here was Hollywood in the flesh, and he was my dad, and he might as well have come from Mars. We went toward him. He took my mother in his arms, and I could see a bruising kiss. Then, in mock confusion giving way to a big smile, he looked at me and said, "Which wan are you? You must be Tomeen. Jesus, Mary, and Joseph, you look like a tinker."

I nodded but I couldn't speak. How can you speak when you've just met a film star from Hollywood, come down from the silver screen?

We went to Tom Jerry's. Dad walked up to Tom Jerry, who was behind the bar, and they shook hands and exchanged pleasantries. Tom was a good host, and he knew Dad was a good, if irregular, customer. Dad ordered a pint of Guinness for himself and a half one for my mother. A "half one" was a shot of whiskey. I knew it's okay for Mom to have a half one because that was considered to be an acceptable indulgence for a woman. I got a glass of cidona. I was excited and happy. This was my dad, and he didn't look a bit like anyone around here. My mother and father talked about little things: the crossing over, the family at home, the neighbors, and the just-arrived fine weather. "By Christ, I hope it holds up," Dad said. My mother wasn't nervous any more. She was relaxed and smiled at him in a way that she never smiled at us. I didn't know him, but I was proud that he was my dad.

A couple of men in the bar knew Dad and welcomed him home. He asked them what they were drinking and bought them a couple of pints of Guinness. Mom knew that this was the time for her to excuse herself—she didn't belong in the company of men in a bar. She asked me to come with her to the "snug," a small enclosed room next to the bar. The snug, or "lounge" to those who considered themselves to be a better class of people, was mostly for women who could quietly gather for a little gossip, while enjoying a glass of Guinness or a half one. I took my glass of cidona off the bar and followed Mom into the snug. I'd much rather have sat on a high stool at the bar with my dad and these other men whom I'd never seen before—even if I had nothing to say, which I didn't.

After what seemed like ages, Mom went back into the bar to see if Dad was ready to come home. Through the open door, I could hear him say that he's going to have one for the road and then he'd be ready. I knew Mom was worried. The two men who had joined him were still with him, and there was a lot of laughing. I heard loud praise for my father's boxing skills and his flute playing, but when I joined Mom in the doorway, I could see that they were all a bit giddy. I knew it was the drink. Mom told Dad that it was time to go home, and he looked from her to me and said, "Jesus Christ Almighty! You too." I looked down at the floor because I couldn't look up. "All right," he said, "we need some fresh meat for a decent meal when we get home."

We left The Ideal Bar, my father a little unsteady and my mother holding him by the arm. I walked behind, wheeling the bicycle. We went over the bridge and up Church Street to Tom Tripp's butcher and grocery shop across from the church. It was really Mulligan's shop, but as there were a lot of Mulligans around, these Mulligans were known as Tripps. I didn't know why they were called Tripps, but that's what the country people called them. Dad bought steaks with blood still running out of them. While Tom Tripp was cutting and trimming the steaks, he and Dad were making small talk. They knew each other from way back and Tom knew that my father had had a couple too many, but this didn't bother him in the least. The Tripps had known hard times too, when they lived in the country, but now things were improving. The shop was doing well. They still had land out in Sonnagh on which to raise bullocks for slaughter, and Tom had become every inch the businessman. I knew he was a business-man because he was wearing a shirt and tie inside his white, blood-stained apron.

He wrapped- the steaks first in white tissue paper then in brown wrapping paper, quickly tied the package length-wise and cross-wise with white twine, broke it cleanly between well-practiced fingers, and handed it to my mother. Mom bought some groceries, a loaf of brown bread, a pound of butter, some sugar and tea, a jar of Chivers marmalade, and a tin of Batchelors peas to go with the steaks, and for breakfast, a pound of Donnelly's sausages and some rashers. My father gave her money to pay for them, and we left for the journey home.

Horkan's hackney car took us home, and my father paid Martin Horkan half a crown. I wondered why there weren't any full crowns. I figured it was because they would be so big and heavy that they'd wear a hole in your pocket in no time at all. I'd never seen a farthing either, but then I'd never seen anything for sale anywhere with a farthing rounding out the price—lots of pennies and ha'pennies but no farthings. We were dropped off on the Main Road by our boreen. Dad asked Mr. Horkan to take us down to the house but he said that the boreen was too wet and slobbery and that if he tried to go down he'd get stuck for sure. He took the bicycle out of the boot, turned the car around, and headed back to Charlestown. We made our way down the wet, slobbery boreen to the house, avoiding the worst spots. "Suffering Jesus Christ," said my father, "this is a God-forsaken place." My mother told him that he'd feel better after he's eaten. He said he'd feel better when he was back in Birmingham on dry, solid streets and no one telling him what to do.

I knew that everyone would be waiting for us when we got home—the whole family. I knew that the house would have been cleaned especially well for the occasion, and although furniture was scarce, we had electricity in for about two years and it was a great convenience. I remembered turning on the switch that first time and seeing the shaded bulb, suspended from the kitchen ceiling, light up. It was fantastic. I kept flipping the switch on and off. I couldn't figure it out. Electricity for us meant electric light at the flip of a switch. Before that we had a single, oil-lit mantle lamp for the kitchen and before that an old wick lamp. For the other rooms, there might be a candle at night, or we could use a lantern. Now we had electric light in the kitchen and in the two front rooms—and we had a single outlet in the kitchen for a plug-in electrical device. We all knew what this electrical device would be when we could find the money to buy it: A radio.

Before long, Jimmy had found a secondhand radio for five pounds. He built a shelf for the radio, taking most of the day with a hammer and punch, boring holes in the concrete wall for the shelf. We all waited, breathless, including Mom, when Jimmy plugged in the radio and turned it on. It took a little while to warm up—then the first sounds we heard were music and song: "Davy, Davy Crockett, king of the wild frontier." We might still be the Grantums or the Morans, but now we were the Grantums or the Morans who had a radio with long wave, medium wave, and short wave. We could listen to Radio Eireann broadcasting from Dublin, and the BBC from London, and Radio Luxembourg and the American Forces Network over in Germany. We could listen to music and songs and news and all manner of programs and know what was happening in the world. We paid for it in installments, and in a year or so the radio was ours.

Shortly after we got our radio, Jimmy, while taking our cows to Dad's place for grazing, met Annie O'Donnell, a neighbor on Madogue Road. The McIntyres also had a radio, and she had been visiting there the night before and had listened to a popular Irish program called Dinjo. She said to Jimmy, "Dinjo was great in McIntyre's radio last night, Jimmy; was it anny good in yeers?"

"No," said Jimmy, known for his embarrassing honesty as much as his wit, "it was no good in ours, but that's because we have only a secondhand radio."

"Arrah, God help us, but sure a secondhand radio is better than no radio at all," said Annie.

And off she went, learning that programs on secondhand radios just weren't as good as programs on new radios.

A couple of months after I was born, we moved from my father's farm in Madogue to the vacant, larger, and more arable farm in the neighboring village of Culmore, where my mother was born and raised. The house in Culmore was a bungalow and much larger than the place in Madogue. The bungalow had four rooms, a large kitchen, and a hallway inside the front door connecting the two front rooms. The kitchen was the main living area in the house. All of the rooms had their own fireplaces for heat in the wintertime, but only once in a blue moon could we spare the precious turf to warm any of these rooms. The big fireplace in the kitchen was a working fireplace. It had hobs on each side to store things like the kettle and teapot. A crane that could swing in and out was used to suspend pots and ovens over the fire. The crane was used for most of the cooking and for boiling water.

Someone once wrote that in Irish country homes the kitchen fire had not burned out in over three hundred years. It symbolized life itself. It burned all day, and at night the last thing that the last person to bed had to do was rake the fire so that it would burn slowly through the night and leave a few hot coals by morning, from which a new fire would be started. Raking the fire meant taking out the coals and putting them on one side while the ashes underneath were cleared away. Then a few sods of damp turf were placed flat on the grate, the hot coals placed on top of the sods, and the ashes placed on top of the coals. This produced a very slow-burning fire, with no flames, that would last until morning. Then the ashes would be taken out and the surviving coals used to start a new fire. The cycle continued, day after day, month after month, year in, year out, generation upon generation.

A good fire was a glorious thing. A good fire was a fire with well-seasoned turf in it. The coals were plentiful and red hot. Flames were happily dancing, and the fire was making nice crackling sounds, like a cat purring away in happy slumber. It warmed the kitchen and it warmed the heart. It made you feel good about yourself, about the future, about life itself, and about God in Heaven. There could be no cheerfulness in a home without a good fire. God help the poor people with bad turf, or not enough turf—so that it must be spared. You couldn't feel good walking into a house like that. If it was a neighbor's home, you didn't feel welcome when you saw in the hearth a wretched little fire, without a single flame, comatose, silently begging for more turf so that it could live.

Sometimes we had bad turf, gathered in a wet summer, or where, after stacking near the house, it got wet and stayed wet because of too much rain. And sometimes we didn't have enough turf because we didn't cut enough or couldn't save enough or didn't use it wisely enough. Then hard times got harder...and colder.

When we got to the house, the door was already open, and my brother, Eamon, and my sisters were standing around in the kitchen. Best of all, there was a great fire on, and that lifted my spirits. Dad, steady now, greeted everyone individually and got every name right: Maureen, Eamon, Patricia, Kathleen, Eveline, Anne, Angela, and Christina, the youngest, a little over a year old. Age-wise, I'm in between Kathleen and Eveline, Kathleen a year older than me and Eveline a year younger. Jimmy, the oldest at sixteen, had recently bailed out and was working in England. There was great excitement, especially from the younger children. I knew that they felt the same way I felt when I saw him get off the bus in Charlestown. He looked as if he didn't belong to us at all, and not to Culmore or Mayo either.

While Mom and my older sisters set the table for the tea, Eamon got the steaks started in the big iron frying pan, placed on top of a three-legged stand over hot coals that have been pulled out a little bit from the fire. The peas were heated too, and soon the meal was ready. The smell of the fried meat made my mouth water, and I'd love to taste it. In our family, where food, especially meat, was almost always scarce, the logic was simple: the ones who had to work harder needed more meat and got more meat. Therefore, most of the steaks went to my father and Eamon, who was four years older than me. My mother and the rest of us got a smaller share, and no share if there was none to be had. The younger ones had to wait until they were older when others, like Jimmy, had left to make their own way in the world. That's the way it was. There was nothing to complain about. And besides, we all had tea and bread with butter and marmalade to spread over the bread. The marmalade was a real treat.

After the meal when the dishes were washed and put away, we knew this was the time to ask Dad to play the flute. The people of Culmore and Madogue and Corthoon and Sonnagh and other villages knew that Eddie Grantum, like his father and grandfather before him, was a great flute player. Dad learned to play the flute from his father, who learned from his father, who learned from God knows who. He could not read a note of music but he could play a tune perfectly after hearing it a couple of times. When he was younger, he used to play in country dance halls like Tom Nell's in Kilaturley and at house dances. I remember Mom telling us once that when she first heard Dad play the flute she was a goner; he was her Pied Piper. He was thirty-three years old, tall and handsome, and built like a boxer. He had a head of black, curly hair; laughing, brown eyes; and a smile that would melt a fair chunk of the North Pole. My mother was twenty-one at the time and one of seven sisters, all beauties according to neighbors, and strangers establishing that they weren't strangers at all. My mother loved to sing and dance, and my father loved to play the flute. For better or worse, this star-crossed couple loved and wed, and obeyed God's commandment to go forth and multiply.

Some years before my parents began going steady, my father had been to America, by way of Canada. His brother, Tom, was already in Philadelphia, as was his Aunt Catherine. At home, on the land, my father was something of a perfectionist. Whatever he did had to be just so. Ninety-five percent was not good enough. This characteristic was passed down to each of us. Whether it was cutting turf, mouling spuds, making hay, stooking oats, or reeking turf, we did it with style and pride. We were proud when a neighbor or a stranger passing by on the Main Road would complement our work. Still, Eddie, like his sons and daughters in their turn, could not find spiritual union with the soil and longed to join his brother in America.

Unfortunately, he failed to pass the physical examination required for admission. My father, the perfectionist, was born with a small imperfection: the little toe on his right foot was slightly bent toward and partially sitting on the next toe. A minor operation would have corrected the piggy-back problem, but Eddie Gallagher couldn't wait. As Canada didn't care about his little toe, he immigrated to Montreal in 1927. Later, he would cross the border into Detroit and make his way to Philadelphia. Even in the midst of the Great Depression and signs that still said "No Irish Need Apply," Eddie loved America. He worked all sorts of jobs in Philadelphia, from working in a lumberyard, to railroad maintenance to tending bar in Irish pubs in Germantown.

> Whoever wrote it, wrote it well
> But the same is written on the gates of Hell
> No Irish need apply.

Before Dad went to America, he had a reputation locally for being very good at ending a fight if one came his way, and quick to break up a fight that might start in a pub or at a dance or a fair. In Depression-era America whenever the opportunity arose he would volunteer to fight experienced fighters whose promoters or managers would call out to the audience for a volunteer to challenge the man in the ring. The purpose was to entertain the crowd, but to Dad it was to make a few dollars. Often he would win. He was no heavyweight, but he was quick on his feet and he could punch. My father was not a stand-your-ground, toe-to-toe fighter. In or out of the ring, he was a dancer and saw no reason to stand and fight when he could move and fight, especially when the other guy was a lot bigger than he was. Dad would dance around the ring, moving in quickly to throw one or two well-aimed punches, then quickly back away before he got hit.

He lost his last fight in America because he gave in to pressure from the crowd to fight like John L. Sullivan. He fought a fellow Irishman by the name of Jack Kelly, who was much bigger and heavier than Dad. With no time limit on the fight, Dad and Kelly fought toe-to-toe for more than an hour before Dad went down and couldn't make the count. Promoters pleaded with him to turn professional, using his own style of boxing, but the life of a fighter was not for my father. On his return to Ireland, his reputation as a man who could take care of himself in dicey situations was still well known, and when he played flute in country dance halls and at house dances, as he had done before leaving, there were no fights. Just knowing that Eddie Grantum was there was enough to keep the place peaceful.

In the United States, while people went hungry and stood in soup lines all over the country, my father was having the time of his life in Philadelphia. In early 1933 his mother wrote with very bad news: his father had cancer, and she wanted Eddie to come home. Perhaps knowing that if he did, he would never return, he was reluctant to leave. His Aunt Catherine, sister of his father, relieved him of the decision, notifying the authorities that Eddie was an illegal alien. He was promptly deported—and advised that he could return, provided he do so legally. He never did return, and his father, Jim Grantum, died in October 1933. Accompanying him on the voyage home were his most prized possessions, five long wooden flutes.

"Dad, please play the flute for us," Patricia asked.

"Ah no, sure I haven't played the flute in ages, Patrisheen."

"You played it for us when you were home last time," Kathleen offers.

"Aye, Catleen, but that was a year ago; I don't know if I have the wind for it now, or the memory."

"You do, you do. We know you do," says a chorus of insistent voices.

Christina, sitting on the floor with gooey black liquorice drooling down each side of her mouth, chirped in. "Fute, fute, fute."

"Sweet Jesus, what can I say to that? All right, all right, where are my flutes?" Dad asked.

Triumphal excitement: "They're in Grandma's box."

"Ah, all right then, bring one out."

There was a mad dash to the front room where Grandma's box, a simple rectangular, wooden box on four inelegant legs, where we used to store extra clothes, stood modestly in a corner. Reeking of camphor mothballs, Dad's flutes were hidden underneath the clothes. One was quickly rushed to him. He looked it over and decided to go see for himself. He brought them all out into the light of the kitchen and chose one. The others were returned to the bottom of Grandma's box. Dad inspected the flute carefully. It was much longer and heavier than the fifes I've seen in the Charlestown band. And the fifes have just six holes like my Clarke's tin whistle that I was learning to play with some difficulty. Dad's flutes were far more complicated. They had all kinds of little silver keys and caps in addition to the holes, and they opened and closed over other holes.

Dad took the flute outside and dipped it into a barrel of water by the gable. He said this gave it a softer, sweeter sound. He dried it off a little and then positioned his fingers on the flute and raised it to his lips. He repositioned the flute by his mouth a few times to get it right, and then the music came. Dad played the flute, and we were all suddenly in another world, a world of laughter and happiness…and sadness, but a sweet sadness. Except for the music, there wasn't the slightest sound in the house. His wind was not broken, his memory not gone, and his fingers move at a blur, sometimes shimmering and lingering to coax out the perfect note. The tunes come pouring out: "If I Met Maggie in the Woods," "The Rocky Road to Dublin," "The Geese in the Bog," "Give Me Your Hand," "The Elizabethan Serenade," "Down by the Sally Gardens," "Danny Boy," "Hath Sorrow Thy Young Days Shaded"—jigs and reels and hornpipes, and even American tunes, like "Shenandoah," that he learned in Philadelphia.

He was standing in the middle of the floor in the kitchen, and we were all around him, my younger sisters sitting on the floor, staring up at the music man in wonderment. We were enthralled. I understood what Mom meant when she had said that he was her Pied Piper. He could make the flute talk and sing and laugh and cry. In his hands it was alive, doing what he wanted it to do. We didn't want him to stop, but it was already past bedtime for some of us. In the morning the hard work that my father had come home from England to do would begin — but there would be no more babies. And after the accident, there would be no more music—but not yet. We still had magical nights ahead of us when my father would play those happy and haunting melodies and take us away to another world.

CHAPTER 3

———— ❧ ————

THE NEXT MORNING my father and Eamon, *slean* and spade in hand, headed for the bog to begin the cutting of the turf. It was mid-March, and we hoped there would be no more frost. Frost could be terrible on freshly cut turf. You might not see it at first, but as it dried in the sun, it could turn to mud. The bog was at the north end of our land on the other side of the railway. The turf banks had to be cleaned before any turf could be cut. This meant taking off the rough, spongy, heathery surface of the bank to a depth of three or four inches. This was Eamon's job. Dad would teach Eamon how to cut turf and, in time, Eamon would teach me. When Dad had cut a bank of turf, you could look at the new face of the bank, from top to bottom and lengthwise, and see a beautiful piece of work. Every sod had been cut cleanly, and the face of the bank was smooth and shiny, and as even as a brick wall—only the bricks were standing almost upright, rather than horizontal. You could see the outline of every inside sod cut, all the same size, all cut at the same angle. Eamon said that no one could cut a bank of turf like Dad, and I knew he was right because I'd seen others. I'd seen some so badly cut that part of the turf-bank had even collapsed. That was a disgrace.

With back bent from morning till night, over two weeks, Dad would cut the year's supply, a sod at a time. Cutting eighteen thousand or more sods of turf, one at a time, was no easy task, but neither was spreading, *groiging,* gathering, and hauling them by cart from bog to house where they would be reeked nearby. In a good, dry year, we might save 90 percent, in a bad year maybe 65 or 70 percent. Dad couldn't worry about what happened after the cutting was done. He had to move on to other things. Over the next four to five months, saving the turf would be a family effort—in between many other tasks. There were very few male-only and female-only jobs here. We all worked equally hard, in the fields and in the bog, and I'd learned that our sweat smelled the same. I was no stranger to housework either. The only jobs reserved for Dad and Eamon—and later for me—are those that were physically too hard for Mom and my sisters.

We had a pony, Molly, and she and Maureen were great pals. Maureen loved to ride Molly, and Molly never went faster than when Maureen was on her bareback. We all knew Maureen was a little crazy, and when she was on Molly she was out of control. They'd go like the wind. Yet there was a magic between them. But Molly had a real job, and it wasn't galloping with Maureen on her back. Molly pulled a cart, and she ploughed and harrowed fields, and much more. To plough a green, grassy field, Molly needed a partner. Dad would pair Molly with Sean Kenny's horse, a big black stallion named Jack. Sean Kenny was a neighbor, and he and Dad sometimes helped each other with big jobs. Pulling a heavy Pierce iron plough through a grass-covered field required two horses. The green field, ploughed black with upturned sod, formed into ridges, would be this year's potato field, and last year's spud field would be this year's oat field. This was the way it was because it's the way it's always been.

Dad and Sean Kenny would plow an acre for oats and an acre for potatoes. The spring's work proceeded, and I was dreading the day when Dad would leave. After he left we would sow the potatoes on the ridges and spread cow manure over the covered seed. Next, Eamon would plow the *seochs* on each side to make the *moul* to be shoveled on top of the ridges. Eamon and I would finish spreading the manure over the bare meadows and I would watch him shake the "special," a foul-smelling fertilizer, which we could sometimes afford, with bucket in hand as he walked up and down the fields. The oat seed was put down the same way, walking up and down the ploughed field, shaking the seed left and right from a bucket. The oat field was then harrowed and rolled with a heavy roller. Harrowing the field let the seed get well into the soil, and the roller smoothed and compacted it, while concealing most of the seed from hungry birds.

The evening before Dad was to return to England, he went into Swinford to attend a funeral service for someone he knew long ago. He would not be able to attend the funeral mass and burial next morning because he would be leaving for England, but he must pay his respects by attending the service, which included accompanying the coffin into the church where the body would remain overnight. He came in from the fields in the afternoon to clean up and get ready. Mom got him a basin of water and boiled the kettle so that he would have hot water to shave. He left for town on the bicycle, looking almost exactly as I saw him when he got off the bus in Charlestown. I didn't know it then, but we would never see him quite the same way again. We knew that after the removal service for Dad's friend, some of the men would go to a pub in town for a few drinks. We weren't sure what time Dad would get home, but we knew he wouldn't stay out late because he had to catch the bus to Dublin in the morning. We waited for him to come home, Mom getting more worried and looking often at the clock on the mantelpiece over the fireplace.

As always, when the worry was on Mom, we'd say the rosary, this time dedicating it to the Blessed Virgin. When Mom dedicated the rosary to the Blessed Virgin Mary, we knew it has something to do with Dad. Mom told us that Dad had great faith in the Blessed Virgin. Unable to sleep, I could hear Mom and Eamon and Maureen talking in hushed voices in the kitchen. I knew something was wrong. My mouth was dry, and I had a queer feeling in my belly. I wanted to get up and go outside, to be alone, to beg the Blessed Virgin to bring Dad home safely. I desperately wanted to hear Dad come around the corner of the house and hear the sound of the bicycle being left against the wall outside the bedroom. Finally, sleep intruded. I awoke some time later to hear the murmuring sounds still coming through the closed door. I put my trousers and jersey on and came into the kitchen, where Mom, Maureen, and Eamon were sitting by the fire. Their faces told me that Dad had not come home

"Tommy, go back to bed, what are you doing up," Maureen said crossly

"Where's Dad?" I asked.

No answer.

"Where's Dad? Did Dad come home?"

"He hasn't come home yet," Eamon said.

"It's all right, Tommy," Mom added. "He probably stayed at Groarkes."

I felt better for a moment. The Groarkes are our first cousins in Swinford—Mom's sister, Mary, is married to Jimmy Groarke. Jimmy and Mary Groarke are also my godparents. The Groarkes have a pub and grocery shop, and it was logical that Dad might have stopped in there to pay his respects to our relatives. And if he'd had one or two too many, it was also logical that he'd be invited to stay the night and sleep it off. I wanted to believe this as much as everyone else did, but I knew that Dad was very proud and he and Jimmy Groarke were not close. I knew that they were polite to each other but they were on different sides long ago, and memories were long in Ireland. And I knew that Dad had to catch the bus to Dublin in the morning. He could get on the bus in Swinford where it stopped for a few minutes, but that wouldn't work because his suitcase was at home.

We learn our history early. I knew that Jimmy Groarke was a member of the Irish Republican Army (IRA), fighting British occupation forces during the Troubles. After the War of Independence, which resulted in the creation of the Irish Free State in 1922, the Gallaghers, like most of the country, tired of war, supported the Free State government, including its military commandant-in-chief, Michael Collins. Many IRA fighters also accepted the Anglo-Irish Peace Treaty and joined the new Free State Army. Many others did not. After so long a struggle, having to accept a treaty that left Northern Ireland still part of the United Kingdom was too bitter a pill to swallow. Adding insult to injury was the continuing requirement, though modified, of swearing allegiance to the British monarch. Jimmy Groarke's hero, Eamon de Valera, who was president of the Irish parliament, rejected the treaty, which led to a Civil War. We learned about Ireland's heroic fight for freedom in school, but we learned about the Civil War at home and in other people's homes and in pubs. Today, we still heard people being described in terms of whether they or their families were Republicans or Free Staters back in those days. I didn't care which side anyone was on back then, but I knew that the old people cared, and some of them cared deeply. The long and the short of it was that I didn't think Dad could or would stay at the Groarkes overnight—and Mom knew it too.

Next morning a guard came to our house. Police are bad news in general, and this one, too, brought bad news. Dad was in the County Hospital in Castlebar. He had serious injuries and was in critical condition. He was found a couple of hours earlier in a ditch at the bottom of Cossu—the local name for a stretch of Main Road that consisted of a long, steep hill, angling to the right at the bottom. At first, the guards thought that Dad had been hit by a car, but if this were so, the bicycle would have been damaged, and it wasn't, except for the handlebars, which were twisted off-center.

We learned later from Dad that there was no vehicle involved. He had been on the bicycle coming down Cossu. It was dark, he had no light, and he was going fast on the steep slope. Near the bottom, as the road banked to the right, he lost control of the bicycle and hit the pavement headfirst. His forward momentum took him off the road and into a ditch, his bicycle landing in a field. He had been to a pub with some neighbors and old friends following the service, but had left long before closing time to get home so that he could get a good night's sleep before the twenty-seven-hour sleepless trip back to Birmingham. The accident occurred around 9:00 p.m., and Dad lay in the ditch for more than twelve hours. When he was found by a passerby who noticed the bicycle in the field, he was nearly dead from a head injury and exposure.

The house was now frantic. The younger children were crying because they saw the awful fear in Mom's face. The older ones were white faced. I felt like a huge stone was sitting in my belly. My mouth was dry and my head was spinning. I had to escape from the house. I ran to the bog and hid in a covered dugout that we used for shelter when we were working there. I prayed to the Blessed Virgin to not let Dad die. Mom said that Dad has great faith in the Blessed Virgin, and now I begged her to make everything the way it was before he left the house yesterday. I desperately wanted time to go back to yesterday afternoon so that we could stop this from happening. I stayed in hiding for hours, praying that when I got back to the house, the miracle will have happened: that the Blessed Virgin will have interceded, that Dad will be home, that there was no accident, and that this was just a nightmare.

But my father wasn't home. He would not be home for several weeks. He did recover but he was never himself again. When he came out of the hospital, he stayed home with us for a while, but he was no longer the Dad we knew. Neighbors and relations came to see him, and I heard the expression "Ah, poor Eddeen, his nerves are gone." Dad, who loved having us all around him, even if only for a few weeks each year, now could not bear loud noises. Sometimes he could not remember our names, or he'd get them mixed up. I would be Eamon, and Anne would be Angela. Once, before returning to England, he asked Patricia to bring him his favorite flute. I think he needed to see if the gift was still there, but his fingers wouldn't do what he wanted them to do, and the music didn't come. He put the flute down and turned to the wall. But we had our tears too, because the magic had ended. Dad never picked up the flute again. Eddie Gallagher's sons and daughters loved the music but did not inherit the gift. Over the years the flutes disappeared, one by one, given away to would-be flute players and pretenders claiming a profound affection for my father.

Back in Birmingham my father got a job in a bakery that was easy on his nerves, and again the money started coming, once a week in the blue registered envelope. Dad would come home again in the spring but only to cut a few banks of turf. Mom said that he didn'tt have the strength—and by this time Eamon was helping him with the cutting, and a neighbor, Mick Burns, was going around the country with his Massey Ferguson tractor ploughing fields for pay in a fraction of the time it would take a couple of horses. I was working more and harder and moving up the food chain. When my father would return to England, I'd still miss him terribly, even though the music was gone. He always left on a Friday morning, and I couldn't bear going to school that day.

Before he'd leave for the bus to Dublin, he'd still give each of us a five brand-new English threepenny bits. He hadn't forgotten this. He'd bring them home especially for the morning that he would leave—to ease the pain. I loved these coins. They were not round like all the others but had twelve equal edges with Queen Elizabeth on one side and what looked to me like a twelve-paned window on the other. The color was different too; they looked as if they were made of brass, or maybe bronze. I always saved mine for as long as I could because they helped me to remember Dad, but then I'd spend them, maybe to buy some toffees at Tom Horkan's shop or maybe to buy a jotter or a pencil for school.

Jimmy came home from England for a while and got a job working for Vet Ruane in Swinford. He had gone to England at fifteen and was barely able to make enough money to live on. Back at home it was a little easier, and the extra money was a God-send for the family. Vet Ruane and Jimmy went around the country in the vet's Volkswagen, carrying out the government's order to test all cattle for TB. People were supposed to have their cattle in the barn when the vet came but often they didn't:

"If ye want to give my cows an injection, ye can round them up yeerselves, so ye can."

"Fianna Fail should be testin' people for TB and not wastin' my time."

"Sure, who ever heard of a cow gettin' TB, but ishn't Margit O'Brien abow in Merlin Park with the consumption, ishn't she?"

"Why didn't Fianna Fail give her an injection?"

"Feckin' hell, injectin' cattle for TB. Have you ever heard the likes?"

Rounding up and holding in place big, heavy bullocks for Vet Ruane to shave a little spot on their necks and then shove in a syringe was a dodgy and dangerous task, and Jimmy often came home black and blue. He said that the *milch* cows and heifers weren't too bad but that the bullocks, in particular, seemed to have a special dislike for Vet Ruane. Jimmy believed this was because the bullocks remembered that it was Vet Ruane who destroyed their balls with the "squezzers," a big steel instrument like a scissors, except that it doesn't cut, it crushes or squezzes a bull's balls into mush. After several ball crushings, the bulls are changed to bullocks, depriving them forever of the pride and pleasure of siring their own offspring.

Jimmy said that real bulls always knew when one of their own kind was no longer one of their own kind, and they had no respect at all for the bullocks. They didn't know that their own sorry day was coming. Even the young heifers and old milch cows ignored these unfortunates with whom they had to share the same field. Bullocks with no balls had a miserable life—and a short one, too, for they were definitely going to wind up in the slaughterhouse before their third birthday.

It was against the law to own a full-grown bull, and only specially licensed farmers were allowed to have them. These bulls had the life of Riley. Their only job was to service all the cows and heifers in the area when they were "around." You always knew when a cow was around because she would start acting crazy, running around and trying to mount other cows or even a despised bullock, thinking they were bulls with whom they needed to communicate in a way that God and nature ordained. Then it was often my job to get the poor, confused animal to a real bull as quickly as possible before the confusion wore off. I could either go to Kennedy's in Cloonlara or Moffit's in Killeen, but either way, it was a two-and-a-half-mile walk with a crazy cow, or worse, a really crazy young heifer on her first visit to the bull.

We had to pay a fee of ten shillings to Kennedy or Moffit for the service—this was because they had to pay an annual license fee to the government. And they also had the expense of having to keep the bull in his own well-fenced field, all by himself. He could not be with the other cattle because he took his servicing job very seriously and could easily make a nuisance of himself. Sometimes it could take a while for the bull to do what he was supposed to do. He might have been tired tired because it was a busy day and all he wanted to do was sleep. Then Moffit or Kennedy would try to get him interested by making a strange kind of whirring-whistling sound, which seemed to work by reminding the bull of his duty.

Once we didn't bring the vet in time and let one of our bulls grow almost to maturity, past two years old. We brought the vet when he began to bother the other cattle. We tied him into a stall in the barn and the vet went to work. The poor bull stayed on his feet, legs apart, paralyzed with terror and bellowing in agony. His balls were big and drooping. I couldn't bear to watch and went outside. Afterward, our new bullock lay down in the field and did not get up for two whole days. When he did get up his balls had shrunk to a bloody lump about the size of a crabapple. It was a lot less painful to make a bullock out of a bull when his balls were the size of marbles. We never let this happen again.

Taking the tacklings off of our pony, Molly, after a day's work, Jimmy noticed that there were drops of blood falling to the ground from the bottom of her tail. Under the long, bushy hair at the base of the tail there was a lump: raw, red, and oozing blood. At first he thought that Molly caught her tail on barbed wire while swinging it back and forth to keep the crowers and horse flies off her behind. He put a little of Dad's Snowfire Vaseline on the open wound, and this stopped the bleeding, but only for a while. Mom was worried and told him to take Molly to Vet Greeley in

Swinford. Vet Greeley was older than Vet Ruane and had more experience with horses. His diagnosis was immediate: Molly had a growth near the bottom of her tail and it was cancerous. The only hope was to cut off the bottom of her tail. Otherwise, the growth would continue up the tail and into Molly's spine, and then she would be finished.

Vet Greeley told Jimmy that he must take the growth off right away. Jimmy walked with Molly all the way home, and he looked sick. We looked at Molly's tail and we knew why. The shiny, bushy hair was gone. There was a stump left, bandaged at the bottom and looking bloody and sore. It was easy to see that Molly was in pain. She kept turning around trying to see what had happened to her tail. We took turns stroking her face and whispering to her, and she made little snorting sounds.

After a few days, she improved. She was eating grass again, and we gave her some of our precious oats as a special treat. Without her full tail, she looked strange and a little scary, but soon she was pulling the cart again. Then the bottom of the stump began to swell up, and it was back to Vet Greeley. The growth had returned. Another piece of Molly's tail was cut off and we and Molly had another reprieve. The growth came back again and Vet Greeley told Jimmy there was little hope. Molly wasn't just the hardest and most willing worker on the farm; she was also a big pet. The thought of losing her was almost unbearable. And if we lost her, Mom knew we wouldn't be able to replace her with another pony. Jimmy asked Vet Greeley to cut one more time. He did and now Molly had no more tail. We said the rosary, asking God to spare Molly – and spare us. We waited and hoped. Soon we knew that it was no use. Molly was having difficulty with her hind legs. She didn't want to walk. Mom told us that Molly was in terrible pain and that we had to send her away. I knew what this meant. It meant that the Burnhouse lorry would come.

On the way home from school, we would often see the Burnhouse lorry pass by. It was unforgettable because of the dreadful smell of animal meat and carcasses inside, bound, we were told, for the Dublin Zoo to feed the animals. The smell was so bad that we had to hold our noses until it had well passed, and sometimes we'd throw stones at it. Now, it would stop by our boreen, for our pony. Jimmy and Eamon lead Molly up the boreen to the Main Road. Maureen wanted to go too, but Mom wouldn't let her. The rest of us stayed in the kitchen, waiting. Mom sat by the kitchen table, staring out the window. She didn't want us to see the worry and the tears. She was with Dad and Grandma long ago when they bought Molly. We stood around, not talking and not looking at each other. Maureen said in her usual scolding voice that we must be brave. We didn't know exactly what was going to happen, but we know that we'd never see Molly again.

The Burnhouse lorry arrived and the driver got out—just another pickup for him. Burnhouse lorry drivers were licensed to carry a revolver for these horrible occasions, and soon we hear a gunshot, half-expected, yet heart-stopping. It was the first time that any of us had ever heard a gunshot. It was so sudden and loud and it echoed across the fields. We knew that Molly was dead, and the tears came. Later, Jimmy told us what happened. We wanted to know and we didn't want to know. The Burnhouse man got out of the lorry, all business: no comforting words; just another job. He lowered the lift at the back of the lorry and told Jimmy to position Molly by the lift. Molly, ever willing, didn't object. She trusted Jimmy as she had always trusted him. The Burnhouse man then took his revolver from the lorry and quickly placed it to Molly's forehead and pulled the trigger. The bullet went through Molly's brain and she collapsed partially onto the lift. The Burnhouse man then asked Jimmy and Eamon to help him move her more fully onto the lift, and then she was hoisted into the smelly lorry. Jimmy said that Molly felt no pain. He said she died instantly.

Jimmy returned to England in 1958, this time for good. Maureen went shortly afterward. Two less mouths to feed. Eamon, at sixteen, was now the man of the house, doing everything that Dad used to come home from England to do. I was twelve years old and his number-one apprentice. He was happily out of school, having left at thirteen, same as Jimmy. Maureen was able to do a few years at St. Mary's secondary school in Swinford and, as a result, got a job in Birmingham, putting her natural bossiness to good use as office manager for Hayes & Finch, Church Furnishers & Candlestickmakers, Ltd. I was helping Eamon in the afternoons, along with my sisters. The tools we used on the land were as familiar to them as they were to Eamon and me, even if they couldn't use all of them. When my turn came, I would clean house — which I didn't mind at all. It was a nice change from shoveling cow muck out of barns or spreading turf. I didn't bake bread, though. My mother and sisters did this well, but I tried once and that was that. The cake wouldn't bake and it wouldn't rise, preferring to stay as a lump of gooey dough. I gave it to Rover, one of our dogs, who eyed it very suspiciously and then eyed me very suspiciously. He let his belly decide for him, and he ate the whole mess. He then returned to his sleeping place behind the reek of turf and didn't do very much for a day or two.

CHAPTER 4

❧

WE HAD TWO dogs—well, three if we counted the pig who thought she was a dog. Our dogs' names were Rover, a big black male, and Flower, smaller, more intelligent and part hound with an almost yellow coat. The pig was another story altogether. Working dogs on Irish farms were more than pets; they were real members of the family, so our dogs' full names were Rover Gallagher and Flower Gallagher. Our neighbors' dogs were Carlow Kavanagh, Bruno Joyce, Rex Drennan, and Captain Kenny.

Rover and Bruno were brothers, and they had hated each other since they were pups. We needed to find a home for one of these two almost identical pups, and we were happy when Frank Joyce agreed to take one, whom he named Bruno. Unfortunately, separating the growing pups by a few fields didn't keep them apart. Soon they would be at each other's throats in ferocious fights. Eamon and Frank would only half-heartedly try to pull them apart. They thought it was fun, but I didn't. Frank would often take Bruno down to the bog atop Dolly, his mule, Bruno sitting astride Dolly in front of Frank, panting away happily and probably not even thinking about Rover. Rover probably hated Bruno all the more for this shameful showing off across Dolly's broad back when he had neither horse nor mule to ride on.

By the time the dogs were full-grown their fights are terrible to see. Once in the middle of a fight, I grabbed Rover's tail with both hands and dug my feet into the ground and tried to pull him off of Bruno. In a flash they both turned on me, and I was lucky to get away with only bloody hands. Sometimes they would howl out to each other across the fields and then take off for battle. If they happened to meet in the middle of Drennan's land, that's where the fight would be. Mrs. Drennan often complained about Rover and Bruno trying to kill each other on her land while she had to lock up Rex to keep him out of the fight. Rover usually won, meaning that Bruno quit and took off for home. Rover rarely pursued Bruno after a fight because he was so exhausted and bloodied himself. He would just just lie down in his sleeping place behind the reek of turf and lick his wounds. Sometimes it took Rover weeks to fully recover from a bad fight, but as soon as he was fit again, he'd send that challenging howl across the fields to Bruno. My only hope was that as they got older, they'd begin to see that it just wasn't worth all the pain.

Late one night a neighboring dog, Dickie Forkin, made the fatal mistake of coming to our land. The Forkins lived several farms away from ours, and as far as I knew, Dickie always stayed around his own place. Why he chose to commit suicide that night I'll never know, but running into Rover on our land was indeed suicide for poor Dickie. He was a small, scrawny, *sess* male dog—friendly but weak. When you'd approach Dickie, even on his own land, he'd lie down and roll over in total surrender, baring his teeth in a sickly smile—as if to say, *Take anything you want, just please don't hurt me.* He had no chance when Rover confronted him down near our cow barns. I heard the terrible cries, grabbled a flashlight, and ran as fast as I could toward the barns, but I was too late. Dickie Forkin was dead, his small, sad, lifeless body covered in blood. I shone the flashlight around and spotted Rover. He came up to me, head down, looking the perfect picture of shame and guilt. In rage, I kicked him in his chest, aiming my kick between his front legs, so hard that I lifted him off the ground. He limped away from me yelping in pain. He had killed a dog half his size who probably offered no defense at all.

The next morning I buried Dickie where he lay, Flower lying by my side, her paws stretched out in front of her, her head lying on top of them, whimpering, as I dug the grave. Flower was not involved, and she wanted me to know it. Then I had to go to Bridget Forkin and tell her what happened to her dog. I didn't tell Mrs. Forkin that I found Dickie a few feet from the door of the henhouse where our chickens were locked up for the night. It didn't occur to me the night before when all I could see was the cruel and heartless murder of a small dog. In the light of day another possibility stared me in the face. Was it hunger that drove Dickie to our land, and to the barns where we sheltered our cows and calves—*and chickens*—at night? Maybe Rover was doing only what Flower had taught him.

Unlike all of our neighbors, our barns are not close to our house. The main cow barn had been part of the house where Mom was born and raised, along with her ten brothers and sisters. When the new house was built in 1935, it was built closer to the Main Road and on a rise where the view was more pleasing to the eye. The disadvantage was that we had to walk a distance to milk cows, clean muck out of barns, feed chickens, and do so many other things where closer proximity would have been more convenient. There was also a greater risk. A fox or maybe a small dog, hungry for too long, might feel encouraged to try a quick raid on the chicken coup. Flower always stayed by the house at night while Rover was the roving patrol, walking regularly during the night between house and barns. Could this be how he encountered Dickie Forkin? I couldn't be sure, but I wanted very much to give Rover the benefit of the doubt. We quickly made up. Dear Rover: all heart, never a grudge, always forgiving.

Flower was much better than Rover at catching rabbits. I had never seen a rabbit on our land in Culmore, but Dad's place in Madogue was full of rabbits and rabbit burrows. Flower loved to go to Madogue, and she would often take off by herself. When she was not around the house during the day we knew where she was and why. She was light, sleek, and fast, and far more clever than Rover at sneaking up on an unsuspecting rabbit. Once she spottted her prey, she'd use the terrain around her like a field marshal surveying the lay of the land before a battle. As quiet as death, she would conceal herself behind tall grass, brooms, whins, bushes, hills, and hollows—anything that provided cover as she moved closer to the rabbit. When there was little cover available, she would lie down on her belly, head flat on the ground, hind legs gathered underneath, and crawl forward, inch by inch, until she was close enough to pounce.

With Flower the chase was usually brief, and unless the burrow was very close by, the rabbit didn't have a chance. Rover, on the other hand, was full of enthusiasm, but not very smart when it came to catching rabbits. He was unconcerned about concealment and knew nothing about the art of the chase. The moment he spottted a rabbit, he'd let the entire village know that he, Rover Gallagher, had one of man's and dog's great pests in his sights. With streams of excited barks and howls, he'd take off for the kill. The rabbit almost always made it to his burrow at a leisurely run, leaving poor Rover, in great frustration, pawing frantically at the entrance to the burrow, trying to dig him out. On those rare occasions when he was lucky enough to catch a dumb rabbit, he would treat himself to the meal. Flower, without fail, would bring the rabbit home and leave it on the doorstep so that we could decide whether we needed the meal more than she did. Mostly it's us, but we shared.

When old age began to slow down Carlow Kavanagh, it was a sad time because we knew what it meant. Carlow was everybody's friend. Though a male, he had such a gentle nature and he'd been around for as long as most of us could remember. But around here few old dogs get to die of old age in the company of the family they loved and served. Old dogs, especially ones in failing health, are done away with to make way for a replacement that will be trained to take over, becoming the apprentice of the doomed teacher. Dogs must be useful and earn their keep. On the big, rich farms of the midlands and in towns and cities, maybe old dogs can live out their final year or two in peace and comfort, whatever their condition, but not on small farms in Ireland's poor West. That's just how it is. No one looks forward to the time when an old dog must be put down. Mostly it's dreaded because the dog is part of the family.

Sometimes the dog knows what's going to happen, knows that the unbreakable bond is broken, senses the invisible barrier that was never there before. I've heard of old dogs leaving home just before the fateful day, never returning and never to be seen again.

Drowning was the most common means of killing a dog around here, but if a neighbor owns a shotgun or a rifle, this is quicker and reduces the pain to both dog and executioner. Carlow's fate was to be shot. In Ireland, by law, you may own a shotgun or a rifle no more powerful than .22 caliber. Even then you have to get a license, which you won't get if you've ever given the guards any trouble, or if the local sergeant doesn't like you for reasons you will never know. There is another way to get a rifle: to join An Forsa Cosanta Aitiuil (FCA) or Local Defense Force. Many of the farm lads join the FCA when they're about fifteen or sixteen. Of course they're supposed to be eighteen to join up, but when the FCA took your measure, it wasn't your age they worried about; it was your measure – whether you were tall enough and have enough meat on your bones to fill sufficiently their smallest uniform so that you wouldn't disgrace it. Some of the fifteen- and sixteen-year-olds don't meet this requirement—hard farm labor can slow the growth—but those who do are in. The FCA is a part-time army: you get to go on "field days" on the occasional Sunday after Mass to drill and train, and you also get to go away to camp for a couple of weeks in the summer and winter, for which you get paid. Jimmy was in the FCA and so was Eamon, and when my time comes, I'll try out too—to see if I measure up.

The FCA gives you a rifle, which you can keep at home, but they are careful not to give you any ammunition for it—unless you are able to pocket a round or two while at the firing range. Eamon told me that this is very dicey because there is strict accounting of every bullet fired, and you don't want to be in the embarrassing position of being asked by an officer or an NCO if you're quite sure you haven't accidentally put a round in your pocket. The rifle you get is the English Lee Enfield 303, and it is much more powerful than the .22.

As Carlow was having more and more difficulty walking, we knew that his days were numbered. Frank Joyce, who is in the FCA, let Marty

Kavanagh know that he had quite innocently, but fortunately under the circumstances, come into possession of a 303 bullet, and the means of Carlow's death was settled. Neither the younger Kavanagh children, nor the younger Joyces, nor the younger Gallaghers were told of the event. I knew it was going to happen, but I didn't know when until I heard the rifle shot on a quiet Saturday morning. Everyone heard the rifle shot. Even though it was farther away, it was still much louder than the revolver that killed Molly.

Later we heard the story of Carlow's last moments. He was lying on the grass snoozing near the house when Frank Joyce and Marty Kavanagh approached. Marty coaxed Carlow to his weary feet. The idea was to walk the dog a distance from the house so that the children would not witness his sudden, violent death. Out of sight of the house, Frank placed his one misappropriated bullet into the chamber of his FCA 303 rifle and pushed the bolt forward. Instinctively, Carlow Kavanagh knew that this was the end.

He tried to run—and reached an earthen fence about twenty yards away. The five-foot-high fence was too much for Carlow, though he tried frantically to get over it. Climbing up halfway, then falling back down, he gave up after a few attempts, too exhausted and in too much pain to continue. He turned to face two humans he had known all his life, one a friendly neighbor, the other he loved, as only dogs can love, without reservation. Frank knelt on one knee and aimed at a spot under Carlow's neck and between his shoulders—and fired his one bullet. It tore through Carlow's body, killing him instantly. The deed was done. There was sadness felt for Carlow Kavanagh in more than one home, but life moved on, and Carlow's replacement-in-waiting became top dog. His name was Jet, named after the jet planes that were increasingly seen high in the sky above the stony, boggy, piss-poor fields of County Mayo.

Once in a while, we would buy a baby pig at the market or fair and raise it until it was ready for slaughter. Pigs were fairly cheap to raise because they rooted around so much with their snouts in the ground that they more or less took care of themselves, while making such a mess in the process that you hardly needed to plow where they had been foraging. The problem was that we all made pets of many of our animals—or they made pets of us—and this made it very painful when it was time for Dad or Eamon to take the pig on that last lonely walk to the barn, from which she would not return, when the pig thought that this was just another walk with a pal. One pig went way too far. She was so little when we bought her that the dogs took a liking to her and sort of adopted her.

At first we just thought it was funny to see all three of them palling around together—so we named the pig Polly. Polly didn't do what pigs are supposed to do, root in the ground finding all kinds of grub to eat. Polly thought she was a dog, and so she behaved like a dog. Rover and Flower knew that they could come into the kitchen in the late evening and sit by the big open fire for a couple of hours but only if they were unobtrusive, taking up the least space possible. Otherwise they'd be told to go outside or out of the way under the kitchen table. It was comical to see the dogs try so hard to make themselves invisible by the fire—until you reached down to acknowledge their presence, and then they were in heaven, accepted in that most honored place.

Polly, having accepted boiled, watery banner potatoes and buttermilk for dinner, thought that she too should have a place by the fire. She would follow the dogs into the kitchen in the late evening when the fire was going strong, taking a place directly in front of the fire while the dogs tried to merge themselves into the wall on each side. Poor Polly stuck out like a very sore thumb, but she didn't care. She would sit down on her arse, like a dog, front legs upright, and grunt happily into the fire. It was hard to put her out and she would object with squeals of outrage at the unfairness of it all.

As Polly grew she would try to keep up with the dogs in the fields. Following their lead, she would try to help in rounding up the cattle but preferred to just run them down to the railway at the end of our land. She would chase the chickens and challenge neighbors' dogs. She would try to keep up with Rover and Flower as they ran through the fields, playing and mock-fighting. She wanted to join in but couldn't keep up with them and would eventually lie down in the field exhausted and angry, squealing in frustration. Polly was one confused pig, but so were the cattle she chased and the chickens she tormented and the neighbors' dogs she kept at bay. Polly was one of a kind, and we all loved her, or at least as much as you can love a pig—but her time was coming, and no one wanted to think about that.

Eamon was the one who must turn Polly into a supply of meat that will last as long as we can make it last. And I must help him. We walked Polly into the barn, our sisters outside, tears rolling down angry faces. Polly, happily grunting at the attention, thinks that this was a lovefest, Eamon and me walking her gently into that long good night, as someone said, and everyone around watching. Soon the girls leave; they don't want to watch, and we don't want them anywhere near our temporary abattoir. In the barn Eamon straddled Polly, over her shoulders, stroking her softly on her forehead. Polly was completely at ease; we were her pals. Eamon looked at me and nodded toward the sledgehammer by the wall. I handed it to him. He took it in his right hand while continuing to stroke Polly's head with his left hand. Polly was quiet, grunting away happily, but probably not quite sure why she was in the barn, where she had never been before.

My mouth was dry and I felt sick, like I was about to vomit, but I knew that if I did Eamon would never let me forget it. I looked at my brother and wondered how he felt at this moment, but he was concentrating so completely on what he must do. I watched and I see him in slow motion raise the sledgehammer over his head with both hands. He squeezed his legs around Polly's neck to hold her steady, then brought down the hammer hard on her forehead. Polly groaned a long snoring groan and collapsed, unconscious. Polly looked dead, but she was only knocked out. Now we must work fast. The worst thing that can happen is for Polly to regain consciousness. Then she would fight ferociously for her life and her screams would wake the dead. A pig's screams of terror are hauntingly human. When you looked into a pig's eyes, you wouldn't see the love so evident in a dog's eyes, or the indifference equally evident in a cat's eyes—but you will see intelligence looking out at you, and you will want to look away.

We quickly pulled Polly's limp body onto the washed barn door that we had removed to use as an operating table. Once Polly was on the door we placed bricks under one end at a time, to give us a little elevation. I held a freshly cleaned, white enamel basin under Polly's neck, and Eamon cut her throat with the sharpened butcher knife. I watched him cutting roughly, almost frantically, through flesh and muscle. We don't want Polly to even begin to come around. She made one last guttural noise. Her eyes blinked open and she was staring straight at me. I looked away in total fright. We were murderers. The steaming, smelly, hot blood gushed out all over me. I felt the vomit again coming up in my throat, and I fought it back. Eamon looked sick but screamed at me to catch the blood. I recovered and repositioned the basin under Polly's neck. We needed the blood because Mom will make blood pudding from this precious liquid.

It took ten minutes for the blood to drain from Polly's body. To help the process, Eamon lifted up the arse end of the barn door. When the blood was drained, I took the almost full, still steaming, smelly basin to the house where Mom took it from me and, in return, gave me a pot of boiling water. Eamon poured the boiling water all over Polly's body, softening the skin and making it easy to shave off the hair. We used sharp knives to shave Polly clean of all body hair. Then Eamon gutted the pig, cutting her from between the shoulders, down through the belly to the tail end. The dirtiest job now was to remove the guts—hot, steamy, and smelly, pouring out a sickening sweet smell. Jesus! I'm going to have to do this by myself in a couple of years.

Eamon knew how to cut the pig up, section by section, piece by piece, because he was Dad's helper. Now, I'm his helper, and I can only pray to God that I can do this when it's my time. We carved the pig up completely, saving every part that could be eaten. We washed and salted each piece so that it would keep through the winter and spring, except for the heart, lungs, kidneys, and liver, which don't save well, salt or no salt—and these must be eaten first. We wasted almost nothing. Even the blood is used to make blood pudding, which is delicious but doesn't last very long. Some people use parts of a pig's intestines for food and some people even eat the brain, but we don't do this. We didn't use the head at all, we just buried it. Polly deserves some dignity.

We stored the heavily salted meat in a tea chest that Aunt Mary in Swinford gave us in return for a piece of Polly. Tea chests are great for this purpose, not really sturdy but strong enough, and lined on the inside with a waterproof metallic foil. These chests are used to transport tea from India. Aunt Mary then packs the tea in half-pound and one-pound packages for sale in her shop. Our sisters soon get over their anger. They still miss Polly but happily eat the pork and bacon that Polly provides. And I do too, and so does Eamon—and so does Mom.

CHAPTER 5

—— ❧ ——

TOM HORKAN WAS a bachelor who lived alone in a nice bungalow. He had a small shop by the Main Road at the far end of Culmore, just the Swinford side of Culmore School. Tom also had a farm of land and some cattle. He didn't like it one bit when someone showed up at the shop in the middle of the day, especially in the spring or summertime, to buy a half pound of tea or a couple of pounds of sugar or some cigarettes. No one gave up when there was no answer at Tom's door. They knew that he was probably down in one of the fields behind the house working, so naturally, the customer would just go find him. Sometimes, I was the unlucky customer having to do this, and had to put up with Tom's anger, leaving his work to return to his shop and sell me a package of Sweet Aftons for Mom. I didn't mind Tom giving out to me, saying that we had no respect for a man at work on his land and that we should do our shopping at Jimmy Greaneys in Swinford after Mass on Sunday like sensible people. By the time we got to the shop, he's himself again and I'm "Tommy Lougheran" again.

Tommy Lougheran was a boxer in America donkey's years ago, and Tom Horkan liked to call me that name. Sometimes he'd call me the Georgia Peach, though I was no Ty Cobb, and sometimes Young Stribling. Tom read everything he could get his hands on. Sometimes I would see American newspapers and magazines in a pile on the floor inside the shop door, but the date told me that they were weeks or months old. Not old for Tom, though, and he especially loved to read boxing magazines, whatever their age. He got these newspapers and magazines from relatives in America. He knew of every great boxer that ever was, and every great fight. He could describe, round by round, the world heavyweight championship fight between Gentleman Jim Corbett and John L. Sullivan in 1892, and between Gene Tunney and Jack Dempsey in 1926 and 1927, and between Joe Louis and Rocky Marciano in 1952.

Tom's shop was a meeting place at night for the lads of Culmore and Cloonaghboy, the next village over on the way to Swinford. While we were there we might have a penny toffee or a threepenny bar of Cadbury chocolate or a bottle of cidona or cola. The older lads might buy a package of Players or Sweet Aftons, or if they couldn't afford these brands, they'd get ten Woodbines, the cheapest cigarette there is. We regularly visited Tom Horkan's shop for the *craic*: to have fun, to tell jokes, to solve riddles, to talk about everything under the sun, including important things happening in faraway places.

Tom knew something about everything, and that was why I loved to visit his shop at night. Often he was like a schoolmaster: lecturing, scolding, encouraging, and always challenging us to use our brains more and make something of ourselves. If he'd had the opportunity when he was younger he might have been be a professor of history or politics or philosophy at some fine university. I learned more in his little shop than I did at school, and it was a lot more fun. More than anything he loved to tell stories. He said that we should pay attention because there was a lesson in every story, and maybe there was, but sometimes I just saw the humor and missed the lesson.

One night he told the story about a fishmonger in town who also had a shop that sold groceries and other stuff, including vegetable seeds. An old farmer who was a bit simpleminded came into the shop to buy turnip seeds, and instead of giving him turnip seeds, the fishmonger gave him dried herring eggs, which looked a lot like turnip seeds. The farmer went home and sowed the herring eggs. Later in the day, a neighbor of the old farmer overheard the fishmonger relating to a couple of townspeople the joke he had pulled on the daft farmer. It's a big joke and everyone laughed. The neighbor told his simpleminded friend what has happened. Together they decide to teach the mean-spirited and dishonest fishmonger a lesson. A couple of weeks later, the farmer rushed into the fishmonger's shop in a terrible state. He pleaded with the fishmonger to come with him back to the farm where something unbelievable is happening. Perplexed, the fishmonger drove out to the farm where, in the little garden behind the cottage, he sees row upon row of herring heads just beginning to break the surface of the ground. In complete terror, he runs from the farm, leaving his van behind.

I didn't really believe this story, but I liked it because, in the end, the country mug of a farmer came out on top.

In the spring we must spread out the turf, sod by sod, flat across the top of the bank and the lower cutaway ground where the bottom spits have been laid after cutting. After a few weeks of good weather, the turf will be *groiged*—four or five sods standing on one end and leaning together with another sod or two placed on top to anchor the others, repeated by the thousands. Standing turf will dry more quickly if there was good drying weather. If there wasn't good drying weather, it could be a cold winter. Nothing was as dismal or as uninviting as a fire with half-dried turf because we didn't get enough good drying weather.

Sometimes, even in good weather, it was a dicey proposition bringing turf out of the soft bog by ass and cart—and more than once I had the terrible experience of a capsize, the ass and cart turning completely upside down on a steep incline. The idea was to go over the incline at a slow, measured pace, holding back the cart with all your might, but if the donkey loses control of the pace and allows the cart to push him down the slope, the game would be over quickly as the cart capsized, turning the donkey, who's harnessed between the shafts, upside down too. This was the kind of entangled mess that no one would want to deal with. First was to make sure that the donkey was okay. If he's okay you must calm him down because at this point he is frantic, eyes wild and all four legs thrashing in the air. Then you must unbuckle the donkey from the upturned cart, talking to him gently every step, because he is trapped and terrified. After freeing the donkey, you must upright the cart, which meant removing the huge, heavy wheels and turning the body of the cart right side up. Then the almost impossible task, if you're alone, to reattach the wheels and reassemble the cart, then reload the scattered turf, and proceed on—and tell no one of this feck-up because it is you who didn't prevent the capsize.

Unfortunately, as was sometimes the case, a cart shaft is broken, bringing about a delay and an expense, both of which we could ill-afford. To replace the cart shaft costs about two pounds, which must be found somewhere—but a donkey's broken leg is far more serious. The donkey must be put down and a new donkey bought. The Gallaghers were lucky—broken carts but no broken donkeys. Still, I've unhitched terrified donkeys from an overturn, and it's taken a while to coax them into being a beast of burden again.

Each summer was hay-making time and later the harvest—cutting and saving the oats. The turf must be gathered, too, and taken out of the bog before the rain softens it too much. If the bog was too soft for donkey and cart, we would have to bag the turf out. This was a miserable job, filling old fertilizer bags with turf, sod by sod, and carrying them on our backs out of the bog and onto dry land where the cart could be used to haul the turf the half mile to the house. In a good growing year we'd be able to save about four acres of hay, which would feed seven cattle, plus Molly's replacement, through the winter months and into spring. It was not a sin to work at saving hay or oats on a Sunday. This was because God knew that we have to work like mad while the weather is good. I don't know why it was a sin to work in the bog saving turf on a Sunday, but it was.

One warm summer's evening, after a long day's work with the hay, most of the family was sitting outside by a field of freshly lapped hay. It was getting dark, and soon the cows would have to be milked, but there was a cool breeze, and we were all enjoying a brief rest, looking over our handiwork. This was a good time—a hard day's work done and no rain in sight. Mom was happily smoking a Sweet Afton. Suddenly we heard the drone of engines in the sky, but off in the distance toward the north. Angela quickly spotted the plane. We could see red and green lights flashing on and off. This was very unusual, for we could very rarely hear the sound of a plane overhead—they were just too high. In the past we never even saw any planes flying overhead to or from America. It was only with the Boeing 707 and DC-8 that we could see the jet trails across the sky on a clear day. Seeing these brand new jets was hugely exciting to us. Following the jet trail back to its origin, we could see the plane itself, small but visible, appearing silver in color, with swept-back wings and trails of white smoke streaming out from each wing.

Often I would fantasize about what it would be like to be on one of those planes, looking out the window at the world below. I wondered if I would be able to make out our small farm. Once in a while, I would think, what if one of these planes crashed into the bog near us? I knew of course that we would all be heroes, rescuing people from the wreckage. Saving lives would be our Christian duty—but we'd also have opportunities to help ourselves to whatever else was scattered around the crash area if it might be useful or valuable. Maybe this would be a mortal sin because it would be stealing, maybe even stealing from the dead, but I wouldn't mind, just once, Old Nick presenting me with the temptation so that I could then decide.

Now, as we watched the lights of the plane in the distance, we contemplated its fate. We knew it was flying lower than any other plane we had ever seen, and that could only mean one thing: it was in trouble. We watched the lights go back and forth and concluded that it was flying in a circle. Clearly, the plane was either looking for something or its steering apparatus was stuck, causing it to turn continuously. We all watched, each offering considered opinions as to what was happening up there. Only Mom was concerned about the fate of the people on board. After a while we agreed that it wasn't looking for something on the ground because in twilight there wouldn't be much on the ground that would be visible to the plane except maybe the lights of Charlestown and Swinford. Finally, the lights seemed to straighten out and turn toward the Ox Mountains, the long crest of which was still visible against the darkening sky. The noise grew fainter. Then, as we saw the lights merge with the Ox Mountains, the lights went out.

We watched in horror. The plane had crashed into the Ox Mountains, and we were probably the only people on the face of the earth to watch this tragedy unfold before our eyes. We all knelt down on the grassy ground and said a decade of the rosary for the poor souls who were lost on that unfortunate airplane. I didn't sleep all night. I wanted to hear the news of the tragedy next morning on Radio Eireann. But there was nothing—nothing! Not a single word about a plane crash in the Ox Mountains. After some thought we came to the inescapable conclusion that the Ox Mountains were intact, unmolested by flying objects. Obviously, we didn't tell anyone about this experience. As for me, I wasn't at all happy with the outcome. For a while there had been the possibility of great excitement—a plane crash. For weeks, maybe months, it would be the talk of the country. Instead, there was nothing: no endless news coverage on the radio, no newspapers full of pictures of the crash scene, no excitement, no fun, no nothing. I was so disappointed it took me two days before I was myself again.

Every morning the diesel train passed through at the end of our land on its way to Swinford and beyond. Every evening it passed in the other direction. There were also two daily luggage trains that traveled in each direction. That's four trains every day on a single track. The diesel was a passenger train: beautiful, long, glassy, green carriages, fast and elegant. In the wintertime when it got dark at 4:00 p.m., I sometimes went to the railway to watch the diesel zoom by. All the carriages were lit up, and I could see the people inside. They were reading newspapers, drinking tea or maybe even coffee, or sipping a hot whiskey. Some were looking out the window but probably couldn't see me there in the darkness, staring at them. They may have been thinking what a Godforsaken place this must be, with not a light to be seen, just blackness. I wondered who they were and where they were going. They flashed by me in a few moments, another world passing through mine without as much as a "Hello there, poor farmer."

I had never been on a train. I had never gone anywhere. The luggage trains weren't as exciting. They were pulled by a steam engine, pouring black smoke out of a black turret. They were mostly box carriages, but once in a while there would be a platform carriage with a motorcar sitting on the platform. When this happened everyone in the bog stopped working and stared at this strange sight, a car on a train, going to some buyer somewhere.

The seven-mile railway stretch between Charlestown and Swinford was maintained by two men who rode their bicycles along the narrow path that ran along each side of the track. These were Culmore men, neighbors: Jim Horkan, brother of Tom, my informal teacher; and Tom Tunney. They lived down Hull Road in a part of Culmore called Hull. Their job was to ensure that the track was always in good condition and safe for the trains. This meant making sure that the huge nuts and bolts that joined the rails together and the rails to the sleepers beneath were fully tightened and that the raised bed of crushed limestone supporting the track was staying intact. Because a fair length of railway between the two towns was built mostly on top of the bog, the ground underneath was soft, causing the railway bed to tremble, rising and falling in rapid succession, as the train thundered by.

Over time this motion would cause the limestone bed to lose stones as they were eventually shaken loose and fall down the sloped sides—and this alone could cause the track to become unstable. Far more serious was that the regular passage of trains in each direction on a rising and falling track stressed the rails to the point where nuts would begin to loosen at the joints. This situation is aggravated in the summertime when the rails heat up and expand during the day and then contract at night.

Jim and Tom's work was mostly inspection and doing maintenance that only requires hand tools. For bigger jobs more equipment and men were needed and sometimes we would see a strange contraption coming over the railway between train times. It was a flat platform on four wheels rolling along on the rails, being propelled by two men using levers, kind of like riding a bicycle, except instead of pedals they had levers. On the platform was the equipment they needed—and more men too if it was a big job like removing rails and sleepers to repair a section of the limestone bed, or replacing a damaged or rotting sleeper.

Beside the track was a sturdy wooden hut built with sleepers like the ones on which the rails were secured. We called it the "Green House" even though it was mostly black except for the roof. Jim and Tom used this hut to store their tools and take shelter in rain, sleet, snow, or frost. The hut also had a pot-bellied iron stove inside to provide heat in the wintertime and boil water for a nice pot of tea. How did I know all this? Because the hut was close to our land, and I knew where the key to the thick wooden door was hidden. It was just under the door, usually on one side or the other—and when Jim and Tom weren't around, I could use the hut for shelter too, or just because I was nosey.

The tools they used included sledgehammers, shovels, crowbars, and heavy, long-handled wrenches. I had often seen Jim and Tom working on the rails with these tools and knew exactly what they were for. The wrenches were to retighten the huge nuts that join the rails together, and the sledgehammers were to tighten or knock out and replace the turf-sod-sized wooden blocks that kept the rail lengths firmly in place from one rail connection to the next.

Looking at these tools one day, a fearful idea came into my mind. I could probably use these tools to loosen a rail and cause a derailment. I was both horrified and wildly excited just thinking about it. After a few moments, I noticed I was sweating. My mouth was dry and I had a queer, uneasy feeling in my belly like when I'm very scared or very anxious. I suddenly needed to get out of the hut and run like hell away from there. I did run away that day, but the terrible thought returned again and again until I knew that I had to do something about it. I had to see if

I could loosen a rail enough to make it wobbly enough to cause the diesel train to slide off the rails, bringing the cozy and secure world of those inside crashing into mine and stopping, eventually, in twisted, mangled wreckage.

One night a couple of weeks later, I returned to the hut. The sky was clear, the moon was rising, and there wasn't a soul within a mile. I found the key, unlocked the door, and went inside. I knew exactly where the two tools were that I would need. I wasn't sure if I would have the strength to loosen the big nuts, but I did. The huge lug wrench was about three feet long and heavy, providing just enough leverage for me to loosen a couple of the nuts on each end of a single rail length. The next step was just as easy, loosening a few of the wooden blocks with the sledgehammer. I didn't loosen all of the nuts on each end of the rail, or loosen all of the blocks on the rail length. I didn't have to. I *knew* now that it could be done and *it was dead easy.*

If I left things as they were at that moment, the next morning the fast diesel train might be in some danger of running off the rail but probably would not derail—but it surely would in a few days or a week as the track became increasingly unstable. I sat down on a sleeper, my heart pounding, and tried to visualize the horror that would quickly unfold if the diesel did slide off the rails. I began to get sick again, like the first time I thought about doing this. My stomach felt like someone took it in both hands and twisted it in opposite directions, like Mom does when she's squeezing water out of washed clothes.

I must fix the rail and no one would ever know of my act of lunacy. Panic struck again when I picked up the lug wrench to undo what I had done. What if I can't tighten the nuts sufficiently, I thought. What if a bolt breaks? What if I can't hammer in the blocks? God Almighty, what if I can't undo this? If not tomorrow morning, it would only be a question of time before the rail would give, and if Jim or Tom didn't quickly discover the loose rail, there would be a disaster. I knew that if I couldn't fix the rail, I'd have to run along the railway into Charlestown, wake up the stationmaster in the middle of the night, and tell him what I had done so that he could stop the train before it reached the Green House.

And then I would be handed over to the gardie, and my crime would be in all the newspapers in Ireland. I could just hear the news on Radio Eireann: "Good evening. This is Charles Mitchel reading the news. We begin in County Mayo, where a dreadful crime was perpetrated by a young boy, the unspeakable results of which were mercifully averted by his own guilty conscience…" My family would be disgraced and shamed forever and would have to leave Ireland, and I would be locked up for years—until I was deemed sane enough to be returned to civil society.

I did fix the rail and there were no mishaps. Using all my strength, I tightened the nuts, hammered in the loosened blocks, and returned the tools to the hut, being careful to put them exactly where I had found them. I locked the door and returned the key to its hiding place and went home. I did not close an eye for the rest of the night. Twice I got up—to return to the scene of the crime to make sure that the nuts and the blocks were as tight as they could possibly be. But I couldn't bring myself to return to the scene of my insanity attack. I never entered the hut again.

Next morning I stood in the middle of the Hill Field overlooking the railway five hundred yards away. I could hear my heart going thump, thump, thump. I was almost positive that everything would be okay, but there was still a terrible fear. Right on schedule I heard the piercing horn of the diesel as it approached Sonnagh Bridge a mile away. In less than a minute, it flashed by the Green House and seconds later our land. I stared at it until it went under the next bridge at Hull Road. It had never looked more beautiful. I was relieved beyond words.

C H A P T E R   6

❧

SEASONAL TASKS CAME and went. Harvest time. Eamon cuts the oats with the scythe and Mom follows behind, gathering the felled oats in sheaves. I follow behind Mom, tying each sheaf around the middle, in a way that only a farmer knows, with a thin strip taken from the sheaf. My sisters follow behind me, stooking—that is, standing the sheaves upright in groups of four and tying them together near the top with another strip. Here the oats will stay for a week or two, depending on the weather, until the grain dries out and hardens. Unfortunately, the crows and jackdaws and magpies and blackbirds—and just about every other winged creature that flies—don't wait for the oats to season. This is what they've been waiting for all summer. This is their harvest, too, and they will not be denied.

While the oats are growing, the birds can't get to them because to be able to pluck grain from standing oats, they would have to be able to eat on the wing, so they wait patiently, chattering noisily on the overhead electric wires and trees nearby, probably speculating as to the quality and quantity of the bounty below. When the field is cut and stoked, they will swoop down, land on top of the stook, and gobble up every grain they can find. We have tried scarecrows, but scarecrows are a joke. They serve only one purpose: to provide the birds a place to rest after they've eaten a bellyful of oats, while they wait to make room for more. Whatever the birds have left us we will stack in the hay garden—which, for us, is the hay and straw garden, the straw being what's left after the grain has been removed.

In the fall the potatoes must be dug out of the ridges and placed in pits and, before winter, covered with a foot-thick layer of soil to keep them from frostbite. If they get frostbitten, they are worthless and cannot be eaten. Blight can also attack the potatoes while they're still growing, and even though we spray the stalks with chemicals to prevent the blight, we are not always successful. Sometimes the potatoes look perfect when we are putting them into the pit, but they may be already infected. We find out a few weeks or months later. Touching a fully infected potato is a memorable experience. I could feel my hand sinking into rotting pulp and the smell hits my face. It is, I imagine, like thrusting your hand accidentally into the guts of a plump, dead rat that has been in this unhappy condition for some time.

Everyone in Ireland knows that the Great Famine was caused by the potato blight and England's horrific indifference to it. I don't know for sure if England made a bad thing worse or not, but I do know that one of the few things the people can agree on is that John Bull is responsible for just about every misfortune to befall dear old Ireland. It doesn't matter one bit, thank you, that half the fathers in the West of Ireland are across the pond in England earning money to keep families from going hungry or winding up in the County Home, blight or no blight.

Fall is also the threshing time. A *thrasher* comes around from village to village, and we find out for sure how much oats the birds of the air have left us. The grain is bagged and placed in the barn where the next battle is to try to save what the birds have left us from the rats and mice that are also waiting patiently for their turn. At Mass and at school, we heard that greed and gluttony are mortal sins and that God provides for all, including the birds of the air and the rats and mice hiding in our barns. He provides for them by giving them a fair helping of our oats. What's left over He provides to us.

Wintertime is the least hectic, without much heavy work to be done on the land. Eamon cuts hay from the stacks in the hay garden, and I help him put the hay in the barn so that it is easier to feed it to the cattle when the fields are bare. Periodically, we have to open the potato and turnip pits to bring supplies into the house. When the pits are completely frozen, it takes ages to break through the rock solid soil—and every time we pray that the frost has not reached the potatoes or turnips. If it has and we try to cook them, the smell will drive us from the house. Eamon and I repair fences and do the things that need to be done all year round, like cleaning the cow muck out of the barns every day and milking the cows every morning and evening—unless they're "in-calf," in which case they have no milk to give.

We all learn how to milk the cows, but Mom and Eamon do most of the milking because they can coax the cows to give all the milk they have. Sometimes you think you've milked a cow completely, but you haven't and she's just holding back. Sometimes a young heifer can be very hard to milk because her tits are still small and your hands keep slipping off them. Or a cow's tits can be cut and bleeding because she went over a barbed-wire fence or she might have gone through some bushes or whins. She must still be milked, and that was definitely a job for Mom or Eamon. A swift kick from an angry cow could send me and the bucket and the stool flying.

Often, When Eamon was milking in the evening and it was dark and I'm standing there holding the flashlight or a lantern, we'd sing songs. The cows didn't seem to mind and sometimes they would start lowing softly, kind of in harmony, when we sang Elvis Presley and Buddy Holly songs. When we sang Irish rebel songs, they didn't participate at all. I reckon the cows could tell that Irish songs were sad. Eamon liked to squirt milk from the cow's tits right into my mouth. He said this was the freshest milk I'll ever get. Mostly he misses though, and I end up wet. When all three cows were in-calf at the same time, there was no milk. When we had no milk from the cows, we bought condensed milk in a can that tasted awful. We didn't drink it as we would regular milk and used it only for our tea.

When we were sick of condensed milk, we'd sometimes buy real milk from the Peytons, our nearby neighbors in Madogue. They had lots of cows and sold milk to the townspeople in Charlestown. It was my job to go to the Peytons' with my big, brown Bulmer's bottle. I would sit and wait in the kitchen while the Peyton boys were milking the cows and their mother, Maggie, was bottling the milk in the scullery in back. While I waited, I enjoyed a mug of tea that one of the girls usually made for me—if they were home. I know that their mother didn't charge us the full price for the milk, and when I didn't have the shilling, Maggie Peyton didn't ask for it. It's was our secret.

Christmas was a happy time for us, not just because it was Jesus's birthday but also because we all got to eat practically as much as we wanted. This was as close as we ever got to committing the sin of gluttony. Mom said that this was a "feast in a famine" and, therefore, not a sin. On Christmas Eve we'd have our high tea in the late afternoon, about 6:00 p.m. There was raisin bread with caraway seeds, and there would be strawberry jam and thick, fruity marmalade, some Galtee cheese, and maybe even a little sliced ham from Morrisroes. Our Santa Claus was Uncle Tom and Aunt Nellie in Philadelphia. Santa didn't always come, but he came most of the time. Uncle Tom and Aunt Nellie knew how many of us there were, and when they could they'd fill up a box with toys and send it over the ocean to us a few weeks before Christmas. None of us had ever met Uncle Tom or Aunt Nellie, not even Mom, but they were very special to us. Because of them Santa Claus visited our chimney more often than not at Christmastime, bringing us enough presents for all to share.

Our presents weren't just toys like little music boxes, racecars, dolls, and brightly colored bouncing balls; they also included clothes, shoes, and pencils and notebooks for school. Aunt Nellie didn't worry about clothes size or shoe size—she knew that whatever size it is, it was going to fit someone. They wrote letters to Mom and sometimes slipped in a ten-dollar bill. They treated us like family because Mom was Eddie's wife and we were Eddie's children. Eddie was Tom's younger brother, and from their letters we knew that Eddie was very dear to them. Dad had lived with them when he was in America during the Depression. We had a good idea of whether Santa was going to come or not because we usually knew if Jim McNicholas, our postman, had quietly delivered a parcel from America. Jim McNicholas knew everyone's business, and he kept it to himself. If Santa wasn't going to come, we weren't too disappointed because we already knew.

Christmas was also the time of the year when we heard from other relations. Mom's sisters in New York—Aunt Jo, Aunt Ann, and Aunt Eileen—never forgot to send a Christmas card, usually with a letter inside telling us all the news, and sometimes there would be a five- or ten-dollar bill tucked inside too. We had another Aunt Jo in New York. She was Uncle Pat's wife, and Uncle Pat was Mom's brother—and even though she was not related to us by blood, she wrote to Mom regularly and, once in a while, slippped in a little money. Uncle Pat and Aunt Jo and their daughter, Peggy, visited Ireland once and came to see us. We were thrilled. They were real Yanks, friendly and kind – no airs and graces. Uncle Pat walked every foot of the farm in Culmore. I walked with him, but he didn't say much. He looked so sad, and I didn't know if I should say something or just be quiet.

He stopped for a while at the cow barn, and that's when I saw the tears. This was the house where he was born and raised, and like Dad's place in Madogue, had a similar simple design. The middle section, once the kitchen, was now a flag-stoned passageway. The larger bedroom of long ago now had four stalls, one for each of our cows and one for a promising cow—a young heifer. The smaller room at the other end was now the shed for the cart. Two other buildings rounded out the cluster, the original cow barn of Uncle Pat's time, now used to house our few bullocks in the wintertime. A loft overhead was used then and now to store farm tools and hay. The smallest barn was the henhouse. I could only imagine the memories flooding Uncle Pat's mind as he gazed at these places and scenes of his childhood. Their daughter, Peggy, had the time of her life, running through the fields and chasing calves and chickens.

For Mom and Uncle Pat, the yanks' visit was a very special time. They had not seen each other in almost thirty-seven years, since Pat left Ireland for America at the age of seventeen when Mom was seven years old. They had little memory of each other. He told us about putting a few possessions in a cloth bag and strapping it over his shoulder. He walked and hitchhiked the one hundred and ninety miles to Queenstown in Cork. Sometimes he would get a ride for a mile or two in a horse and cart, sometimes in a jaunting car, and once in a while in a real motorcar. At Queenstown he boarded a ship to New York, traveling steerage class—"In the bowels of the ship," as he said. His journey to Queenstown was the biggest adventure of his life, but he knew that ahead of him lay a much bigger adventure and a bigger challenge than even he had anticipated.

Way off in the distance was the Statue of Liberty in New York harbor. Uncle Pat told me of the incredible experience of passing Lady Liberty, all passengers on all decks, laughing, crying, and waving—some almost hysterical at the prospect of coming ashore in the most prosperous and freedom-loving land on the face of God's earth, and some in fearful silence, dreading the medical inspection that they would face at Ellis Island, where they would either pass or fail. Those who passed the test had all of their dreams intact and now just needed time and hard work to make them come true. Those who failed had no more dreams. They were returned to the misery and poverty they had hoped to leave behind forever. Some failed but most passed, including Uncle Pat.

A few years after Uncle Pat arrived in the "land of milk and honey," the Roaring Twenties came to a shattering end with the stock market crash in October 1929 and later the onset of the Great Depression. The Depression brought harder times than my uncle had ever seen in Ireland. On the streets of New York, he saw respectable men in suits, wearing shirts and ties, begging for money to buy food for hungry children at home. Like my father, Uncle Pat also saw signs that said, "No Irish Need Apply," and, like my father, they didn't slow him down a bit. He was rarely unemployed through the Depression, doing jobs so menial that he couldn't even talk about them, telling me so many years later that anything was better than being in the soup line. His Irish pride wouldn't let him do it. He told me that he didn't leave hard times in Ireland to get in a soup line in America.

No matter how much or how little money we got, at Christmas or any other time, it always went for necessities. Luxuries were things we saw advertised in magazines and newspapers and could only dream about having one day—things like a gas cooker, or a refrigerator, or a clothes washer. We didn't save any money, and we never had any reason to go into a bank. I did go into the bank in Swinford one time, but I had no business there. It was the Fair Day, and I had helped a neighbor walk a bullock the three and a half miles to town so that he might be sold on the town square where most livestock are sold.

The Fair Day in Swinford was the first Wednesday of each month, and the Fair Day in Charlestown was the first Thursday of each month. So if you have no luck selling your pig or heifer in Swinford, you could try Charlestown the next day, but couldn't count on having too much luck there either because the Charlestown fair was almost never as well attended as Swinford and the deals weren't as good. What you were guaranteed at each was a very messy town square, and God help you if you had the bad luck to slip on all that cow shit because you couldn't just go home and change your clothes. When you saw an otherwise respectable farmer or cattle jobber covered in muck from head to foot and completely ignoring it, you knew what happened.

On this occasion I was helping a neighbor, Jim O'Reilly, bring his two-year-old bullock to the fair for sale. It was a hard walk to Swinford with a wild bullock who was desperately trying, at every opportunity, to turn around and return to his own family—even if he had been disowned for losing his balls. Near the town the jobbers were already coming out to meet us, to make the quick, easy deal, but O'Reilly wasn't having any of it. The jobbers wanted to do the deal before we got to the square, where there would be more competition, especially for a good-looking, well-fed bullock like O'Reilly's. We made our way slowly to the square. There were several more offers along the way, but O'Reilly sticks to his price:

forty-five pounds and not a bob less. When a bargain looked in the making, a crowd gathered around, some on the jobber's side—or pretending to be on the jobber's side—and others on O'Reilly's side, or pretending to be on O'Reilly's side. The to and fro continues:

"You're offerin' me forty pounds for this fine bullock. Look at his belly, will you? Sure he's eaten more than forty pounds worth of grass and hay, and the mash too."

"I'll give you forty-one pounds and that, sur, is me final offer."

"Now, now, don't walk away like that," says an onlooker. "There's only a couple of pounds between ye. Now, sur, will you take forty-two pounds and be done with it?"

The bargain was made at forty-two pounds, and the jobber and O'Reilly spat in their palms and shake hands to seal the deal. In keeping with custom, the jobber gave O'Reilly a half a crown "lucks money," and with his blackthorn stick put his mark on the bullock's back with cow muck from the street—which was getting muckier and pissier and smellier by the minute. I'd have hated to be one of the street cleaners who'd have to clean up this sea of piss and shit after the fair. O'Reilly paid me ten bob for helping him and, even with the walk to Swinford and then back home, it was an easy ten bob for half a day's work. The bullock was taken away to someone's back yard, which the jobber was using as a holding pen for the cattle he's buying. When all the dealing was done and the fair over, the jobber would load his cattle on a lorry and take them to God knows where. He may have kept some for a month or two to fatten them up some more on land that he owned or rented, but sooner or later most would be shipped to England. A small few would have the honor of dying for Ireland and wind up on Irish dinner tables rather than English ones.

O'Reilly needed to deposit the proceeds of the sale into his bank account, and he asked me to go along with him for company—or to let me see that, unlike most farmers, he had a bank account. This was a whole new experience for me. We had never put money into the bank, and whenever we sold a heifer or a bullock, it was because we had so many bills to pay that they had be paid down or we wouldn't have any credit left in town. Next to the church, the Bank of Ireland was the most impressive place I had ever seen: mahogany, brass, and marble all over and self-important tellers secure behind glass walls with little openings so that they could take your money. O'Reilly removed his hat and cautiously approached a teller. I saw two other men come into the bank, and their voices immediately dropped to a whisper like they'd just entered the church for Mass or confessions. It occurred to me that maybe this was the way you're supposed to behave in a bank.

Still, I was surprised that O'Reilly, a kind and comfortably well-off old man, was so meek before the teller, a woman of about twenty to my reckoning. Here he is, depositing more than forty pounds in the bank, for which he would receive a modest interest of maybe 2.5 percent per annum. (We had learned about interest rates in school and how to calculate simple interest and compound interest. Apart from that, all I knew was that banks charged a lot more to loan you money than they paid you to loan them money.) The teller showed little respect for O'Reilly, looking disdainfully at the dirty banknotes, then back at him like he's a tinker instead of a customer loaning the bank money. Of course she ignored me completely. There she was looking down on him like she's the cat's meow. And why did he accept this treatment, hat in hand, looking down at the floor? She was probably from the country herself, blessed with having had the opportunity to complete her five years at the convent school and was now lording over her own people. I decided then and there that I didn't like banks.

Dad's weekly seven pounds, and the occasional extra dollars from America, helped us to catch up a little bit. I was always happy when we could pay down our debt in town. For a while I'd feel better about going into Charlestown, where we do most of our shopping. The extra money from relatives at Christmas meant celebrating the birth of Jesus the way we see in Christmas cards: jolly, laughing rich people seated around a fancy table feasting on huge legs of lamb and roast beef, surrounded by mistletoe and holly. Well, maybe not exactly like the happy picture in the Christmas cards, but at least we could look forward to Christmas Dinner after Mass on Christmas Day. There would be a roast goose or turkey, roasted potatoes, peas and carrots, Mom's delicious stuffing, and for dessert, Bird's custard and jelly. We got to repeat the feast again on Small Christmas Eve with high tea on the fifth of January and a big dinner after Mass the next day. Then we were back to much leaner times and not much to look forward to for months.

CHAPTER 7

WE WEREN'T ABLE to replace Molly with another pony. Horses were expensive to buy, asses not so much, so we bought a donkey instead. On his annual pilgrimage home from England, Dad bought us a second-hand ass and a second-hand ass cart to go with him. Molly's cart was stored in Dad's old house in Madogue because it was too big for a donkey, especially this puny excuse for a donkey. The ass my father bought was the worst ass in Ireland. Mom said the ass jobber saw Dad coming. After Molly, it was hard to like the ass anyway, but he could have made it easier. He could at least try to take Molly's place, but he didn't. He was as clever as he was lazy. We gave him no name because he didn't deserve a name. He was the no-name ass. That first day we tackled him up for a trip into Charlestown, we were hoping for the best with our untried donkey. All the way into town, he walked slowly, head hanging low. He would not run and he would not hold his head up like any self-respecting animal. The worst part was in town when his lazy walk slows to a crawl. People asked, "What's wrong with your ass?" Eamon stared straight ahead, and my face got hot and redder than its usual unhappy state.

We went down Church Street, me leading but mostly pulling no-name by the bridle. Eamon sat in the cart facing backwards. We had a stick in the cart, but we can't hit the ass going down the middle of Church Street. The ass knew this, of course. Hitting no-name would be shameful, and people would feel sorry for the ass and say that we were no better than the tinkers who are well known for beating their asses and ponies. Soon, we found a way to ease the embarrassment. Just below the church, we turned left by Henry's chemist shop and sneaked down the back way, behind all the shops and houses that front on Church Street. We had to come out when we reached the river, turning right up by Eamon O Hara's, painfully pulling both ass and cart over the bridge. Then we turned left down by Jim Phillips's and again sneaked down the back way to Joe Mahon's.

If going into town with this sorry excuse for an ass was embarrassing, coming out of town was absolutely mortifying. With bags of flour and pollard and bran and yellow meal and groceries in the cart, we dreaded our exit. I remembered seeing in the cowboy pictures the rancher coming into town for supplies. The cowboy is riding high on the buckboard of a big, four-wheeled wagon, being pulled by two magnificent horses. He hits town at a gallop, then slows and pulls up to the general store, where he steps down, looking proud and prosperous, hat pushed back a little on his head. Handsome and tanned, he had nothing to be embarrassed about. When he strolls easily into the store to buy his supplies, he's able to take out his money right then and there and pay for them—not like Eamon and me, where we have to ask Joe Mahon to mark it down. That's what Eamon says after Joe Mahon has loaded the cart and Mrs. Mahon has filled up bags of groceries: "Mark it down, please." The Mahons were saints; they never complained. Once in a while they'd ask if Mom could pay down our debt a little. And once in a while we can—when we had a bullock or heifer reasonably ready for sale.

We used to do most of our shopping at Baby Chuumer's in Church Street, but Baby told Mom one day that she couldn't just keep marking it down, that she had to pay her bills too. From then on, she said, it would be strictly cash and carry—no more credit. When Eamon was born, Mom took out a life insurance policy on him. The insurance man, Jim Foy, came to our house once a month to collect ten shillings. Often we went without to make sure we had the ten bob for Mr. Foy. When Eamon turned fifteen, the policy was paid up and we received the incredible sum of one hundred pounds. Much of the money went to pay off our debt to Baby Chuumer, and we never shopped there again.

We started shopping at Joe Mahon's, and the debt started piling up again. "Mark it down, please." I didn't want to live this way. Why couldn't I have been born in 1886 in Montana or Texas, where people have ranches as big as Mayo and thousands of head of cattle and horses to ride on and pull wagons at a gallop? Between Dad's place in Madogue and Mom's place in Culmore, we had about twenty acres of land, much of it not worth the time of day. On it we had a few head of hungry cattle and a half-dead ass who felt that it was perfectly all right that my brother and I should pull the cart ourselves. Jesus! There had to be a better way to live.

I felt ashamed standing in front of Mrs. Mahon as she gathered the groceries we needed and placed them on the counter, and wrote each item down on a pad: sugar, tea, a loaf of bread, salt, maybe a pound of sausages, and some black pudding—if I could muster up the courage to ask for these extras. Mrs. Mahon added up the bill in her head, column by column, first the pence, then the shillings, then the pounds column—if the shillings went over twenty, as they often do. At this point Mrs. Mahon would look at me expectantly and I would either have the money or utter the terrible words, making sure to clear my throat first: "Mark it down, please." Once in a while, I was able to tell her that we would be selling a bullock or heifer at the next fair in Swinford, and this always had the desired effect of brightening her spirits. She knew that we would then pay down the bill—not pay it off but at least pay it down. I knew that like Baby Chuumer the Mahons' also had bills to pay, to stock the shop and the storage sheds out back and just to live.

Not being able to pay our way in the world made me feel like a beggar, not much better than the tinkers who begged from door to door in the towns and villages. The Wards and McDonaghs were the two big tinker families in our area, so big we reckoned that they must have included first cousins and second cousins and maybe even third cousins, all together in their caravans and tents. I know for sure that they didn't feel any shame in begging and stealing, and since we would pay off our debts when things were finally getting better and staying better, we were not like the tinkers, whose circumstances never seemed to improve—or so they were quick to impress upon us.

When you thought not having the money to pay for groceries couldn't possibly get any more embarrassing, it got more embarrassing. I wasn't always lucky enough to have Joe or Mrs. Mahon attend to me in the shop. They knew that it is mostly a hit or miss as to whether I had money in my pocket, but the first time I encountered their daughter, Pauline, I practically panicked. I was fourteen and she was maybe a year or two older and there she was behind the counter by herself, pretty and different in that special kind of way that a young lad is happily beginning to notice—but for me, a bit shy and awkward in this coming awareness.

My face rapidly heating up to furnace temperature, I mangled the simple words: "Mark it down, please." She didn't understand and is embarrassed—which made me even more uncomfortable. I uttered the hateful words again. After ages she blurted out, "I'll have to ask Mammy." A few moments later, she returned and says, almost with pity, "Ah, sure, that'll be all right." It wasn't all right. It would never be all right—until we were debt-free. When we were debt-free, I would be anyone's equal; I would be everyone's equal. It would be, I imagined, like being let out of prison. I would ride my bike down Church Street in Charlestown with my head high. I would fear no one. I could look anyone in the eye because we will owe nothing to anyone. We'll be paying our own way in the world.

There was no problem coming up the back way from Mahon's. A few good whacks of the stick and no-name takes off, full of gusto and brimming with energy. Then we came out onto the street by Jim Phillips' Imperial Hotel and started over the bridge. We didn't get very far before the ass realizes that he was out in full view of Charlestown, at the single best location for everyone to see him from all directions. He lay down on the bridge, the two shafts of the cart scraping into the pavement. This was mortal embarrassment. I wanted to leave the scene and deny any connection with it. Eamon cursed Dad for buying this worthless animal. People came closer, laughing and making jokes, then moving on. People we knew didn't come closer because they were afraid we'd ask them to help us get no-name on his miserable feet. We lifted the shafts off the street while saying politely, "Get up, ass; please get up." Eamon gave him an acceptably gentle little kick to get his attention. Nothing doing. He was the town celebrity and in ass heaven.

I looked up Church Street and wanted to die. Coming down toward us, on both sidewalks, in little clusters of twos and threes and fours, were the schoolgirls from the Marist Convent secondary school. "Jesus Christ," says Eamon, "this can't get any feckin' worse." There was only one thing for it: total denial. We are not associated in any way with this pathetic scene. We just happened to be crossing the bridge at the time and now, if you don't mind, we'll just tarry awhile and enjoy the serenity of the babbling brook flowing gently under the bridge while someone's ass rests on his belly beside us. The girls were approaching, giggling and laughing and pointing at us. We ignored them. What do they know about serenity?

After what seemed like years, the schoolgirls pass, and we reclaimed ownership of the thing in the street. We decided to unhitch the cart from the ass and back it away. We were proceeding nicely with this when Guard Flaherty arrived on the scene. He knew Eamon, and he didn't like him. It was Guard Flaherty's job, in addition to his regular garda duties, to see that children went to school. Eamon missed a lot of school and got on Guard Flaherty's list. He hadn't forgotten, nor had he forgotten that Eamon wasn't afraid of him.

"What's your feckin' ass doin' lyin' in the street?" Guard Flaherty asked.

"Takin' a rest," Eamon says, "An' he's not my feckin' ass."

"Who's feckin' ass is he?"

"He's Tommy's feckin' ass."

"Who's Tommy?"

"I'm Tommy," I say.

Guard Flaherty turns back to Eamon. "Are you blackguarding me?

71

I know who you are, Gollaher, an' I know where you're from."

"I know who you are an' I know where you're from too," says Eamon.

"Get your feckin' ass and cart off this bridge; you're inthurferin' with thuraffic."

"Will you give us a hand?" asked Eamon.

"I'll give you the back of my hand across your smart aleck mouth, so I will."

Back in Montana, the rancher might also have encountered the law but it would have been an entirely different kind of experience:

"Afternoon, Mr. Buckley."

"Howdy, Marshal."

"In for your monthly supplies, I see."

"Yup, but I need to get back pronto. Just picked me up an extra two hundred fifty acres near the north slope. Gotta be fenced."

"You got a good foreman in Hayes; he'll handle it."

"Yeah."

"How's Mrs. Buckley and the family?"

"Fine, Marshal, just fine. And your family is well, I hope."

"Indeed they are, Mr. Buckley. Thank you."

"Well, have a good day, Mr. Buckley."

"You too, Sam."

Guard Flaherty, face flushed with anger, walked away, and we got back to the thing in the street. Mercifully, after we backed the cart off of the ass, we were able to get him to his feet. I don't believe this: there was nothing wrong with him and we had to lift him up onto his feet. I begged God to kill this memory, to wipe it from my brain forever. We connected ass and cart again and gently coaxed no-name over the bridge and down the back way by O'Hara's shop. We knew and no-name knew that there would be no trouble moving quickly along the back way, where we could apply a little corporal punishment. But we still had to come back out onto Church Street up by Henry's chemist shop. "God, I don't ask you for much," says Eamon, "but I'm asking you now, God: please get us out of this friggin' town without any more shame." We did get out of town, me pulling no-name by his bridle and Eamon pulling alongside by the front crossbar. It was black dark when we got home, and I never, ever, ever wanted to do this again.

But I did—and worse, I had to do it alone. Eamon swore to God on High that he would never again be seen, dead or alive, anywhere near this worthless ass when there was the slightest chance that he may be seen by townspeople, passing motorists, and especially young ladies from the Marist Convent secondary school. It was torture for me going into town with no-name. I wanted to wear a mask or a cover my head and face, pretending to have some highly contagious illness. I saw other farmers going through town in horse and cart, mule and cart, even ass and cart, all riding comfortably in the cart, practically like the Montana rancher. I saw Sean Kenny, my neighbor, sitting on top of a high load of turf that he was going to sell to someone in town. Sean's horse, Jack, was practically trotting. I was walking in front of no-name, pulling him by the bridle and trying to keep his nose off the pavement. Sean Kenny says, "Mandear! Tommy, that's the laziest ass I ever saw."

I was terrified that No-name would lie down in the street in front of the church. He had come to a standstill by Tom Tripp's and seemed to be seriously considering this. As we hadn't reached the back-way entrance by Henry's chemist shop yet, I couldn't use the stick in the cart. No-name dropped to his knees, the first step in a lie-down. He didn't even have the excuse of a loaded cart; we were still on our way into town, for God's sake. Now he was on his knees. He wouldn't lie down and wouldn't get up. One of the Caseys asks if my ass might be praying because we're in front of the church. "He is praying because he knows that I'm going to kill him," I said.

And I was deadly serious. At this moment I wanted to kill him more than I wanted to live. I wanted to run into Tom Tripp's and grab the biggest butcher knife I could lay my hands on. I wanted to decapitate no-name right there in the street in front of the church. I wanted to hack him to pieces. I was past rage. There was a fury inside of me, and I was afraid of what I might do. I cursed Eamon for not being here to share my humiliation. I cursed the church for looking on in silent, mocking grandeur. If Joe Morris, the church caretaker, was around, he could ring the bell and bring all to see this sorry spectacle. I cursed the world for being the miserable way it is. Another passerby offered his considered opinion that my ass may be kneeling in remembrance of the many bullocks slaughtered by Tom Tripp out behind the shop.

That's it! Suddenly, the rage was gone. It burst like a bubble of soapy water, and I felt it draining out of me. I wanted to laugh and cry at the same time. I sat down on the sidewalk and laughed out loud, no longer caring about anything. I looked at this silly scene in front of me: an ass, tackled and with an empty cart behind him, kneeling in the street between a church and a butcher shop/slaughter house. I got up and went over to No-name and lifted up the cart by the shaft. Half laughing and half crying, I say, "Get up, ass; please just get up." No-name looked at me with those big, sad, dumb eyes and got up with no more fuss, and we headed for Joe Mahon's through the back ways of Charlestown.

No-name would lie down again, in town and out of town, with an empty cart and a full cart. He would lie down on our farm, on potato ridges, and in fields, on boreens and in the bog—where gathering the turf and bringing it home is my paid-in-full penance in Purgatory. He would kneel on his knees sometimes, and sometimes he would lie on his belly. I did not know what he was thinking or why he was doing this. He did not seem to know or care that it was improper and indecent and shameful for an animal to lie down under harness. No-name taught me humility on a scale that would even embarrass Pope John XXIII, the only real saint in the Catholic Church, according to Mom.

I almost felt like becoming a priest – for every schoolgirl between the two towns had seen me in situations demanding either suicide or the priesthood. Eamon decided that we must get rid of this ass and I was grateful because, after all, I was the one who'd been robbed of his self-respect. Sometimes in the quiet of night I wondered why this lazy ass behaved as he did. I was afraid that he knew more than we did, that he was laughing at us and maybe grieving for us too. Eamon gave him to the tinkers for the princely sum of one pound and he called this luck's money: good luck for him, bad luck for the tinkers, he says.

Now we needed another ass. We sold a yearling heifer at the Fair Day in Swinford for twenty-eight pounds, and the same day Eamon bought a new ass for eight pounds. The balance paid down our debt at Mahon's and bought food, Wellingtons, and clothes. Someone in the family always needed Wellingtons, and often it was me. I hated Wellingtons. They weren't too bad when I had long, wooly socks that come up to just below my knees, held in place with elastic bands that you could buy. Then the Wellingtons wouldn't rub against my bare legs until they were red and sore and ready to bleed. Mostly I didn't have elastic bands because mostly I didn't have long socks. When my legs got too sore from the Wellingtons rubbing against them, I'd roll down the tops, and this helped a little until a new ring of soreness developed at the point where they had been rolled down to. Then I would roll the Wellington tops up a bit or down a bit or so that no spot got too sore.

I didn't like Wellingtons and I didn't like corduroy trousers because they both immediately identified you to all but American tourists as an agricultural lad. And they both quickly gave up the struggle with farm work. In no time at all, the Wellingtons would be ripped, torn, and leaking. Corduroy trousers, like Wellingtons, didn't last long. The once-soft, brown velvet-like rows of fabric were soon threadbare with knees sticking through. I preferred blue jeans because they didn't say, "Hello there, I'm occupied by a poor farmer"—at least when they were new and still clean. They didn't last long either, though, and I figured it was because they were probably made in Ireland and not in America where blue jeans were invented. I'm sure our Corduroy trousers were made in Ireland too, as well as the useless Wellingtons.

Tom Gallagher

In school we were constantly reminded to "Speak Irish, Buy Irish, Be Irish." On Radio Eireann we heard the same thing over and over—even admonishing us over the airwaves at the close of a program sponsored by Walton's Music Shop in Dublin, "And if you feel like singing, do sing an Irish song." I wondered why we were always being told this when anyone who wasn't a complete *eejit* knew that we had no choice in the matter anyway. In school we had to learn Irish. We bought Irish because that's mostly all there was to buy and we certainly couldn't change the fact that we were Irish. I knew from school and from the radio that we exported our best things: linens, whiskey, crystal, racehorses, cattle, tweeds, wool, and people. We were told in school that we should be very proud of this—that our linens and tweeds, our racehorses and Waterford Crystal are highly prized abroad. I'm sure that there are people in Ireland who benefit from all this exporting. Maybe we do too, like when we sell a bullock at the fair and he ends up on an English dinner table.

We also exported foods like butter. Jimmy told us that Irish creamery butter sells in Birmingham for much less than it sells for in Ireland. He said this was because Irish butter sold in England must compete with English and French butter, but in Ireland, because of high import tariffs and endless reminders to only buy things that are made in Ireland, there was little or no competition, so we paid four shillings and nine pence a pound for butter made in Ireland while the English, who were far better off than we were, bought the same pound of butter for three shillings on the other side of the Irish Sea. And it wasn't just butter. The government set the price for most of the foods we bought, plus cigarettes and alcohol. The result was that we had very limited choice in what we could buy, and we never saw Fianna Fail reduce the price of anything. We paid high prices for almost everything and, apart from food, most things we could afford to buy weren't worth a fiddler's fart. Buy Irish, my arse, I wanted to say. I'll buy Irish when it's made as well as it's made in England or Germany or America and is priced the same too.

Our new ass was a big, powerful-looking male, a jack like No-name, but there the resemblance ended. He was almost as big as a mule, and I was happy and grateful. This ass deserved a name, and Eamon named him Coco. Coco was fast and he was willing. He practically didn't know how to walk. He wanted to run and gallop all the time, whether he was pulling a cart or not. When Eamon or I rode on him, he'd go like a bat out of hell. There had better be no fence or barbed-wire gate in the way because Coco would either go through it or over it, but not stop simply because it was there. More than once I had to hurl myself off his back a second or two before he crashed through an obstacle, like a wire fence, that didn't get out of his way. If No-name was clever and lazy, Coco was neither. He was just all heart and seemed to have no brains at all. At least that's what I thought in those blissful early months. Eamon decided that it was okay for him to be seen in town with Coco and was especially pleased when someone complimented him on Coco's liveliness, quickly offering that he bought Coco himself.

No more back ways for us. We went down Church Street at full throttle, pulling back on the reins like a charioteer in ancient Rome. Once we passed Henry's chemist shop so fast that I could barely read the letters MPSI by the shop's name. I asked Eamon what MPSI stood for and he let me in on the secret. He said that MPSI stands for "Monkey's Piss Sold Inside" but that Henry's couldn't put the words up there because some people would be insulted. He told me that monkey's piss had magical healing powers, that you could even pour a tiny drop on an open wound—and, boy, I had these all the time—and it would close up almost right away. He said you could drink it too for all kinds of internal problems like the flu or even TB. But by far the best way to take it, he said, was to boil it and inhale the steam coming out of the kettle snout. He said that this cured just about any kind of sickness you had and gave you a rare good feeling too. I didn't know how much of this to believe, but he blessed himself and swore on a pretend Bible that it was true.

One day in town, he told me that he needed a pint of monkey's piss because he said he was now old enough to take the cure. Across the street from Joe Mahon's and up a bit was Luke Colleran's chemist shop, and it too has the letters MPSI beside the name. Eamon gave me a shilling and told me to go into Collerans and get him a pint of monkey's piss. He said that I should just go in and ask Luke Colleran for a pint of monkey's piss and that if there were other customers there I should ask Luke quietly, kind of like only he and I knew about this. I didn't want to do it, but I knew that if I didn't I'll get belted, so in I went. Oh shit! Immediately there was a problem. Luke wasn't behind the counter. His daughter, Margaret, a scholar at the Marist Convent, was there in his place. She was pretty and had lovely fair hair and there was no way I could ask her for a pint of monkey's piss for my brother. Just looking at her, I could feel the blood rushing to my face. With a big smile she asked, "Can I help you?"

"No, thanks; I'm just lookin'."

She looked confused. "Do you know what you're looking for?" she says.

"Yes I do," I reply. "I'm lookin' for MPSI."

Jesus! My face is getting redder and hotter. Now she looked totally confused.

I try winking to see if she'll get the idea.

"Are you looking for something for your eye?" she asked.

Without answering I walked out, mortified. I told Eamon what happened, and he said that I was a real feckin' *amadan* to believe a cock-n-bull story like that about MPSI. Then he demanded his shilling back. Eamon could be a real bastard sometimes. The embarrassment I had just endured was worth a lot more than a bob.

Soon my brother realized that going into town with an ass and cart, when you are eighteen years old and having to deal with convent schoolgirls, isn't quite as impressive as going into town with a horse and cart, whether the ass is big and fast or not. An ass is still only an ass. He decided that it was time for me to take over this job on a permanent basis. I didn't mind a bit because for me it was practically a pleasure to be with Coco.

CHAPTER 8

DICKENS BEGAN HIS epic novel about the French Revolution with the words, "It was the best of times, it was the worst of times." I think this fairly described childhood and its terrible twin, school. The extraordinary thing about childhood is that not only do we survive it, more or less, but in later life we tend to look back upon it with a dreamy nostalgia, as a time of endless carefree days when life was simple and uncomplicated. The truth, of course, is that at the time it wasn't at all simple or uncomplicated. To our young, developing minds, it was a time of confusion, anxiety, stress, and pain—as well as joy and excitement and laughter. In these momentous years, we felt and tasted the full range of emotions and experiences that, in large measure, would shape us into the grown-ups we would become. It was here we learned to love and hate, to fear and fight, to be kind or cruel, to bully or help, to ridicule or defend, to go along or stand apart, to be counted in or counted out.

We heard ourselves described by adults as cute or sly, or clever in a devious kind of way—these were considered admirable and desirable characteristics. Woe to the child who was open and honest, and not cute or sly, for he or she was often thought of as daft or soft or an amadan. It is likely that this kind of labeling was a carry-over from long generations of foreign rule when cuteness and slyness were survival traits. In any event, helped or hindered by a smattering of genetics, it was here that we learned to be what we are. Fortunately, most of us are blessed with selective memory, the ability to remember the happier times while forgetting or blanking out the not-so-happy ones. For others, sadly, some experiences were not too painful to remember; they were too painful to forget.

Tom Gallagher

Whether caused by a parent, a teacher, a priest, or someone else, these childhood scars and labels could remain for life. In Ireland I think all of us knew such people. Some had done well, perhaps even overcompensating to prove their worthiness in society. Others have remained in the shadows of life, marginalized, barely coping or not coping at all. We could debate until the cows come home as to whether or to what degree in later life our childhood experiences affect our perceptions of ourselves and the world in which we live. I expect that most practitioners in the field of human psychology would agree that there is clear linkage, but it's also probably fair to say that we sometimes exaggerate the connection. Whatever its effects, there is no escaping childhood. We have to go through it.

The day I was supposed to start Corthoon School, I was five years old and all dressed up for the occasion. I was wearing my new short trousers, a shirt inside a red jersey and a pair of shoes and socks. I probably would have been wearing Wellingtons, but they didn't make them that small. I didn't start school on the day I was supposed to because my grandmother died that day. My education was put on hold just like that. I didn't quite understand what all the commotion was about, but I knew that something big and sad had happened. There was a wake for my grandmother that night in our house, but only the oldest children were allowed to stay at home. The rest of us spent the night at a neighbor's. The next day we returned to see our house full of people and others coming and going. The coffin was still sitting on a stand in the kitchen, and I thought it looked so grand—stained and polished wood and lovely, shiny brass handles, but it was too high off the floor for me to see into.

There was a lot of crying as people said their last good-byes to Grandma. Then my mom and dad leaned over the coffin and kissed my grandmother, and some men helped my father put the lid on the coffin and screw it down. My dad, our cousin, Jim Conway, and two other men lifted the coffin onto their shoulders and slowly walked up the boreen to the hearse parked on the Main Road. All the people followed behind. The funeral was huge. I had never seen so many people and so many motor-cars. Mom said that Grandma was loved and respected by everyone, and when she left this world in 1952, I got to stay home from school on my very first day.

Corthoon National School had two rooms, the missus's room and the master's room, and a chimney in the middle with a back-to-back fireplace in each room. In the wintertime we'd have a turf fire in each fireplace so that we wouldn't freeze to death. Some farmers in Corthoon and Sonnagh with more turf than they need would sell the schoolmaster a cartload now and then through the winter, happy to make the easy pound. The load of turf would be dumped on the side of the road by the little entry gate to the schoolyard. Then the schoolboys would carry the turf, a few sods at a time, around to the back of the school where there was an enclosed and roofed shed for the turf. When the job was done, the door to the shed is locked and the key returned to the master. No one was going to steal the school's turf.

The schoolmaster got reimbursed for the turf he bought by the Department of Education—I think—or maybe by the Canon in Charles-town. I'm almost sure that the pound didn't come out of his own pocket. In Mom and Dad's time, scholars were required to bring a sod of turf to school each day during the winter, one sod per family, per day, and there was no pay or reimbursement. If the turf is bad, the scholars were asked to gather firewood, mostly withered old sticks, on their way to school. The sticks helped get the fire started and keep it going longer. No one minded gathering bits of firewood because the sooner the fires got started in each room, the sooner the rooms warmed up. You didn't want to arrive at school too early in the wintertime. It was better to let those who wanted to be the teacher's favorites get there first and light the fires. Black smoke pouring from the chimney was a bad sign, for it meant that the fire was still struggling. Gray or white smoke was a welcome sign because it meant the fire was going strong. We didn't keep the fire going throughout the school day because we'd go through our turf supply in no time at all, and reimbursement had its limits, I'm sure. So by noon the fire was well on its way to sleep.

You had to stay in the missus's room from low infants through second class, and then you moved to the master's room for third, fourth, fifth, and sixth classes—and seventh class, if your parents made you go. When I started school, Mrs. Cassidy was the teacher in the missus's room, and her husband, Mr. Cassidy, was the master in the master's room. My first day at school was eventful. Out in the yard during playtime, Mr. Cassidy came up to me to say hello.

"Hello, young man. What is your name?"

"Tommy."

"And, Tommy, is this your first day at school?"

"Yeah."

"Good. Well, Tommy, I'm going to give you something just because this is your very first day at school."

"What are you going to give me?"

Pat Cassidy, who looked to me to be well over one hundred years old, put his hand in his pocket and took out two pennies and gave them to me. I looked at the pennies in disbelief. They were my own pennies. Maureen had given me these pennies that very morning. They were old and worn and had the image of King Edward VII on one side, who looked even older than Mr. Cassidy. These pennies were in the pocket of my coat, which was hanging up on the porch wall. I was speechless. How could this be? He's giving me back my own money. I didn't know what to say and he was waiting for me to say something. Finally, the words come.

"You stole my money!"

"I stole your money?"

"You stole my money!"

"Now, now, Tommy, I didn't steal your money. I would never do that."

"But these are the pennies Maureen gave me."

"No, Tommy, they cannot be the same pennies. Where did you put the pennies your sister gave you?"

"I put them in my coat pocket, but you stole them."

"I didn't steal them. Where is your coat?"

"In the porch."

"Well, young man, let us go and see if the pennies Maureen gave you are still where they're supposed to be."

We went into the porch and, sure enough, the two pennies Maureen had given me as a present because it's my first day at school were in my coat pocket. I was afraid to look up at Mr. Cassidy. I wanted to cry. He carefully inspected all four pennies and declared that they were, indeed, identical and that anyone could have made this mistake. He then burst out laughing and laughed so hard he almost fell over. I had just doubled my money, and I felt anything but good about it. I was off to a dubious start.

I liked the story where the young lad was asked if he likeed going to school and he replied that he didn't mind going to school one bit, then volunteered that coming home from school was even nicer, but the part that he didn't like at all was being there. I didn't like being there either, and I envied Eamon, because he didn't have to go anymore. I would have preferred to stay home too, and help Eamon on the land. I had just one more year to do, and I could hardly wait. Then I would be free of all this compulsory nonsense. I did not understand why we had to go to school. It was mostly a waste of time. I knew it was nice to be able to read and write and do sums so that people knew you weren't a dunce or simple-minded, but you didn't need to go to school five days a week to prove that. Just Wednesdays would be enough, I thought. When I finished sixth class I would happily turn my back forever on Corthoon National School, I would be treated like a grown-up and get more respect. I would be working on the land with Eamon, eating more bacon and qualifying for a bigger piece of chicken, and enjoying the luxury of being able to feel sorry for the less fortunate who must still go to school.

We start school when we're about five and go until we're thirteen or fourteen. By the time you're thirteen, you should be in sixth class, unless the teacher kept you back a year or you started late. When you finished sixth class in June, you could take the Primary School Examination. If you passed you received the Primary School Certificate, which said that you had passed national written tests in Irish, English, and Arithmetic. The Primary School Certificate was printed in English on one side and Irish on the other side. Some pupils took the exam and some didn't. Some passed it and some didn't, and no one cared much either way, except for the teacher, who was anxious that those who sat for the exam pass. If someone was not likely to pass because he couldn't come to school regularly or she had a problem with the Irish language or maybe someone was just a bit slower than the others, they were not encouraged to take the test, because failure was a bad reflection on the teacher.

For most pupils in sixth class, the important thing was that you could leave school at the end of the school year in June and the guards couldn't do a thing about it. You could still go on to seventh class if you wanted to or your mother made you go, but almost no one completed the final primary school class. What was the point? You weren't going to learn anything new, except that you might be doing the sums toward the back of the sixth-class sum book that you didn't get to when you were in sixth class. Or you might be asked by the teacher to help teach the lower classes, like third, fourth, and fifth. I watched Paddy Mulligan go through seventh class. All he did was help other pupils and, occasionally, do sums from the back of the sixth-class sum book.

We didn't learn only English and Irish and sums in school. We also learned Irish history, world geography, and Bible history. At Big Play, meaning lunchtime, we played soccer in the hard-packed dirt yard that surrounds the school. Those who didn't have any lunch in their satchels could start the soccer game right away, and when the others had finished eating, they could join in the game. The girls had their half of the yard on one side, and we had ours on the other side. They played their games, and we played schoolyard soccer. Schoolyard soccer isn't real soccer, but we abided by soccer rules as far as possible.

Mostly, we used a solid rubber ball about the size of an apple. It was a waste of time and money to use an air-filled ball because in no time at all someone was going to kick it over the school wall and into a blackthorn bush, and that was the end of the ball. The yard we play in was not even half the length or width of a real pitch, and it angled around the school so that from one goal you couldn't see the other because it was out of sight. Still, no one complained, and we had some great games—even the schoolmaster joined in sometimes. It was the only chance we ever got to punish *him*—by *accidentally* kicking him in the ankles.

I didn't know how learning Irish was going to help me get on in the world since no one outside Ireland speaks it and few people inside Ireland speak it. And if I had to learn history, why couldn't we learn more than just Irish history? Irish history was mostly about Ireland's almost eight-hundred-year struggle against English rule, and it was depressing. All we ever did was memorize dates of significant events and the names of battles and when they were fought. Mostly, we lost battles but sometimes we won, like the Battle of the Yellow Ford in 1598. Here, Hugh O'Neill and Red Hugh O'Donnell, leaders of Ireland's two most famous fighting clans, met and defeated an English army under Marshal Bagnal. I got goose bumps reading about how the two Hughs and their ragtag army outfoxed Bagnal and his professional soldiers.

Another victory was in my own county, Mayo, in August 1798. In the spring and summer of that year, there were several uprisings throughout Ireland. Inspired by the American and French Revolutions, Ireland made another bid for freedom. The uprisings were supposed to have been coordinated and carried out in a very military fashion, but they weren't. Everything that could go wrong did go wrong, helped as usual by the ever-present informer. Lord Lieutenant of Ireland in 1798 was General Cornwallis, who personally took command of English forces in the field. Cornwallis was determined that these Irish rebels would not humiliate him as the damn Yankee rebels did at Yorktown over in America.

For a while the rebels had smashing victories in County Wexford against mostly local militia units called yeomanry, but when Cornwallis committed the regular army, the rebels were slaughtered wholesale. The other uprisings of 1798 also failed, but in Mayo there was a sweet victory in August. A combined army of professional French soldiers, under General Humbert, and mostly untrained but highly motivated Mayo volunteers surprised the English garrison in Castlebar and routed them in panic. The English soldiers ran, we read, as fast as they could go along the Main Road that runs by our land in the so-called Races of Castlebar and didn't stop until they got to Athlone. Boy! I was so proud of this, to think that an English army, panic-stricken, ran right by where our house is now, being chased by a bunch of screaming Mayo men armed with pitchforks and pikes and the odd musket.

Sadly for Mayo and for Ireland, the victory in Castlebar was soon reversed in the bog at Ballinamuck in County Longford. Here, on September 8, General Humbert surrendered to General Lake after a semi-respectable shoot-out with a regrouped and reinforced English army. Why, in God's name, couldn't the French have sent Napoleon! The French prisoners of war were shown every courtesy and quickly repatriated back to France. General Humbert was treated with respect and professional consideration by General Lake. And, after all, why not? They were both pedigreed gentlemen—and gentlemen, whatever their uniform, are gentlemen, and they know how to deal with rabble.

Humbert probably used the Mayo men as a shield for his advancing troops, a tactic that Lake, no doubt, would have considered entirely appropriate. Lake very likely sympathized with Humbert for his bad luck to have been selected to lead this reckless and futile expedition. They probably enjoyed tea or sipped some fine brandy before Humbert was sent on his merry way back to France. Meanwhile, the volunteers of Mayo were massacred as they tried to surrender, or drowned in the surrounding bogs as they tried to escape. None received mercy, for they were rebels, not prisoners of war. Their leaders were hanged and a few decapitated heads returned to Castlebar, scene of England's earlier humiliation, where they were hung out in public for all to see, to discourage such foolishness again.

I think what angered the English so much about these rebellions was that they had been able to conquer entire continents thousands of miles away but they couldn't quite keep down the unruly natives on a small island visible to their west on a clear day. No matter what the English did or didn't do, there was always another Irish rebellion in the works, even as the last one ended in crushing defeat. The English just couldn't understand why the Irish kept on rebelling against their rule, rather than behaving like reasonable people, like the Welsh and the Scots, who gave up the struggle against England centuries ago. I think the English believed that it was their God-given right to bring civilization and their superior way of life to the barbarian world, and if the barbarians didn't like it, well, that was just too bad. The Irish resisted through the ages so they were considered by the English to be irredeemable barbarians and, therefore, subject to brutal suppression.

If the English couldn't civilize us to their liking, they had the means to treat us like the savages they preferred to believe we were, even if we looked just like them. They needed to believe that the Irish were completely incapable of governing themselves, so that they could then steal the whole country, replacing our civilization with theirs, without feeling the burden of guilt or shame. That's what I thought.

We learned in school that the English had no business coming to Ireland in the first place, even if they were invited by an Irish king and had the pope's blessing. Dermot MacMurrough, an Irish provincial king, ruling Leinster, had a falling out with Rory O'Connor, high king (*Ard Ri*) of Ireland. It seems that Dermot had refused to pay his taxes to O'Connor, which the high king needed for the upkeep of his army and the royal household. Rory marched into Leinster and threw out Dermot. In a terrible state, having lost his kingdom and his honor, Dermot fled across the Irish sea to ask Henry II, the Anglo-Norman English king, for military assistance to regain Leinster, and maybe the rest of Ireland with a bit of luck. Henry obliged by sending over the Earl of Pembroke, Sir Richard FitzGilbert de Clare, nicknamed Strongbow, to assess the situation in

Ireland. The year was 1169. Not completely trusting the handsome and ambitious Strongbow, Henry himself arrived later with an army.

Pope Adrian IV didn't have a problem with this intervention by one Roman Catholic country in the internal affairs of another Roman Catholic country. On the contrary, Adrian thought it was altogether a good idea because the Irish Church needed to be cleansed anyway. The pope had heard disturbing reports that despite St. Patrick's heroic efforts centuries earlier, the Irish were still mostly savages living rough in the wilds, having few towns and villages like civilized people in England, and worst of all, were still practicing pagan rituals. The Irish Church was not only turning a blind eye on this un-Christian behavior but was actually celebrating ancient pagan feast days by giving them Christian names. These sinful practices had to be stopped and Henry was just the man for the job.

Henry II was a generous man and liked to reward his friends for their loyalty by giving them large estates of land. He was so generous, we learned, that he had given away much of England and Wales but, alas, there were still landless friends saying, "Where's my ten thousand acres?" He relished the prospect of acquiring brand-new baronial estates in Ireland, and now Dermot MacMurrough had given him an engraved invitation to come in and help himself. As for the pope, well, Adrian IV was the first and last English pope, and he and Henry were probably pals. And so began a tangled and tortured history between the two islands.

I loved history. I just didn't like reading about so many defeats and failures. Who wanted to learn about being beaten and humiliated over and over again? I wanted to read about epic battles ending in magnificent victories. I wanted to read about Irish heroes who won, who stayed in Ireland to continue the fight rather than giving up and going to the continent to fight for France or Spain or the pope. I wanted to read about Irishmen who preferred to live for Ireland, not die for it. I thought dying was the lazy way out of a bad situation. Tom Horkan told us one night that the American general, George Patton, said that wars are won and nations saved not because of our willingness to die for our country, but because of our absolute determination to make our enemies die for their country. Strewn throughout Irish history were men who sought glory and martyrdom by dying for Ireland. I knew this much: Irish history would not be so depressing if there were more of the other kind.

I loved geography, too. The atlas showed me the physical and political structures of the world, and my geography book tells me the population of each country, its capital city, what its main industries were, what it exported and imported, and what kind of government it had. I knew which countries had democratic governments and which ones didn't. I knew points of interest like the tallest mountain and longest river. I memorized all this. I knew the rivers and mountains of Ireland and England and Europe and America and Africa. I knew the capitals of dozens and dozens of countries. I could draw maps of countries and continents practically with my eyes closed. Best of all, I could dream about visiting them one day. I wanted to visit exotic capitals in faraway places. I wanted to meet people who looked nothing at all like me. I wanted to hear and maybe even learn strange and wonderful languages.

In fifth class and with a year to go, it's fair to say that Mr. Brannigan, our schoolmaster, and I were not the best of friends. Most pupils were afraid of him, and he had little compassion for those who were a bit slow. Mr. Brannigan didn't believe that anyone could be a little slow or maybe unable to learn well on an empty belly—or maybe because they were too scared of him. They were either bright or lazy, no in-between. And if he deemed you to be lazy, you would have an abiding and most unhappy relationship with Willie. Willie was the teacher's willow cane, a three-foot-long instrument of fear, curled at one end. I was a little better than average as a scholar, so I didn't get walloped much, but neither was I a stranger to Willie. Mr. Brannigan was as skillful with the cane as a champion football player is with the ball. Even when he wasn't walloping someone with it, he would sometimes walks up and down the classroom practicing wallops. He'd raise it over his head and bring it down hard. It swished through the air and made a smacking sound as it hit his right trouser leg.

When it didn't get that far and instead crashed onto your outstretched hand, the pain was intense. Punishment was usually either two or four slaps, one or two on each hand. Occasionally, you might get just one, maybe for a small spelling mistake, but mostly Willie deliverd the pain evenly, so that you wouldn't feel lopsided. Afterward, you wrapped your burning hands around the cold iron legs of the desk.

One Friday afternoon, Mr. Brannigan was reading an article to us, received from an Irish missionary order. The story was about the sad and grim conditions in some part of Africa, where war and plague were devastating the country and children were starving. In his most serious tone, Mr. Brannigan read on, telling us that a group of these children was waiting patiently in some hellish place for a lorry that would bring them a meager amount of food and water. Instead of reading, "The children waited patiently for their slice of bread from the lorry," he misread the text as "The children waited patiently for their slice of lorry from the bread." Unfortunately for me, my imagination ran wild, and I instantly visualized a gigantic knife slicing through the lorry. I burst out laughing. Thank God for those cold iron legs; they eased a lot of pain.

The best part about going to school was coming home from school. If Mr. Brannigan knew the kinds of things we sometimes got up to on our way home from school, we'd have no hands left at all after he and Willie got done with us. The afternoon bus to Swinford often stopped at Corthoon School at about the same time that we were getting out, three o'clock. It stopped to let people off who lived nearby or to let some-one on who's going to Swinford. Mostly, it's to let someone off because, at three o'clock in the day, there's no sensible reason for anyone to be going all the way to Swinford, about four and a half miles away and in an entirely different parish. It didn't stop for us because we walk home. All the buses in Ireland looked the same, and they were all owned by Corus Iompar Eireann, which also owned all the trains. CIE was owned by the state—whatever that meant. I think it meant that you would have to pass a civil service exam or know someone who was well connected and, therefore, has some pull before you could drive a CIE bus or train, or even be a conductor. All the conductor did was collect fares and crank out tickets from a machine suspended from his neck by a leather strap. The ticket machine looked like a Kodak camera with a few extra knobs on it. I very seldom got to ride on the bus, but when I did, I enjoyed it immensely, especially when it was pouring rain outside and I'm inside sitting on a nice soft leather seat.

For a while I wanted to be a bus driver. When I was old enough, I thought, I would pass my civil service exam and my driver's exam and then drive a bus all over Ireland. I would see everything there was to see and never be bored because the scenery would never stop changing. If I wanted to change the scenery faster, I would speed up. If I wanted to enjoy a particular sight, like crossing the River Shannon, I'd slow down. Then, I remembered that I would have to keep stopping every quarter mile or so to let someone off or pick up someone, and I didn't like that idea at all. What if I wasn't in the mood one day or wanted to reach the Shannon in a hurry, and didn't stop? Old-age pensioners waiting for the bus would stare, eyes wide and mouths open, as I sped by at seventy miles an hour splashing water and muck on them. Inside the bus, people would be causing a great commotion because their stop was miles back and getting farther back every second. I decided that driving a bus was not for me. I'd get the sack in no time.

The bus had a ladder on the outside at the back. The ladder went up to the roof, where baggage and parcels and, in the spring, day-old chicks and all manner of things were stored. I got the idea one day that if I could climb onto the lowest rung of the ladder when the bus stopped at the school, I could crouch below the back window and not be seen by the conductor or passengers inside. Then I could steal a ride home from school. I would have to plan the operation carefully. First, the bus would have to stop at Corthoon School. Next, I would have to very quickly scan the windows to make sure there was someone on the bus who would need to get off at Madogue Road, close to our house. Then I would have to be sure that Mr. Brannigan and Mrs. Cassidy had already left in their car. To do this while Mr. Brannigan was still on the scene was more dangerous to my health than hanging on to the back of a bus.

The day came when all three requirements were met. School friends promised not to tell but didn't really believe I'd do it. I did. There was no time to think about it. By the time I had confirmed that the bus would stop at Madogue Road and that the teachers had left for Charlestown, the bus was already moving off. I grabbed the ladder and lifted myself off the road and squeezed both feet onto the bottom rung. The bus picked up speed and I could see the road passing beneath me in a blur. It was an exhilarating ride. And it was scary. Soon a car caught up and was following close behind. I couldn't see the driver because I didn't dare twist my body around enough to look, but I could see part of the car and it was way too close for my liking. I wondered what the driver must be thinking, no doubt that I was the greatest eejit in the West of Ireland. When the bus stopped at Madogue Road, Ellen Jane Smith got off, and I got off practically beside her. Ellen was a bit startled and had no idea where I'd come from—and I did not feel compelled to tell her. I did not repeat this caper. The thought of falling off and being run over by a thoughtful motorist was too much for me.

Sometimes, when coming home from school, we would lie in wait behind a fence by the Main Road. Armed with stones, our purpose was to ambush certain kinds of vehicles that passed by. Targets of opportunity were lorries, large panel vans, and petrol tankers. Cars were not targets because we didn't want to break windows, and we especially didn't want to hurt anyone. We wanted to have a little fun before we got home to eat our spuds and cabbage and go to work. The Charlton Bros van from Kiltimach was a regular target because it passed our way about the same time once a week. On each side of the van, it says CHARLTON BROS and underneath KILTIMACH, CO. MAYO. I did't know what BROS meant, but if it was a surname, I knew it wasn't Irish. The Christian name didn't sound Irish either and, except for Charlton Heston, the film star, I never heard of any real person having a first name like that. The Charlton Bros van delivered confectionery to shops in town. It was the color of chocolate and probably had loads of chocolate bars inside. It was a nice target. Its sides were already well dented by our stones and we shared a feeling of pride when it went by with our marks all over it.

The Caltex petrol tanker was not a good target because, although it was big enough to easily hit, its oval shape deflected our shots. Still, we did our best, not wanting Patsy Pudler, the driver, to get away scot-free. We had a particular dislike for the Burnhouse lorry because of the dreadful smell of its cargo: animal carcasses. I hated it because of Molly. Tom Horkan said that the awful smell was caused by the preservative that was used to keep the meat from rotting on the long journey to Dublin to feed the inhabitants at the zoo. I reckoned if it was meat the animals would eat it regardless of how it smelled. It was very hard to have any effect on the Burnhouse lorry. For one thing, we had to hold our noses with one hand while we let fly with the other. For another, the lorry had cast-iron sides, and we weren't strong enough to throw anything big enough to make a mark. Nevertheless, there was no lack of enthusiasm, and our efforts were commendable. At least we thought so.

CHAPTER 9

❖

SOMETIMES WHEN MOM got sad or depressed, she'd talk about selling out and buying a house in Charlestown or Swinford—or even moving us all to England. She was tired of the land, the backbreaking work in the fields, a house where the paint peels off the walls in colored streams because of dampness, the miserable weather, often not enough food or clothes or shoes for the family, and no man by her side to share the responsibility. She would say terrible things about Dad for leaving her alone to raise a big family. Sometimes she would get so angry over the way things were that I was afraid she would hurt herself or one of us. She would rage around the kitchen, screaming at us, throwing things, putting Dad down and saying that she wished she was dead and six feet under in Kilconduff graveyard, that she was robbed of her girlhood and her dreams, that all she has gotten from Dad each spring is another mouth to feed. I knew—we all knew—that the anger would pass, that she didn't mean the things she had said. The rage gone, she would ask God to forgive her and tell us that Dad is doing the best he can, and that lots of Irish dads have gone to England and deserted their families completely.

Exhausted and spent, she'd cry her heart out and tell us over and over that she would never hurt us. We would crowd around Mom because we, too, were afraid, for her and for us. I felt so sorry for her. I wanted to put my arms around her and tell her that it would be all right, that things weren't so bad, but I couldn't. We love, we care, we ache, but we don't hug—not in our family, not in Irish families. That's how we are. When it was more than I could bear, I'd head the bog, my place of refuge, and smother myself in its bleak loneliness. I often stayed awake at night dreading that something would happen to my mother, that she might give up on us and go away or even die and leave us all alone in the world.

When I was six years old, Mom was taken to the hospital in Castlebar and then to a hospital in Dublin. I didn't know what was wrong, but I knew she was very sick. She had been in bed for a couple of days, not able to get up, and at night we could hear her moaning through the wall that separated her room from the room where my brothers and I slept. Jimmy and Maureen were going in and out of her room but wouldn't let anyone else go in. The older ones were asking, "What's wrong with Mom? Why can't she get up?" Maureen, at eleven and always the bossy one, said, "Mom is very tired and doesn't need any of you bothering her. Now be quiet and stay out of the way." Next thing I knew, Jimmy was rushing out of the house and off across the fields like a hound. Maureen told us that Jimmy was going for Margaret Joyce, a neighbor and friend of Mom's. Soon Margaret arrived and went to Mom's room right away. She shouted at Maureen to bring warm water in a basin.

A pot of water was quickly hung on the crane over the fire. Margaret then yelled at Jimmy, "Go to John Thomas; tell him to bring Dr. Cawley. Hurry, hurry." Jimmy was off again across the fields in the other direction. John Thomas owned the only hackney car for miles, and right now we needed him to go to Swinford for the doctor. We were all terrified, and I was beyond fright. I knew that something was horribly wrong. Margaret Joyce came out of Mom's room with the basin in her hands. She tried to hide it from us as she took it outside, but I could see that the water was now red. We heard Mom moaning, and Margaret returned to the room, telling Maureen to bring more water. I went outside to watch the Main Road, praying that each car from Swinford would be the one that would slow down and turn into our boreen. Finally, Dr. Cawley arrived with his big brown leather bag and went into Mom's room. Maureen and Jimmy joined the rest of us in the kitchen.

We were all too frightened to say anything. Even if I tried I knew no words would come out. We heard low voices in the room: Dr. Cawley talking to Mom and then to Margaret Joyce. A little later Margaret came out and told us that Dr. Cawley had already called for the ambulance, and it was on the way from Castlebar. She said that Mom would be going to the hospital. John Thomas had told Dr. Cawley what Jimmy had told him and he immediately phoned Castlebar, then left his patients in the waiting room and headed for Culmore. Jimmy went up to the Main Road to flag down the ambulance because the driver had only rough directions and wouldn't know exactly which house was ours.

It took ages to arrive. Like Dr. Cawley, the ambulance came down our mucky boreen all the way to the house. Two men in white coats got out and removed a stretcher from the back. They went straight to Mom's room and a few minutes later came out, slowly guiding the stretcher down the hall and out through the kitchen to the ambulance. The woman on the stretcher didn't look at all like Mom. She looked so old and worn out. For a second I felt a wave of relief sweep over me because I couldn't believe that this was my mom. It had to be someone else.

It *was* my mother, though, and she was now in critical condition. We learned later that Dr. Cawley did not think she would survive the journey to Castlebar, twenty miles away. At the age of six, I didn't know where babies came from. Mom had told us that an angel from Heaven brought each one of us into the world. She was in her sixth month of pregnancy when something went terribly wrong. A month earlier John Thomas had taken her into Swinford to see Dr. Cawley because she was feeling pain. He warned her that she must take it easy and stay away from the fields, but that was easy for him to say. First she began to feel intense cramps. She went to bed hoping they'd go away, but they got worse. By the time she told Jimmy to bring Margaret Joyce, she was hemorrhaging. By the time she reached the hospital, she was unconscious. She lost the baby and for days hovered between life and death. When she was strong enough, she was transferred to a hospital in Dublin, where she slowly regained her health and her strength. We would not see her for six weeks.

During this time we were taken care of by Mary O'Malley of Triumph House. Mary was older than Mom but had long been a friend in good times and hard times. She was a widow and lived with two adopted daughters about a mile away as the crow flies. She also had two grown children, but they were abroad somewhere, in England I think. While our mother was in Dublin, Mary O'Malley came to our house almost every day to keep house, clean and bathe us, and see that we had food to eat. She was more strict than Mom, and we learned new house rules: no shouting, no banging doors, no mucky shoes in the house, no mess-making, no arguing, no fighting. We had to speak respectfully to each other and especially to grown-ups—yes sir, no ma'am, please, thank you, may I, and excuse me. Mary O'Malley's task was formidable: taking care of nine children between the ages of two and twelve, none of whom had more than a fleeting acquaintance with the niceties of polite behavior.

Being polite to each other seemed, to us, like such a waste of time—unnatural and silly. Challenging, calling names, baiting, arguing, fighting, taking sides, sulking, and making up were normal everyday activities. Mary quickly saw that the secret to success was to gain Maureen's support. At first Maureen was defiant, resentful of Mary O'Malley's authority, but soon Mary won her over. With Maureen as her right hand, Mary's task became more manageable, and with no Mom to rein her in, Maureen relished her role of enforcer of civil and polite behavior.

For six weeks in 1953, Mary O'Malley became our second mother, and while we didn't fully appreciate her teacher-like approach to mothering, we quickly found her soft spots, and never forgot her kindness. Mary had seen hard times herself when she was younger. Widowed at an early age and with two small children, she had found herself homeless. The people of the village took up a collection, and with their own labor built her a small cottage by the Main Road. The little rectangular glass window over the front door said Triumph House. Mary O'Malley's home was always a welcome place for anyone, friend or stranger, going to or coming from Swinford to stop in out of the rain, or just for a cup of tea.

I loved Triumph House. It was always immaculate, and I don't remember ever being there when there wasn't a happy fire in the fireplace or when I wasn't welcomed like family.

When Mom came home from the hospital in Dublin, I was thrilled to see that she was the Mom I knew, and the neighbors said that she looked better than she had looked in years. Mom said that the long rest was just what she needed, but she grieved for the little baby girl that was lost. As for resting and taking it easy, the moment she got home the rest was over. Soon she was back in the fields, back bent, oblivious to panoramic views that would later be worth many thousands of pounds.

Mom was the youngest in her family and only twelve years old when her mother died. I can't imagine how terrible this must have been for her. Most of her brothers and sisters had left Ireland by this time. At twelve I couldn't bear the thought of losing Mom—even with more brothers and sisters around than I could count, it would still be unbearable. Mom had a few close girlfriends from her school days and, in her time, she too had boyfriends and secret moments in quiet places. She met Dad at a dance where he was a part-time flute player in a part-time band. She and her Pied Piper married two years later, as Hitler's armies marched and conquered without mercy. Despite the war she was optimistic about her life with Dad, at least in the beginning.

With England at war with Germany, and America just beginning to come out of the Depression, Mom was sure that Dad would stay at home, even though it would mean hardship. And he did for a while. After Jimmy was born, Dad went to England, leaving my mother and grandmother to care for the baby. Dad had to go. There was just no money at home while England was crying out for workers to replace the vast numbers of men being drafted into the military services.

I knew how Mom felt about her life and her broken dreams, but I didn't think that things were so bad, and we never talked about not having things that other people had. In school every day, I saw children who were worse off than we were. When I was younger and Mom would talk about selling out, I would daydream about living in town, where I was sure we'd be in better circumstances. We would be townies—a step up in the world from country people. We wouldn't have to save turf or make hay or pick spuds or haul drinking water on foot from a well three farms away when we got home from school. I would walk home from the town school, down real sidewalks, past shops and houses side by side, where if it was raining you could easily stand in a doorway and not get drenched. After tea I could join my new friends in the park or the ball alley for a game of football or handball. Boy! Life would be better.

I enjoyed my daydream about moving to England even more. Living in the big city of Birmingham would be a great thrill. Everything would be new and exciting, and soon I'd forget all about Culmore and Madogue and Corthoon School. Dad had written home saying that his landlord, Paddy Mahoney, was going to get us a house, but he'd been saying this for years. Mom believed that Paddy Mahoney was just fooling Dad, always promising him that he'd find us the perfect house, and Dad always believing. Or maybe not. Paddy Mahoney was Irish, and all of his boarders were Irish. He owned a dozen houses in Birmingham, and rented out all of them by the room. Mom said he made more money by the room than by the house—and the Irish made the best boarders because they didn't complain, no matter how shabby their little rooms were. The Englishman wouldn't put up with it, Mom said.

In a few years, I knew that my turn would come, that I'd be bailing out like my brothers and sisters before me. I wasn't sure where I'd be going, but it would probably be England, where Dad and Jimmy and Maureen already were and where Eamon would be in a year or two, as he liked to remind us at least five times a day. I'd love to go to America, where we have lots of uncles and aunts and cousins, but it takes much more money to get to America. First of all, you have to have a relative in America willing to sponsor you, meaning that the sponsor is responsible for taking care of you if you couldn't find work because the government wouldn't help. I didn't worry about this. Mom said that opportunities in America, where most of her brothers and sisters were, are far better than in England. Still, the obstacles were there. You have to travel to the American embassy in Dublin to apply for a visa. If you got one, you were practically on your way, provided you had money to pay for the plane ticket.

A neighbor of ours, Fidelma Joyce, immigrated to Chicago. There was a big going-away doo for her the Sunday before she left. All the neighbors came and we had a great time. There was great fun: music and dancing and singing and drinking galore. Fidelma's young brother, Brendan, invited me into the front room. Most Irish bungalows had two rooms in front, usually meaning located on each side of the front door, which usually faced the Main Road or a by-road if the house was not in sight of a Main Road, or the most pleasant view if there were no visible signs of civilization anywhere around—and for the odd fellow who wasn't in a mood to welcome visitors, whether neighbor or stranger, finding the entrance to his house could be tricky. Sometimes one of these rooms, the "front room," was designated as a special room, meaning that it was respectable enough to invite a neighbor or even a stranger into. In fancier homes or in the town, whether fancy or not, this room would be called the parlor, but out here in the country we had no such airs and graces.

Front room or not, most entertaining in rural Ireland was done in the kitchen, almost always the largest room in the house. I had never been into the Joyces' front room, and it was very posh. There were rugs on the floor that I'd only seen in movies. It even had a leather-covered settee in it, the first one I'd seen. Mom said that Margaret Joyce, the mother, had brought all of these things from Chicago where she herself had been as a young girl. On the mantelpiece over the fireplace there was a statue of the Blessed Virgin Mary, so beautiful, smiling down at the Baby Jesus in her lap. Brendan said that it was a new addition to the front room. He reached up to take it down so that I could get a closer look at this lovely glossy statue of Our Holy Mother and Child that Brendan said had been blessed with holy water by Canon Stenson in Swinford. Holy Mary! He let it fall and it broke into a hundred pieces. Hearing the crash above the din in the kitchen, his mother rushed in and almost fainted at the sight. There was the Blessed Virgin's head resting on the hearth, looking lovingly at the floor, and the poor Baby Jesus, with only a small piece of a lap to rest in, all alone over by the settee. I was speechless, and Brendan looked like he was about to be beheaded.

For a second I thought he was going to do the understandable thing in a moment of panic and blame me, but he didn't. He blamed an unnamed power beyond this world. His mother looked so shocked and heartbroken you'd think it was Brendan who was in a hundred pieces on the floor. In a hoarse whisper, she asked him what happened. He blurted out that he never touched the statue, that he just looked at the Blessed Virgin and she fell off the mantelpiece, Baby Jesus and all. I thought she'd never believe that looney story, but she seemed to because then, looking even more terrified than her son, she asked him what sinful thoughts were in his head to make the Blessed Virgin fling herself and her infant son off the mantelpiece rather than be touched by him. She looked at me in that knowing way that said, *You shared these sinful thoughts with* my *son, didn't you?* I didn't wait to hear Brendan's confession; it was definitely time for me to rejoin Fidelma's going-away doo, still happily underway in the kitchen and completely oblivious to the terrible sacrilege in the front room.

Doos were the traditional way to say good-bye to someone going to America—because America was so far away. But not as far away as it used to be, because now you could fly across the Atlantic Ocean and be in America in less time than it took to get to England by bus, boat, and train. In earlier times the big send-off doo was a sad event for the family, for often it meant that you were saying good-bye to a son or daughter, brother or sister forever. You would never see them again. In these times the going-away doos were called wakes—which still required a big gathering of neighbors and as much food and drink as the family could afford. The more food and drink, the more mourners would come to grieve and have the craic for the departed soul—or the soon-to-be departed emigrant.

The Joyce family knew that Fidelma would be back for a visit in a few short years, so no one needed to pretend to be mournful. Still we tried, because we were supposed to, in honor of times past. A good way to show that you're mournful was to start a sad sing-song about emigration to get the mourners to pretend to be in the proper frame of mind. Fidelma's older brother, Paddy, began the honors with an emotional rendition of the ballad of Noreen Bawn:

> Now strong youths and tender females
> Ponder well before you go
> From your humble homes in Erin
> What's beyond you do not know
> What is gold and what is silver
> When your health and strength are gone
> When you think of emigrating
> Won't you think of Noreen Bawn.

The song told the story of the fairest maiden in all of Ireland, "Erin's darling, Noreen Bawn," who emigrated to America. Long years later she arrived home to her widowed mother, dressed in the finest clothes and mortally infected with scarlet fever. Paddy was overcome by the loud applause, and tears rolled down his face, either lamenting the sad fate of Noreen Bawn or the coming departure of his sister, or both, or maybe because a nice cry once in a while is a good thing in itself.

Like most national school scholars, Eamon left Corthoon School when he was thirteen. He was happy to be gone. He didn't like Mr. Brannigan, and Mr. Brannigan returned the sentiment with enthusiasm. Eamon didn't attend school regularly, and when he did he was often late. He had to get up early in the morning, milk the cows, and, except in winter, drive them to our land in Madogue before going to school. He had little time to worry about personal hygiene or being properly attired. He would show up late when Mr. Brannigan might already have one of the classes up around his desk in a half circle, reading English or Irish composition or grammar, or doing sums or spelling, or some other equally thrilling subject.

Mr. Brannigan always kept Willie at the ready, either hooked on the doorknob of the cupboard behind his desk or placed on the desk in front of him. You never wanted Willie pointing in your direction; it just wasn't a good sign. Sums and spelling always got Willie a very good workout. Eamon would come in looking a bit scruffy and always with that cold defiance in his eyes, like he was daring Mr. Brannigan to do something about him being late. Mr. Brannigan knew that punishing Eamon—by walloping him with Willie—was a waste of time, except for the practice. Eamon wouldn't flinch. He would just stare coldly at Mr. Brannigan as Willie smashed onto his hands. By the time my brother and Mr. Brannigan parted company in June 1956, Eamon and Willie had not been in physical contact for some time. My brother had become a nonperson, ignored.

It's summer 1959. Patricia and Kathleen finished Corthoon School in June, and I got confirmed in May. After Baptism and First Holy Communion, Confirmation is the next big event in a Catholic's life. Everyone was born with the stain of Original Sin on his or her soul. Original Sin was the sin committed by Adam and Eve in the Garden of Eden. They disobeyed God by eating the one apple that God said they were not to eat. They could eat every other apple in sight but not this one apple. Well, Satan came to Eve and tempted her and then she tempted Adam and the apple got eaten and mankind has been paying for it ever since with the stain of Original Sin. Every baby is born with this black mark on his or her soul but thank God for the Sacrament of Baptism. Baptism removes this stain from your soul and restores it to perfect cleanliness.

At Baptism the baby's godparents come forward and are named. It will be their responsibility to take care of the baby if something terrible happens to the mom and dad. The priest pours holy water on the baby's head, says some special prayers, and in no time at all the baby's soul is immaculate. Bible history said that John the Baptist baptized Jesus in the River

Jordan, which I didn't understand at all. How could Jesus have Original Sin on his soul? And if Jesus was born with Original Sin, does that mean that his mother, the Blessed Virgin Mary, also had Original Sin? But that can't be because catechism says that Mary, the Mother of God, was without sin. Maybe I'll understand this when I'm older.

If you died without committing a single sin in your whole life, you could not get into Heaven if you hadn't been baptized. Babies that died before being baptized went to Limbo, where they stayed forever. They didn't suffer in Limbo, but they couldn't get out either. However, if you count longing to get out suffering, then I reckon they do suffer. From the stories the missionary priests tell us about the hunger and starvation in Africa, Limbo must be full of African babies. I didn't understand why babies and other unfortunates had to spend all eternity in Limbo because they didn't get baptized. And I didn't understand how you could live your whole life doing good works and then, in a moment of weakness, commit a single mortal sin and if you died before you had a chance to confess it and receive absolution, you were going straight to Hell forever and ever. And why did the unfortunate soul have to keep burning in Hell for all time for maybe a single mortal sin—why not just burn up and be done with it? All the prayers and good works counted for nothing. I didn't understand why one apple could cause so much trouble. I wanted to ask questions about why this is so, but I'd probably be denounced as a heretic or something. Brannigan, for sure, would have his close pal, Willie, respond in the usual way.

You received First Holy Communion when you reached the age of reason, which happened when you were seven years old. You were now old enough to know the difference between right and wrong, and the difference between a venial sin and a mortal sin. I'm twelve and I still don't know the difference. I asked one of our parish priests, who visited our school to test us on religious knowledge, if there was an easy way to know for sure the difference between a mortal sin and a venial sin—as it would be nice to know in advance, and there were no lists that I could look up. He looked at me very sternly and said that every boy and girl knew in his or her own heart the answer. Well if that's so then I'm a dunce because I'm still confused. What if I and my pal, Colm Duffy, commit the identical bad deed together on our way home from school, but I believe in my heart it's a mortal sin and he believes in his heart it's only a venial sin—and we're run over by a CIE bus before going to confessions? I'm going to Hell forever while he's going to Purgatory and will get out in a few years. How can that be fair?

We were told that only Christians could go to Heaven because only Christians get baptized into the Christian faith and have the sin of Adam and Eve removed. If you were a non-Christian but still lived a holy life and believed in God but not in Jesus, you didn't get to go upstairs after you die. You're finished. I didn't know where all these non-Christians went—whether it was to Limbo along with the African babies or if they just died and stayed dead. Yet whether you're a Christian or a non-Christian, if you lived an evil, sinful life you will burn in Hell for all eternity. That's the way it is. Rules are rules, as Mr. Brannigan would say.

I feel sorry for the Jews and Moslems and all the other non-Christians because they don't have much to look forward to when they leave this world. Once, a priest, back from the missions in Africa, said from the pulpit in Charlestown that only Catholics can enter the Kingdom of Heaven because the Catholic Church is the only True Church, with an unbroken line from St. Peter. He said Protestants are no better than Jews and Moslems, and that all those outside the One True Church, including heathens, atheists, and the English, are damned. He said that it is a grievous sin—which I think is the same as a mortal sin—for Catholics to enter a Protestant church or even bless themselves with the sign of the cross when passing one—something we have to do when passing a Catholic church or a shrine by the road. I told Mom about this, and she said that he had either been in Africa too long or maybe not long enough. She told us that once when she was a young girl at Mass in Swinford, a priest, also back from the missions somewhere, roared from the pulpit that it would be easier for an elephant to go through the eye of a needle than for a lawyer to get through the Gates of St. Peter. With Michael the Archangel around, Heaven probably didn't need lawyers anyway.

For Catholics the important thing to know is that if you died with only venial sins on your soul, you'll have to do your penance in Purgatory, but eventually you'll get to Heaven—sooner rather than later if your relatives are praying a lot for your soul, having Masses said for you, and contributing as much as they can to the church and the missions. My problem is that, since you didn't get a message from Heaven telling you that your dead grandfather just received the welcome-home nod from St. Peter, you never know when you can stop praying for him and move on to some other poor soul who's still doing her penance. The result is that the list of departed souls you have to pray for keeps getting longer, meaning more time on your knees at home and in church. Anyway, when you receive Holy Communion, you are taking Jesus into your soul, and that means you must be in a state of grace and have been fasting from midnight before receiving Our Lord Jesus Christ.

After you received Holy Communion, you were okay until you committed more sins, usually the same ones as the last time. If the sins were always the same you could memorize them and get out of the confessional box quickly. Then in a couple of weeks, it's back to confessions to confess the same sins again to the priest, promise not to sin again, say a sincere Act of Contrition, receive absolution and your penance, and then go immediately into the pew to do your penance. For small sins penance is usually an Our Father and three Hail Marys, but a mortal sin can easily get you a decade or two of the rosary. For me it's the usual Our Father and three Hail Marys—unless I volunteer that I have had bad thoughts, which I'm beginning to have for reasons that I don't understand, except that I know they're sinful. This is the death knell on a quick getaway:

"An' what were those evil thoughts about?" asked the Father.
"You know, Father..."

"No, my son, I don't know—you must tell me. How can I give you absolution without knowing the sin, my son?"

"They were about girls, Father."

Much later, I am in the center aisle facing the holy altar, a decade of the rosary before me—but at least away from the confessional box I don't appear to be a confessor at all, just a lad who came into the church to pray for his dead relatives like a lot of the townspeople do. They just come in at their convenience to pray before the altar or do the Stations of the Cross. They don't have to worry about pedaling a bike for miles and miles in the wind and rain and frost.

"Dear, I'm going up to the church to say a few prayers for Grandda and Grandma."

"Fine, Love, be off with you, then."

You always knew who the big sinners were because they took the longest to do their penance—except for the sly ones who will leave the church early and finish their penance on their way home. Almost always, they are girls and old women.

Confirmation is a sacrament through which you receive the Holy Ghost to make you a stronger Catholic and a soldier of Jesus Christ. You got confirmed when you're about twelve years old and in the fifth class. For my confirmation, the bishop traveled from his seat at the Diocese of Achonry to Charlestown to perform the Confirmation Ceremony during Mass, so that many could be witness to the swearing-in of a bunch of twelve-year-olds becoming soldiers in the battalions of Christ. The bishop looked very impressive in his vestments—the amice, stole, white cope, and mitre—and he had an enormous ring on his hand, with a huge red stone on top. He held out his hand and each of us, in turn, had to kiss the ring. He anointed all of us on the forehead with the holy chrism—which is probably holy water mixed with some kind of oil—and made the sign of the cross. The ceremony ended when we all knelt down and he laid his scepter on our right shoulder, one by one, and made mumbling pronouncements in English and Latin. We were now soldiers, under the command of Jesus Christ, prepared, if necessary, to die in defense of the faith. I sincerely hope it will never come to this.

We all go to Mass every Sunday and on Holy Days of Obligation. Whether you want to or not, this is a most solemn and serious requirement. If you don't go to Mass and don't have an acceptable excuse, meaning an accident or serious illness or because you're too old and infirm, it's a mortal sin, and if you're struck dead by lightning on a Sunday afternoon, having failed your Catholic duty, you're going to Hell. It's as simple as that. I know a man in our village who didn't go to Mass at all, and I can't even begin to imagine what his punishment was going to be in the next world. If just skipping Mass one Sunday can get you an eternity in Hell, how much worse can skipping ten years of Sunday Masses and Holy Day Masses be? On the other hand, if you overdo it, like going to Mass twice on the same Sunday, that's viewed with suspicion and disapproval. Biddy O'Loughlin, a neighbor down the road, has developed the habit of going to first Mass and last Mass each Sunday. The neighbors didn't like this at all. "Arrah, who does she think she is annyway, St. Bridget?"

There are two big collection days at every Catholic church in Ireland each year: Easter Sunday and Christmas Day. We are all expected to contribute some money each Sunday and Holy Day of Obligation, but we must do better on these two High Holy times. God is not the only observer at these special collections, but also all the villages that make up the parish, meaning all of your neighbors, relatives, and friends, and hundreds of others who may or may not know you. At Mass, a week or two following Easter and Christmas, the priest gets up on the pulpit and instead of the usual sermon begins the long recital of those who have made a contribution to the Holy Church on these holiest of occasions. The recital is name upon name, village by village, and it goes on and on until all names and all villages have been recited. This can take a long time, as hundreds of names must be called out.

Those like Johnny Conlon of Lowpark, usually the highest on the list with a ten-pound contribution, are proud as peacocks, heads held high as if to say, *There, beat that if you can.* The last names called in each village were the ones who had contributed the least. The names were not called alphabetically but by amount—and you didn't want to be near the bottom where the lowest amount worth calling out is a half a crown. To be down at that level was a mark of shame, so the calling out of names was an encouragement to rise to the occasion, whatever the circumstances at home. If your contribution was less than half a crown, your name wasn't called out, and that was the same as not contributing at all, and keen ears would know the uncalled souls. Mom would never allow the Gallaghers at the far end of Culmore to be at the lowest level, no matter what. The church had its ways, and avoidance of shame was a powerful incentive.

In September 1959 I began my final year at Corthoon School. This, I sincerely hoped, would be my last year of schooling. But now I was worried. Patricia and Kathleen finished at Corthoon School in June 1959 and, at Mom's insistence, were now going on the secondary school at the Marist Convent in Charlestown. What if she had some plans for me when I finish next June? Jesus! As if I don't have enough to worry about. Now I've got this cloud hanging over my head. I think about it for a while and I feel better. I'll have a good excuse for not continuing this going-to-secondary-school foolishness. I'm needed on the land to help Eamon. The more I think about it, the more convinced I am that secondary school for me is out of the question. Not only am I needed on the land to help Eamon, I will have to learn how to do everything he does, the jobs that I am not yet able to do, like cutting turf, ploughing seochs, stacking hay, cutting oats, and reeking turf—and that's only some of the jobs he does. Most of these jobs are very hard work, and all of them require skills as well as muscle—and have to be learned so that they can be done properly.

We all worked on the land through the summer, doing the things we always did: saving the turf, saving the hay, harvesting the oats, and checking the still-growing potatoes to see what kind of a crop we're going to have. By July we knew if the potatoes were going to be nice and big and, as far as we could tell, free of blight. If they were still small, like poreens, it was time to start worrying because there's not much growing time left. If the potato crop was poor, it meant lean times over the next twelve months. The crop could be poor for different reasons: not enough fertilizer, too much rain, not enough sun, the stalks being attacked by blight, the soil too poor or too wet, or the seed potatoes themselves not being good. If the crop was good, we could begin digging out new potatoes in August, and this year we were lucky—the potatoes are big and plentiful. We say the rosary in gratitude to God in Heaven. We didn't say the rosary every night like the priests say we're supposed to—and sometimes we will go for a week or two or without going down on our knees on the kitchen floor. But when the worry is on us, for whatever reason, we say the rosary, and when God and nature gave us a good crop, we offered up the rosary in thanksgiving.

We prayed a lot for good weather. Rainy weather was the Irish farmer's greatest curse. We never had to worry about droughts like they had in America and other parts of the world. Every year we worried about the rain destroying much of our hard work. We were very generous with God on the matter of the weather. If we got fine weather, we thanked Him for it. If the rain came down so hard that the turf swam away and the hay rotted in the field and the oat stalks were knocked flat in the field by wind and rain so that they couldn't be cut or saved, the Irish saying was "Ah, sure it could have been worse." No matter how bad it was, "Ah, sure it could have been worse." And God was thanked for not leaving us completely destitute. That wasn't my sentiment, I can tell you. I didn't mind telling God to ease up on the unending tests of our faith and worthiness and to keep a closer eye on the weather so that I didn't have to lie awake at night worrying about what we'll do if we couldn't save any turf or if we lost the field of oats. Mom liked to say that God was good and God would always take care of us, but sometimes I wasn't at all sure of this. I was often reminded that I was Doubting Thomas, and I was.

Most of our potatoes were Kerr Pinks. They had a pinkish skin and tasted good—not great but good. Kerr Pinks were easier than most potatoes to grow because they were less demanding of the soil they were planted in. We also sowed Golden Wonders, Champions, Epicures, and Records. These potatoes were delicious, each kind having its own special taste. When they were boiled, their skins cracked open and you could see the floury, succulent pulp inside. They tasted so good you didn't want to swallow and did so when it was the only sensible thing left to do. We didn't grow many of these pedigreed potatoes, though, because they needed richer soil, which meant we had to put more cow manure on the ridges in which they're sown. As cow manure, like everything else, was scarce, we had to grow what would grow with the least fuss, and that was Kerr Pinks and Banners. Banners would grow almost anywhere because they had no pedigree. They grew big and watery and are tasteless. They were the Woodbines of the potato family, but we were happy to have them when there was nothing else. This happened sometimes in the springtime when we were saving what's left of the better kinds for seed.

But in summertime with the promise of a good crop, we didn't worry about seed potatoes. New potatoes always tasted the best, and in the early weeks after the crop has come to fruition, we would make *cally*. First, we scrubbed the potatoes until they were spotless. Then we boiled them in a pot. When they were well done, we'd drain the water out and let them steam for a few minutes. We then mashed the potatoes in the pot with the pounder, a piece of wood trimmed and pared for the job. Halfway through the mashing, salt was added, along with some milk and a generous slice of our own homemade butter. Now we had cally, and it was a meal all by itself, delicious and filling. You couldn't do heavy work for a while after having a big plateful of cally. You just had to take it easy until the heaviness leaves your belly.

CHAPTER 10

SEPTEMBER 1959. MY final year of school was underway and with it my fervent hope that it would indeed be my final year of schooling. Eveline, a year behind me, was in fifth class, Anne was in third, Angela in second, and Christina, the youngest, would be starting school next year. In March 1960, Eveline won a national award for handwriting, and we were all very proud of her. I could write well enough to keep Mr. Brannigan at bay, but I was incapable of writing in beautiful script the way she could. Her penmanship belonged in another age. My only honor in my last year of school was that Mr. Brannigan read out a composition that I had written, which he deemed to be worthy of mention. I titled it, "My Life as a Postman." I didn't really want to be a postman at all. I wanted to be a pilot and fly airplanes—but I knew nothing about flying planes and I knew a lot about the life of Jim McNicholas, our postman, so my choice of subject was easy.

I wrote about a young boy who dreamed about growing up to be a postman: how he so loved the black uniform and important-looking peaked cap that made him look like a guard, and how he would have to be at the post office at five in the morning to sort his mail by village and family. Then he would arrange the huge pile of mail in bundles in his great big mailbag, which he slung across his shoulder. Then he went out to his trusty bicycle, his rainproof cape around his shoulders if it was raining, and off on a many-mile bike-ride on main roads and byroads and boreens, through villages big and small, returning to the post office late in the day, tired but happy with his life of being the carrier of news—and sometimes, as Christmas drew near, parcels of happy anticipation, from near and far and very far. Mr. Brannigan thought it was a great composition, but it wasn't me at all.

Patricia and Kathleen were first-year pupils at the Marist Convent, riding their bicycles past Corthoon School each day on their way into Charlestown. Secondary school was a different kind of reality for them, and they told us about their experiences in the world of higher education. For one thing, they were studying more subjects. And rather than one teacher, they now had many. There were nuns they liked and nuns they didn't like. There were nuns who loved to teach because that was their passion and there were nuns who grimly regarded this as a most unpleasant but necessary task, and they accepted it because it was God's work and their reward would be waiting for them in Heaven. The nuns didn't have Willies to wallop the girls with, but they had their own ways of punishment and humiliation—the tongue can wound more than Willie. I would listen to Patricia and Kathleen talking on and on about the nuns, and I began to remember their names. They all sounded foreign: Mother Augustine, Sister Philippine, Sister Ignatius, Sister Veronica, Sister Cecilia, Sister Alvarez, and Sister Fancha. These couldn't be their real names because I'd often seen the nuns in town and they were all as Irish as Molly Malone. I reckoned that these were the names given to them, or chosen by them, after taking their final vows and voluntarily committing themselves to a life sentence. They left their old names and their old lives behind.

My sisters' schoolbooks were a lot more interesting than mine, and I liked to steal a look whenever I could. They didn't just memorize poems like we did at Corthoon School; they analyzed poetry to understand what the poet was saying and how poets used language to express both simple and not-so-simple feelings. Sometimes I didn't understand the poetry because, even though I knew the words, they were used in a way that didn't make sense. Then I read that this was a technique that poets sometimes used to disguise what they were really saying. Even the strange words were explained, and there was discussion about each poet in the book. I enjoyed reading the poetry and learning about the poets. I read about Wordsworth, Byron, Shelley, Keats, Tennyson, Frost, and the

Irish poets, Patrick Pearse, William Butler Yeats, and Thomas Moore. I loved Thomas Moore's poem about ancient Ireland and the freedom that was lost at the end of Ireland's Golden Age, before the arrival of the Anglo-Normans in the twelfth century:

> The harp that once through Tara's halls
> The soul of music shed,
> Now hangs as mute on Tara's walls
> As if that soul were fled.
>
> So sleeps the pride of former days,
> Now glory's thrill is o'er,
> And hearts that once beat high for praise,
> Now feel that pulse no more!
>
> No more to chiefs and ladies bright
> The harp of Tara swells;
> The chord alone that breaks at night,
> Its tale of ruin tells.
>
> Thus Freedom now so seldom wakes,
> The only throb she gives
> Is when some heart indignant breaks,
> To show that she still lives.

Patricia and Kathleen were also studying European history. This confirms what I had long suspected: that other countries had their histories too. In Corthoon School we learn that Ireland was history and history was Ireland and nothing else mattered very much. The only English history we learned was the part that affected Ireland—and, of course, that England brutalizes people all over the world and steals their wealth because that's the kind of people they were. It's difficult to read the European history book, though, because it's in Irish. How could you really learn European history and enjoy it if it took most of your concentration just doing the translation in your head. And it wasn't just European history; they also had to learn other subjects in Irish. This made no sense to me at all. I thought it was a trick to make the pupils spend more time on Irish and less time on English and even less time on learning about European history. Maybe next they'll come up with another brilliant idea, to teach English in Irish.

I didn't do much homework because homework was every bit as interesting as watching cows shit. Besides, I didn't have a lot of time for homework, especially in spring when there were more important things to be done. I did my sums and that was about it. If I had extra time, I'd try to read the girls' secondary schoolbooks or I'd read comics whenever I could get them, or maybe a library book if a fresh boxful was delivered to the school. The best thing about comics was that they were short on words and long on pictures, the idea being that the pictures let you see what's happening and eliminate the need for a lot of discussion, and I was all for anything that reduces blather. Whoever said that a picture is worth a thousand words was probably the same person who invented comics.

Most of the comic books I read were cowboy comics. They had names like *Billy the Kid, Buck Jones, The Cisco Kid, Kit Carson, Buffalo Bill,* and *Wyatt Earp,* to mention just a few. I also liked war comics, but there weren't as many of those. The war comics were all about World War II and were almost always about heroic England against evil Germany, in the air, on the sea, and on land. They had names like *Battle of Britain, Fight Back to Dunkirk,* and *The Guns of Navarone.* The Germans called the English enemy "Englanders" or "Britishers," and the English called the Germans "Gerrys" or "Krauts" or "the Hun." No matter how bad it was for England, you knew that by the time you got to the end of the comic, Britain would be victorious—which, in this case, was perfectly okay with me because I knew that Nazi Germany and its Führer, Adolf Hitler, had to be beaten to save the world from brutal, dictatorial fascism. Now we were told that the world needs saving again, this time from Godless communism.

Once in a while, I was able to buy a comic or two for a tanner or a bob at Honans in Charlestown, and after reading them I could trade them to a friend for another couple of comics, ones that I hadn't already read. If a comic was new and clean, still had its cover, and had no tears in it, it could be worth two or even three old and worn comics or ones without covers—unless the old and worn one was a Classic like *The Call of the Wild* or *Hamlet* or *Moby Dick*. These were worth more because the stories were better and many were based on true adventures. Cowboy comics were always about good guys and bad guys and shootouts between them. Sometimes the cavalry was involved, and when you had the cavalry, you had the Indians, and the shootout was somewhere out on the plains or maybe around an army fort. The thing about cowboy comics was that you always know how the story would end. The good guys would win and the bad guys either wind up in boot hill or jail. The Classics were different because we didn't know how they will end. Even the ones that told fictional stories, like my favorite, *A Tale of Two Cities* by Charles Dickens, were so much better than the comics that come from Fleet Street in London.

I believed that the Classics came from America and they all had the yellow Classics label in the top left corner of the front cover. On the back cover of each Classic was a list of all the Classics available, each with its own special number. They were called Classics Illustrated, which meant that they were the comic-book version of great works of literature—and when you read a Classic you knew you were reading something very different than a *Buck Jones* or *Cisco Kid* comic. I would have loved to be able to read and save all of them. I only had a dozen or so, but I'd read about twenty-five. Classics were more than twice the price of a regular comic, and most lads didn't like to trade them unless it was for another Classic in equal condition. If I had read all the Classics Illustrated, I would have been very proud of myself. I could say that I was well read and, therefore, educated, a young man of letters, so to speak—or in my case, a young man of pictures. The nicest thing about being educated this way was that

I didn't have to go to school. I could do it at home in my spare time and enjoy it a lot more too.

The Year of our Lord 1960 was to have been a glorious time for me, a time of triumph and celebration. I had finished my penance at Corthoon National School and received my Primary School Certificate. I could now look over this period of my life as a sentence completed. School for me was over—and not just for the summer, but forever. How I had longed for this moment; just the idea of not having to go to school ever again was intoxicating. I knew, of course, that the vocational priests and nuns would be visiting many homes in June and July. They would have the names of all the boys and girls leaving the primary school, and this would be their opportunity to call on parents for the purpose of seeking new recruits for the religious life of Holy Orders—the priesthood, the convent or one of the many Catholic orders dedicated to helping the poor and impoverished around the world, while also spreading the faith. I was not looking forward to the priests' visit. I knew they would tell Mom what a great honor this would be for the family—that there was no greater source of pride for the Irish family, especially the poor Irish country family—than to have a son a priest or a daughter a nun.

First, there would be the finest education in Ireland's best colleges, seminaries, and convents—free. And there would be a new respectability, and with it the unspoken requirement of neighbors and townspeople for deferential treatment toward all members of the family making this most honored and noble sacrifice. Sometimes a priest or a nun would come to our school to talk to us about the religious life and ask us to pray for the vocation. The girls were told that in becoming nuns they would be the brides of Christ. They would wear a gold wedding ring on their marriage finger, but their husbands would not be of this corrupt and sinful world. They would all be married to Jesus Himself, and there can be no greater honor on earth or in Heaven than to marry into the Holy Family with God as your father-in-law and the Blessed Virgin Mary as your mother-in-law.

I wondered why priests didn't receive any special honor after being ordained. Why couldn't they be the groom of someone in Heaven? I know that Jesus was an only child and didn't have any sisters or brothers, so a new priest could not become a groom of Jesus's sister. But what about Saint Mary Magdalene, who was a follower of Christ? Why couldn't the priests be married to her? We learned that she had been an unclean woman at one time—whatever that meant—but was saved from eternal damnation by Jesus. I think maybe it was because, even though saved by Jesus, she would still be marked, not just for life but for eternity.

I would ask Mr. Brannigan about this, but I'm sure he would consider it an improper question. So I asked Tom Horkan one night, and he told me that I shouldn't worry about such things, and besides, he said, it didn't help very much whether you were a bride of Christ or the groom of someone else in Heaven when you were pondering an empty bed on a cold winter's night—and he should know, he said. I told him that the priests would be coming soon to the house to talk to my mother about my future and asked if he had any advice. He told me to run for the bog. When I was younger, I did think about becoming a priest once or twice, mostly because the priests I saw in Charlestown and Swinford seemed to have a very good life, living in big, fancy houses, driving nice shiny cars, and everyone bowing and nodding respectfully to them on the street. But now I knew this was not the life I wanted.

When the car turned into our boreen from the Main Road, I knew it was them and I headed for the bog. They would want to talk to me too to see if I had the vocation. I knew that I didn't, but I was afraid that if Mom sided with them, I might be persuaded that I did, and if I wasn't persuaded I'd feel guilty for letting Mom down and denying our family the honor and respectability of my sacrifice. I decided that the bog was the place to be at that particular time. I returned to the house after they were safely gone, expecting Mom to be angry and disappointed that I had fled. She wasn't. She simply said she knew they had come to the wrong house. I was happy and relieved that she understood. Then she said, "They do give you a great education, Tommy, and there is no law that says you have to take your final vows. You wouldn't be first one who went for the education and then left by the back door rather than the front." I knew she was right, but the thought of spending another six or eight years in school was almost as bad as the thought of being a priest the rest of my life.

The priests' visit with Mom had a far greater effect on her than I thought—but I would learn very soon afterward. She told me that, no matter the hardship at home, the youngest of her three sons would go to secondary school in Swinford, come September. My sister, Maureen, over in England, had agreed to pay the ten pounds first year's tuition. All my protestations—my appeals to reason, my attempts to avert this disaster—fell on deaf ears. Worst of all, even Eamon, who knew better than anyone what this meant, said nothing. My best hope and he said nothing. Later, when the battle for my deliverance from school was lost, I asked him why he was seemingly struck dumb in my hour of colossal need, and he simply said, "I don't give a shit. All I know is that I'm bailing out next year whether you go to college or not."

To be admitted to St. Patrick's College in Swinford, you had to take an entrance examination. I knew that if I deliberately failed the test so badly that the priests would think I was a mental case, I wouldn't be accepted. I agonized over it but finally decided that I could not deliberately fail. It would be too shameful—even if no one knew it but me and maybe a priest or two. Besides, there was a bright side…well, at least a match light down this dark tunnel. With Eamon going to England the following year, all I had to do was endure one more year's sentence of school. Then there could be no argument, no high-minded nonsense about getting a college education. It's not that I was against education. I wasn't. I'd like to learn many things—history, science, philosophy, poetry, and a foreign language that would be more useful and interesting than Irish. I just didn't like the idea that you had to be imprisoned in a school to do this—and be at the mercy of teachers who believed that regular humiliation and frequent walloping was the only way to make you properly disposed to learning.

I read a story about Abraham Lincoln, America's greatest president. He was born poor in Kentucky and was self-educated, going on to practice law, free the slaves, and save his country from destruction. If self-education was good enough for Abraham Lincoln, it was good enough for me, too.

I was now the dubious owner of the first bicycle I'd ever had, my very own bike. Mom bought it for me at P. Duffy's in Charlestown for three pounds, ten shillings. It looked like it was about fifty years old, but it's mine and that's what counts. Of course the only reason I got my own bike at the young age of thirteen and a half was because it's the only way I could get to school in Swinford. That's why I have mixed feelings about the bike. I was heartened by the fact that I could ride around with my pals at night and not have to worry about whether there would be a bike available at home or not. I'd be able to ride my bike to Mass on Sundays, too, and not have to walk as I'd done for as long as I could remember. Sometimes a neighbor, cycling by, would stop and give me a ride, usually on the bar if it was a man's bike. If it was a woman's bike with no bar I'd have to settle for the handlebars or the carrier behind the saddle, if there was one.

Of the three passenger seats on a bicycle, there is no question at all that the carrier behind the saddle was the safest and nicest ride. If there was a high wind in front of you or rain, sleet, snow, or hailstones pelting down, shielded behind the poor unfortunate doing all the pedaling was the place to be. I would not miss sitting on the handlebars, I can tell you. It was an uncomfortable ride and dangerous too, trying to maintain your balance while keeping your feet out of the spinning spokes of the front wheel. More than once I'd had the painful experience of flying off the handlebars onto the pavement, face first, either because I lost my balance—after hitting a pothole, for example—or because my smart-aleck, pick-me-up friend thought it would be funny to brake suddenly and jettison his cargo.

My bike had a carrier too, not for picking up passengers but for carrying my schoolbooks. We couldn't afford to buy a real carrying case for my books, so we did the next best thing: I asked Jim Terry, the blacksmith in Charlestown, to make me one. He did a lot more than just shoeing horses and mules and asses and fixing broken tongs. He was also a carpenter and made those big spoked wooden wheels for carts and even whole carts. Jim laughed when I asked him to make me a carrying case for my schoolbooks. He said no one had ever asked him to make a school case before, and I was a little embarrassed, but he was good-humored about it and said that he'd give it a try. A few days later, he showed me this wooden rectangular box with a lid, about eighteen inches long, fourteen inches wide and six inches deep. It had a thick leather carrying strap and it looked a bit rough to say the least. I tried to appear impressed but I dreaded having to lug this thing into a classroom. Even empty it weighed a ton. Still, for five shillings, it was a bargain. Jim even offered to sand it down a bit so that I wouldn't get splinters in my fingers—and paint it for me.

I had two paint choices—red or blue—the same two colors he used on the wheels and carts he made. I chose red and that was that. The case was too big. I should have measured the length of the carrier on my bike before I placed the order. I couldn't use the pull-back spring on the carrier to hold the case in place so I had to use a piece of rope to tie it to the carrier. It was not an impressive sight, but I needn't have worried about having an unusual school case for on my first day at St. Patrick's College, I saw all manner of book carriers, from the very fancy—polished leather and brass buckles—to the unpretentious, mostly belonging to the country lads like Rory O'Connor, named for an *Ard Ri* in ancient Ireland, who rode his bike from the far side of Ballaghaderreen in County Roscommon to Swinford, more than twenty miles each way, every day, whatever the weather. His commitment to an education—or his parents' commitment to his education—was more troubling to me than I cared to think about, so I didn't. Of course most impressive were those scholars who lived in the town, close enough to St. Patrick's that they didn't need a school case at all—and simply carried the books they needed for that morning or afternoon under their arms, the way students in America do.

In America we'd be called students, not scholars or pupils, and our college would be called high school. I envied the students over in America. From the magazines that I'd seen, like *Seventeen,* they all seemed rich and sophisticated and had their own huge cars with long fins and no tops. They had big wide smiles showing beautiful even, perfectly white teeth. I'd never seen teeth like that in Ireland—ours are a bit crooked, uneven, with a few gaps here and there, and not very white. They went to the same high school, boys and girls together. Not so for us. If any of us went on to secondary school, it was mostly a convent school for the girls and mostly a college for the boys. The girls were taught by nuns and the boys were taught by priests and sometimes by the Christian Brothers.

There were a few Jesuit colleges in Ireland but only someone who wanted to be beaten to death early in life would want to go there. Survivors of Jesuit colleges were supposed to be highly educated, hopelessly brainwashed, and belonged forever to the Jesuits in heart and mind, body and soul. The Jesuit boast was supposed to be, "Give us the boy at seven and he is ours for life." I heard that the Christian Brothers weren't much better—in their colleges you just change color, from white—or red if you're out in the wind and rain a lot, like me—to black and blue, following their frequent administration of corporal punishment. Still, the Jesuits and the Christian Brothers were highly prized by the grown-ups of Ireland for the fine education they beat into their victims. Thank God I would only have to deal with regular teaching priests.

There were also a few vocational schools around, and Swinford had one. The vocational schools were for boys and girls, but they didn't teach as many subjects as the convents or colleges, and focused more on the trades, with subjects like carpentry, mechanical drawing, and electronics, and, for the girls, shorthand and typing. It took five years to finish at the convents and colleges, taking two comprehensive, national examinations along the way: the Intermediate Certificate at the end of three years and the Leaving Certificate at the end of the fifth year. Every scholar sitting for these exams began them at precisely the same time, on the same day, all over the country, and the results were released about two months later at the same time, on the same day, all over the country. There would be much happiness and relief on this day, and much weeping and desolation too. If you failed either one you could repeat the previous year's studies and try again, accepting the unspoken shame that hung over you like a cold November fog. If you didn't try again or, God forbid, fail the second time around, you were done for and might as well leave the country and not show your face again.

You could finish up at the vocational school in just two years and then go to work for the Electricity Supply Board or a furniture factory or as a shorthand-typist in an office in Dublin or Galway. Fortunately, I didn't have to worry about these exams. I'd do my one year at St. Patrick's and happily leave to take over when Eamon bailed out. I told myself that it wouldn't be so bad. The year would fly by and soon St. Patrick's would be only a bad memory. Besides, there was something that would ease the bad memory: I'd be able to say that I went to college and studied important subjects with strange sounding names, like elocution.

CHAPTER 11

⚜

I SOON LEARNED that St. Patrick's College was much harder than Corthoon School, and there was no getting away from homework, or "study," as we now called it. We had all kinds of new subjects. Sums were no longer sums, they were mathematics and include algebra and geometry and later trigonometry, whatever in the hell that is. In addition to English literature, poetry, and composition and Irish literature, poetry, and composition, we had Latin and with it endless memorization, translation, and composition. There was biology, botany, science, elocution, world history, geography, and religion. And that was just the first year. We had different priests for different subjects, and sometimes the same priest would teach two or three subjects. We also had two lay teachers who weren't priests at all.

One was Mr. Walsh, but he didn't teach first-year students. The other was Mr. Mangan, and he taught Irish literature and poetry. At Irish he was brilliant—a native speaker and totally fluent. More important, he was not hard on us. Mr Mangan was a gentle soul who tried his best to do the impossible: teach us to love Irish. He lived about a mile out the Charlestown road in a small slate-roofed house and walked to and from his home, along the Main Road, head always bent a little to the right, giving him, I thought, a slightly different perspective of things.

Soon after I began my final year of penance at St. Patrick's, I had practically a life-changing encounter on my way home one afternoon. I noticed two girls on bicycles in front of me. I had to slow down because they were cycling so slow and wobbling all over the road I was afraid of a collision if I tried to just zip on by. They were chatting and laughing as though they didn't have a care in the world—and not the least bit concerned that they may be holding back motorists or other cyclists, like me, who did have some cares and needed to get home because there was work to be done. I was about to pass them—so far to the left that I was off the road and on the grassy margin—when the closest one to me turned, and a little startled said, "Oh, hello there; who're you?"

I looked at this lovely smiling face, a mass of beautiful dark curls falling around her shoulders, and I almost fell off my bike. I didn't know God made faces like this. My face became instantly red hot. I could feel the blood pulsating through my cheeks and forehead. Even my ears started to burn. My stomach was suddenly all knotted up. Much worse, I couldn't speak. All I was able to do was focus my entire intelligence on not falling off my bike. I was terrified that I'd start bleeding from the mouth, nose, and ears just to ease the pressure in my bulging face.

When time started going again, I was able to mumble out: "My name is Tommy, Tommy Gallagher; who're you?"

She turned to her friend and said, "See, he *can* speak," and turning back to me replied, "I'm Maura Heany and this is my friend Kate. Are you going to St. Pat's or the Tech?"

"I'm going to St. Pat's," I said. "How about you?"

"We're going to St. Mary's."

And then Maura Heany boldly grabbed the bull by the horns.

"Why is your face so red? Are you shy?"

"No, I'm not shy. I have too much blood."

"Oh, I see. For a minute there I thought the cat had your tongue—or maybe that you were deaf and dumb. Maybe you should give all that extra blood to the Red Cross."

Now she was making fun of me and, as I was in no condition to respond, I did the only thing my barely functioning brain could instruct me to do. I pedaled off furiously to the sound of laughter behind me. I was almost home before my face had returned to its seminormal state—seminormal because it was always too red anyway. Mom liked to tell me that my face wasn't red, it was ruddy—as if there was a difference—and that I was blessed to have such a healthy look. I knew that this was a nice way of saying that I looked like a country mug, out in the wind and the rain and all kinds of weather all the time. I didn't mind saying that I'd happily risk a near-fatal illness if it meant that most of the blood in my face would just drain away, leaving me deathly white.

I had known since I was young that I had too much blood—if only I had two or three pints less there would be no more burning, throbbing face at the worst possible times. I came from a long line of fairly good-looking people, on both sides, except for me, and all because of this blood disease. I was probably the only person in the world who would look much better, maybe even handsome at death's door than when he was disgustingly healthy. The Red Cross…now that's an idea.

But Maura Heany and her friend Kate Maloney, a neighbor of hers, were not finished with me yet. A few days later, I had the bad luck to come upon them again on my way home from St. Pat's. Just seeing them in front of me caused my face to heat up like an electric iron. I could feel my hands getting slippery on the handlebars, and that same queer feeling was back in my belly. At first I decided to stay a safe distance behind them but almost immediately realized that this wouldn't work. They were again cycling so slowly, talking and laughing and taking up the whole road. There was nothing for it but to pass them, and the only way to do it was to do it fast—before Maura Heany had time to make some smart-alecky remark. I caught up to them in no time at all and was about to pass when Maura Heany swerved directly in front of me, leaving me no choice but to swerve to the left and off the road into a fence full of briars. O fecking, fecking Hell! Mercifully, I didn't fall off the bike—my bike and me and my schoolbook case all fell into this briary fence but we stayed intact and semi-upright. Still, this humiliating scene was almost as bad as it could get. I had briars in my wheels and thorns in my clothes, and my left hand was scratched and bleeding.

Why couldn't I have been hit by a car as a result of Maura Heany's reckless behavior? As long as I wasn't killed or seriously injured, this would be a much better outcome for me. First of all, I would be a totally innocent victim, soaking up all of the attention, concern, and sympathy of everyone at the accident scene. Maura Heany would, of course, be in a terrible state, knowing that she was totally at fault. She would be telling anyone who cared to listen how sorry she was. More importantly, she would be telling me how sorry she was as I lay there on the side of the road, in great pain but heroic, being attended to by Dr. Cawley and the ambulance people. But no such luck for me. Instead, here I was stuck in a fence, bloody hand, pounding face, my mouth dry and no hole forming under my feet to swallow me up and save me from this mortification.

Maura Heany did tell me how sorry she was and, happily, even sounded sincere about it. I could see the concern in her eyes. But, God help me, looking into those eyes—beautiful, soft, warm, and worried—for a moment I completely forgot about my burning face. She wanted to clean my bloody hand with her scarf, but I bravely dismissed my injury as nothing, less than nothing. Maura Heany's attention to me was both exciting and embarrassing. I could see that Kate Maloney wasn't nearly as concerned about my health and was ready to leave the accident scene. I wanted to leave the accident scene too because my belly was going up and down and sideways like when we're churning butter. And I was mumbling rather than talking. I knew Maura Heany didn't know what to make of me. How do I escape without her thinking me a complete mental case? I was saved when Kate Maloney decided that she'd had enough of this small drama and cycled off. I took off too, with Maura Heany protesting that I should rest awhile longer, as I didn't look well.

We joined up on the road home several more times, and I began to feel a wonderful excitement getting up in the morning to go to school. This wasn't penance at all. I could happily deal with the priests and the classes knowing that there may be a chance meeting with the prettiest girl I've ever seen. With some effort I was even able to control the miserable and strange things that happened to my body when she said hello. I was hoping that soon she'd realize that Kate Maloney could easily find her own way home so that she and I could be alone to talk about practically everything and anything.

Then one day there was a dramatic new development in my budding whatever-it-was with Maura Heany, and whether it was my handling of it in my own usual grown-up way or events that were soon to unfold anyway I will never know. What I do know is that whatever it was that was keeping me awake at night was about to end. We met, as usual, on the way home from school and, as usual, I tried to speak intelligently, talking about school and my struggle with elocution and the upcoming presidential election in America that was in the news every day. I must have impressed both Maura Heany and Kate Maloney, because they decided to follow me home. I was horrified, speechless. I could feel my face burning and pulsating again. Had they gone bloody daft?

"You can't come home with me."

"Yes, we can," said Maura happily. "We've never seen the far end of Culmore. Are there others like you there?"

Maura Heany's eyes were laughing at me in a nice way, and I would have liked it, but the thought of having these two girls, strangers, come down our boreen to our house was unthinkable. How, in God's name, could I explain to Mom what they were doing at our house?

"What will my mother say if she sees you?"

"You can introduce us and tell her that you've made two new friends," Maura Heany offered as we pedaled on toward the far end of Culmore.

"I'm supposed to make new friends at St. Patrick's, not at St. Mary's. You're girls—you can't come home with me."

"Ah, don't worry about it," Maura said. "Sure it's all in fun, and it's nice that you know we're girls. I was beginning to have my doubts."

Fun! Fun for who? I've heard about panic, I've read about panic, and now I know what panic is. This is panic. I cannot be seen with Maura Heany and Kate Maloney. I pedaled away like mad. If I could make it to our boreen and get off the Main Road before they rounded the turn at the Joyces' gate, they wouldn't know where I'd gone. Brilliant plan, except that they were pedaling like mad too. I couldn't believe that these two girls who rode their bikes like two drunken old-age pensioners were now pedaling like demons possessed. I couldn't believe this was happening. I was trying desperately to get away from two girls, one of whom I liked more than I knew why. All I knew was that when she looked at me or talked to me or smiled at me, I got wobbly and tongue-tied and felt stupid. And this was horribly stupid. Why couldn't Maura Heany and I have a wonderful secret friendship, nurtured each day for a brief while on the way home from school? Instead the two of them had gone looney on me, and I had no choice but to disown them and disavow any connection to them whatsoever. Thanks for nothing, God!

I almost made it to our boreen before they came around the turn at the Joyces' gate and spotted me. Looking behind I saw them and they saw me turning off the Main Road. Jesus! Why didn't I just keep on going, maybe all the way to Charlestown and beyond? Too late now. I rode down the boreen to our house, 150 yards away. I didn't turn around and I was praying hard that they wouldn't follow—that this was the end of their *fun*. It wasn't. They left their bikes at the entrance to our boreen and followed me on foot. Dear God Almighty, what now? I could be seen to be with them. My sisters, all younger than me, would torment me forever, and Mom would ask questions, and I would feel ashamed for bringing about this unexplainable situation. I left my bike and books by the gable of the house and headed for the bog, my usual refuge. If I could divert them away from the house, there was at least some hope that this mortally embarrassing scene would pass into oblivion with no one the wiser except for me—and in a year or two maybe I'd be able to put it behind me.

Our bog was below the railway that marks the northern boundary of our land. The Main Road marked the southern boundary. It was called a "Main Road" because it connected our part of the country, "Mayo, God Help Us"—as it was called by people who didn't need God's help—to

Dublin, the capital, 150 miles away, or about the same distance as the moon, as far as I was concerned. Our farm was long and narrow, like all the others that lay side by side and were bordered by the Main Road on the south end and the Great Southern & Western Railway on the north end. We and all of our neighbors had our bog the other side of the railway and had level crossings from our farms to the bog. "Level crossings." Boy! That was a laugh. There was nothing level about ours. Just ask Coco. Because this part of the railway ran through bogland, it sat on a raised bed of crushed limestone. This meant that our crossing rose steeply on each side of the track. With a full load of turf coming out of the bog, Coco needed help getting up the short but steep slope, and more help in slowing the cart down on the other side.

I remember being terrified when I was very young and standing close to the track, my hand firmly in the hand of a brother or older sister, as a train approached. It would thunder by, and the whole earth would tremble and shake. I could feel myself going up and down and *see* the land around me, left and right, doing the same thing. At first I was convinced that it was just a matter of time before a giant chasm would open up and swallow us—or at the very least that the train would topple off the track, with a fifty-fifty chance that it would land on top of us. Now, I was just proud to say that even though we didn't live in far-off California or Japan, we had our very own earthquake several times a day. Thanks to the government, which owned the railway, the line was well fenced in and we had to go through two sets of iron gates to go to and from the bog. On the first gate was a warning sign:

G.S. & W.R
NOTICE
Any Person Leaving
This Gate Open Is
Liable To a Penalty
Of Forty Shillings

I don't know why the sign didn't just say two pounds instead of forty shillings—it was the same thing. Probably because forty was a much bigger number and, therefore, country people would be more frightened by it. An open gate meant that cattle or sheep or a horse or an ass could wander onto the railway. A few years ago, a farmer by the name of Browne lost several fine bullocks and heifers because someone left the railway gate open and the luggage train made mincemeat of them. Poor Browne not only suffered an terrible loss, but he had to pay the penalty too—and he swore high up and low down that no one in his family would be so careless. Browne believed it was a neighbor or a tinker who, taking a shortcut, passed through and forgot to close the gate, and no one doubted that this was true, but since it was Browne's open gate that led to the slaughter and endangered the train, Browne had to pay the fine. The law is the law. There was no warning sign on the second gate, which lead directly into the bog. I reckon this was because the railway people didn't care much if the second gate was left open or not—as there wasn't anything of sufficient size to wander onto the railway from that direction. A hare or a badger facing down the train wasn't going to give the train engineer a heart attack.

We were fortunate that our bog was so close to home, about half a mile away through the fields, and except for the twenty yards across the railway, we remained on our own land. Every farmer was entitled to a portion of bog so that he could cut and save his turf to boil his spuds and bacon and warm the house in the wintertime. But if there was no bogland nearby, the farmer might have to go miles for his turf. I didn't know what the people in Dublin did about their turf, and I didn't care much either. Anyway, they probably used coal from Newcastle.

Bogs were also a great place to hide, safe from the British Army and the Black and Tans during the Troubles; safe from the guards if you were making poteen, Ireland's favorite illegal whiskey; safe from the family if there was a screaming argument in the house; and safe from St. Mary's schoolgirls gone daft in the head. Lying low in thick heather, I scanned the

Hill Field five hundred yards away. This is where they would first appear if they were still serious in pursuing me. It meant that they have already passed our house, a couple of fields, and the cow barns—and now had a clear view of the bog below but could not see me. Heart pounding, I waited and watched...and then they came into view, their blue-and-white uniforms as clear and unmistakable as my stopped heart.

Dear God, I prayed, *please turn them around. Don't punish them, God. Just turn them around and send them home and don't let my sisters or my mother see them. And if they have seen them, Dear God, please erase the memory from their minds forever. If you do this, Dear God, I promise I'll consider the priesthood again.*

The blue-and-white uniforms came over the Hill Field to the Field of the Fairy Bush and stopped. All of our fields, big or small, had names. There was the Field of the Road by the Main Road. Below that was a rough, swampy field called the Bogeen. Next was the Field of the House, which was in front of the house. Then there was the Side Field to the side of the house, the garden where we grow all our vegetables was just behind the house. And below the garden was the Other Bogeen, then the Field of the Barns. Below the barns was the Hill Field, then the Field of the Fairy Bush, and below that was one long, mostly wet four-acre stretch to the railway. We called this the Field of Rushes. Rushes were a plague weed that thrived in poor, wet ground. As much of the West of Ireland consists of poor wet land, there was a constant struggle to keep the rushes from taking over completely. The only thing rushes were good for was thatching the hay cocks and oat cocks in the Garden by the barns. Our fields in Madogue had names too, but these were all in Irish and date back to a time ages ago when people spoke only Irish. These fields have names like *Talamh Garbh, Glannfathereen, Glannahumpaun,* the *Closheen,* and that ancient piece of earth, *An Fort,* the fort, place of my dreams and fantasies.

In the middle of the Field of the Fairy Bush, but at the end that rose up to meet the Hill Field, there was an old blackthorn bush that had been there since the beginning of time. It had been half dead for as long as anyone could remember, but some of its limbs lived on in grim defiance.

There was a rotted-out hole in its trunk at the base, and once Jimmy even lit a fire in the hole, but the fairies put the fire out, so Jimmy said. It was always called the fairy bush and, as children growing up, each in our turn, we believed that the fairies lived under that bush. At night when the wind was blowing hard and dark clouds were racing across the sky, the fairy bush made the strangest, loneliest sounds—almost human, its bare, dead limbs talking to the live ones. Maybe the fairies did live there. Anyway, whether it was God answering my prayer or the fairies warning off strangers, the girls from St. Mary's turned around and went back over the Hill Field, up the boreen to the Main Road and back to their own village. And I was saved...from what I didn't know.

At home there was no mention of this scandalous incident, and I felt it was only right that I reconsider the priesthood, as I promised God. I did too, but only briefly—you can't create a true vocation out of nothing. If I felt embarrassed about meeting Maura Heany again—and I did. I needn't have, for she wanted nothing more to do with me. I was both relieved and, at the same time, horribly depressed. For me, the best part of going to St. Patrick's had become, like the joke, the coming home part. Now both Maura Heany and Kate Maloney had disappeared from the face of the earth. For weeks I didn't see them at all and figured that *they* were hiding from me. Finally, one afternoon in late October, I spotted Maura in front of me...and, Holy Mary! She was alone.

Thank you, God; thank you! I'm sorry for being angry with you in the past. Now, I beg you, please keep my blood under control and help me to behave like a normal, intelligent human being. Nothing doing. I could feel the same dumb things starting to happen: blood rushing to my face by the bucketful, heart thumping—ka-boom, ka-boom, ka-boom—and my hands already so sweaty that they were slipping off the handlebars. I asked God again to remove this affliction from me so that I could concentrate on mustering up the courage to catch up and say something witty.

My hope was that the unspeakable incident would not be mentioned, that it would be utterly forgotten as though it had never happened. Then, in my heart and soul I would silently forgive Maura Heany for causing me such trepidation and we could get back to building our beautiful, secret friendship. I wanted to tell her how happy I was to see her again, that I had missed seeing her for so long. If she mentioned that awful event, I was prepared to do the honorable and gentlemanly thing: accept full responsibility for what happened, saying that I should have explained to her that it was much too soon to meet my mother, that Kate Maloney didn't need to meet my family, that our relationship was only starting, that my mother would ask questions, and that my sisters would torment me night and day.

And, above all, that I was sorry for my stupid, childish behavior. Maura Heany was a little crazy, but she was special in a way that I didn't understand and couldn't explain. Since meeting her I could not seriously think of anything else. Despite my woeful shyness and despite my pathetic inability to control my mental and physical self in her company, Maura Heany was the most exciting thing that had ever happened to me, and I desperately wanted whatever this was to continue.

Alas, the first great love of my life did not see it that way. When I came alongside, heart still hammering, I offered a cheery "Hello, Maura. Where's Kate?"

Maura Heany did not turn around to look at me or speak to me. She continued to stare straight ahead, her lovely face expressionless. I tried to be humorous. "That was quite a bike race we had the last time I saw you."

No response. She was staring way off in the distance, but I knew she wasn't seeing anything.

"Maura, I'm sorry; please say something. Tell me I was stupid but please say something. Did you really want to meet my mother?"

Maura Heany who, at this moment, held my heart in her hand, now threw it to the wind like a used sweet wrapper. I stayed with her for a minute or two more until embarrassment overcame me, and then I pedaled off, feeling a terrible loneliness inside me, and this time I felt the unwanted tears on my face.

After a while I managed to convince myself that Maura was just being Maura, that she was being unpredictable—or maybe punishing me because I had hurt her feelings. I prayed that this was the reason for my nonexistence beside her. Then there was a chance we could make up. It was not to be. For weeks I pined over her while at the same time telling myself over and over that whatever this new experience was, it wasn't worth it. During this time Maura Heany was nowhere to be seen, but each day I hoped... Again she had disappeared. Eventually I learned that Kate Maloney had stopped going to St. Mary's, and Maura Heany's father had transfer his daughter to a boarding school somewhere in the south of Ireland where they make nuns, the rumor is. Not that I could ever see Maura Heany becoming a nun, but then, sure, who knows? The power of prayer can move mountains, we're told. Maybe, I consoled myself, this was the reason she could not even look at me on that last sorry day—she had been persuaded, probably under duress, that she had the vocation. And now she was going to a convent in Tipperary or Kerry where my lovely Maura, with so much earthly promise, would instead become a bride of Christ. That was the end of whatever-it-was between Maura and me. What was left was only a bittersweet memory of something that was so special but didn't quite make it. My final year of penance resumed.

CHAPTER 12

———— ❧ ————

WE HAVE TAKEN the boy out of the bog, and now our great and holy task is to take the bog out of the boy. God help us in our work. This was the mission of St. Patrick's College, not exactly sign-posted on the way in, but clear enough.

It was November 1960 and over in America Senator John Fitzgerald Kennedy had just been elected president, and there is great excitement in Ireland. Everyone knows that Kennedy is Irish-American, and the way Radio Eireann goes on and on, you'd think that he was 100 percent Irish-born and raised and that we Irish, ever known for our generosity, selflessly gave him to America to save the world from Godless communism—just as we sent saints and scholars all over barbaric Europe during the Dark Ages to Christianize and civilize the less fortunate. Our teacher priests at St. Patrick's were especially proud because Kennedy wasn't only Irish, he was also a Catholic—not all Irish people are blessed with this affliction. In between classes we were encouraged to pray for his election, and now it was evident that God, in His infinite wisdom, heard our prayers and put the world on the right course for salvation.

We were proud and I was proud. Soon, like every other family in Ireland, we would have JFK's picture on the mantelpiece over our kitchen fireplace, book-ending Pope John XXIII on the other side. The pope and the new president would look smashing together: Kennedy, young—at least for an American president—and handsome, and the pope smiling down at us like a saint, not at all like the dour-looking Pope Pius XII. I was glad that his picture was finally gone. Pope Pius XII sat on the throne of St. Peter for donkey's years and his stern, unsmiling face looked down

136

on us year after year until he finally went to his eternal reward in Heaven a couple of years ago. Everyone knew that popes went straight to Heaven when they died—no stop-over in Purgatory for them. At least I hope they did, for if they didn't, it doesn't bode well for the rest of us. Tom Horkan said that Pope Pius XII didn't do much to bring the Catholic Church out of the Middle Ages, never venturing beyond the walls of Vatican City except to visit his summer home in Castel Gandolfo. Tom said popes needed to get out and travel the world, and see for themselves the state of the church in distant lands, and show themselves to their flock.

Pope John XXIII is planning to convene a Second Vatican Council to bring the Church into the world of the 1960s or, as he put it, "to open the windows of the church to let the people see in and the church see out." Tom Horkan wished the pope luck and said that he'd need lots of it. The big shots in the Irish church wouldn't like this at all, Tom said. They liked things as they were, the church all powerful and the poor farmers and peasants of Ireland forever humble, just waiting for their reward of a better life in the next world.

Centered on the wall over our fireplace was a large picture of the Sacred Heart. This would be our own Trinity, Jesus with his hands stretched out, one toward President Kennedy, the other toward Pope John. There was something almost divine about this, I thought, one savior already in Heaven—waiting for the nod from God to return on the Last Day—and the other two on our mantelpiece.

The First Vatican Council, Father Jack O'Neill told us, was held in 1869 and 1870. It was convened by Pope Pius IX, and it was not welcomed by many of the cardinals, who were deeply worried about possible changes in rules and doctrine. A matter of considerable controversy was whether the notion of papal infallibility should be established as absolute dogma. Many of the cardinals were concerned that the church's noble mission of converting non-Catholics to the One True Church would be made more difficult, not to mention great powers like the Austro-Hungarian Empire that might view such a move as a direct threat to their own absolute power.

These rulers would prefer the pope to know his place and stay there. No one likes change, Father Jack said, and the cardinals of the church, along with kings and emperors and popes, were no different than anyone else.

I liked Father Jack. He was my favorite and I was especially happy about this because he was also the president of the college. He treated us like adults and encouraged discussion in class—a whole new experience for me. No question was stupid and there was no Willie in Father Jack's classroom, and no fear. Everyone was at ease and eager to learn. You could feel the excitement. In addition to religion, he also taught biology and botany – and asked us not to use the toilets at school but to go up to the college vegetable gardens behind the school and defecate all over the place because human manure was the best kind of fertilizer for vegetable growth. Father Jack grew everything up there, and he took his vegetable growing far more seriously than I took mine—but we grew vegetables at home out of necessity, not for show.

He also liked to tell jokes, like the one about the old woman on her deathbed and a priest hearing her confessions and giving her the Last Rites—and she says to him in a whisper, "Father, I'm not afraid to go. I've lived a hard life in this valley of tears—my only pleasures being the few fags and maybe the half wan at Christmas to celebrate Our Lord's birth, and the wan thing that kept me goin' day in, day out, Father, was me cuppa tay. Tell me, Father, will there be anny tay in Heaven?" The priest thinks quickly for a few moments and then, holding the old woman's hand between his two hands, he reassured her, saying, "Mrs. Murphy, I have it on the best authority there is, Holy Scripture, that you will have a variety of tays in Heaven—there is Adoramus te and Benedicimus te and Laudamus te, and for those who like their tay a bit stronger, there is Voluntates te"—and with that the old woman peacefully departed for the Gates of St. Peter, knowing that just beyond, waiting for her, would be a lovely cup of bless-ed tay.

One day in biology, Father O'Neill brought in a large picture of the human body, showing the complete skeleton with even the smallest bones identified: all muscle groups, all organs—everything, even the unmentionables, kind of superimposed to show both male and female parts. He looked at it like he was seeing it for the first time and said to himself more than to us, "Dear God, what perfection. How can anyone look at this masterpiece of creation *and* not believe in God?" As usual, when I was embarrassed, my face got redder than normal red, and just looking at this detailed image of the human body was a red alert—and I wasn't the only one, I can tell you. Father Jack noticed the wide-eyed gawking and the awkward silence and said, "Gentlemen, we are adults in this class, and we are here to learn about the divine miracle of our own bodies." I immediately felt much better. We were adults, and we were learning about human biology and physiology.

The hard part for us was that we had to memorize just about all the bones in the skeleton, all the muscle groups, and all the organs, for we would have to draw this picture from memory in an exam and identify all major bones, muscles, and organs. Father Jack left the picture on an easel in the classroom for a few days so that we could memorize it bit by bit. Later in the school year, I won an academic award and once again I got to kiss the bishop's ring when he visited the college to show himself, look important, and present awards. My award was a book in Irish named *Maire*. I left it with my cousins in Swinford—where my Aunt Mary treated me to lunch every school day—and never asked to see it again, for who wants to read an entire book in Irish?

Not all of our teacher priests were like Father Jack, but one came very close. He was Father John McNicholas, and he taught English poetry and literature. Like Father Jack, Father John did not believe in corporal punishment but did believe in encouragement and in making learning fun. Most importantly, he believed that even lads from the bog could study Shakespeare's plays and sonnets and learn beautiful poetry. It was easy to see that both of these priests loved to teach. Yet they had altogether different personalities. Father Jack was always loud, happy, and humorous—"Now, gentlemen, I don't want to see any of you using the toilets; I need that manure for my vegetables." Father John was more reserved and serious, almost shy—until he started reading Shakespearian prose or reciting poetry. Then he came alive like he turned his Ever-Ready on. Marching up and down the classroom, he would charge full steam into a poem:

White founts falling in the Courts of the sun,
And the Sultan of Byzantium is smiling as they run
They have dared the white republics up the capes of Italy,
They have dashed the Adriatic round the Lion of the Sea,
And the Pope has cast his arms abroad for agony and loss,
And called the kings of Christendom for swords about the Cross.
The cold queen of England is looking in the glass;
The shadow of the valois is yawning at the Mass;
. . . .
Don John of Austria is going to the war,
Stiff flags straining in the night-blasts cold,
In the gloom black-purple, in the glint old-gold,
Torchlight crimson on the copper kettle-drums,
Then the tuckets, then the trumpets, then the cannons, and he comes.

Father John suddenly stopped, eyes wide. "Lads, lads, can you hear the drums, can you hear the cannons?" I knew no one would believe it, but I could hear the rattle of the drums and the cannons blasting away. I could see the cannon fire wreaking havoc on the warships below. Father John could take me into the life of the poem, and I was there, far from the classroom, seeing it all. He resumed the stirring poem by Chesterton that told the story of the epic naval Battle of Lepanto, off the Greek coast in 1571, where, as Father John said, the forces of Christendom, under Don John of Austria, defeated the forces of Islam under Ali Pasha. This battle ended the Ottoman Turks' quest for supremacy of the Mediterranean. Next time Father John might launch into *Hamlet* or *The Merchant of Venice*, or Chaucer's *Canterbury Tales*, and we would happily struggle with the strange sounds of Old and Middle English.

Tara's Halls

I love the Irish poems because they touch my heart:

Who fears to speak of Easter Week
Who dares its fate deplore
The red-gold flame of Erin's name
Confronts the world once more

So Irishmen remember them
And raise your heads with pride
That brave men and straight men
Have fought for you and died.

Patrick Pearse was one of the leaders of the Easter Rising in April 1916.
We had learned in school that Pearse, a school teacher by profession, was
a patriot, a hero, and a martyr who wrote poetry and prose in English and
Irish. He became commandant-in-chief of Provisional Forces during the
Easter Rising. In his powerful poem, "The Rebel," he expresses the emo-
tion, the passion, the pure, raw feeling of one who has endured too much,
one who has crossed the line and passed the point of no return. Patrick
Pearse was ready for rebellion:

I am come of the seed of the people
The people of sorrow
That have no treasure but hope
That have no riches laid out
But a memory of an ancient glory
I am of the blood of serfs
My mother bore me in bondage
In bondage my mother was born

The children with whom I have played
The men and women with whom I have eaten

Tom Gallagher

Have had masters over them
Have been under the lash of masters
And though gentle, have served churls

And now I speak being full of vision
I speak to my people
And I speak in my people's name
To the masters of my people
And I say to my people
That they are holy
That they are august despite their chains
That they are stronger than those that hold them
And richer and purer

That they have but need of courage
And to call on their God
God, the unforgetting
The dear God who loved the peoples
For whom He died a-naked
Suffering shame

And I say to my people's masters, beware
Beware of the thing that is coming
Beware of the risen people
Who shall take what ye would not give
For did ye think to conquer the people
Or that law is stronger than life
Or than men's desire to be free

We shall try it out with ye
Ye that have harried and held
Ye that have bullied and bribed

We shall try it out...
Tyrants, hypocrites, liars.

Pearse and many of the other leaders who survived the Easter Rising of 1916 were quickly tried before a military tribunal, found guilty of treason, and executed.

Like Father Jack's, Father John's classes were always fun and interesting, and if it wasn't for some of the other teachers, I would have had a complete change of heart about going to school. I reckon God didn't want to make this too easy for me, and maybe this was the way it's supposed to be. Unfortunately, there were other teacher-priests who were a bit more challenging. Father Leonard taught mathematics and, as he liked to say himself, he was hard but fair, and he was. Father Leonard was brilliant, and we were all kind of in awe of him, but he had little patience for slackers, and he was hard to please. Father Rowley taught history and science. History was my favorite subject until I met Father Rowley. I liked science too but was never quite good enough for him.

Father Lynch taught Latin and elocution, and he was the one with the belt. Inside his long black robe on a hook was a three-foot-long, brown leather belt. On the friendly end was a loop for Father Lynch's hand to firmly grip the monster. The belt was about two inches wide and a quarter of an inch thick. On the outside, in bold black print, were the words "For Toughs Only." Father Lynch introduced us to his For Toughs Only belt as soon as we got into his classroom on that first day of class. Unlike Mr. Brannigan, he did not give it a nice friendly name—its name was already printed on it.

Fathers Leonard and Rowley didn't use belts or canes to deliver punishment; they just walked up to your desk and raised you to your feet by your sideburns, thumb and forefinger by each side of your head. Father Leonard used this method sparingly and only when it was absolutely necessary to get the lad's head right, he said. Father Rowley used it for the pure pleasure of inflicting pain. On that first day of class, he was late, and when he arrived there was noisy chatter in the classroom. It took a few moments for the class to settle down. Father Rowley then headed straight for me in the front row. He lifted me right out of my desk by my sideburns. The assault was so unexpected that, at first, I felt no pain at all. I was just stunned. Then the pain of having hairs pulled out of the side of my head by brute force hit.

I complained that I had done nothing to warrant this attack. "I know, I know," he said, almost gently, then turning to the class, continued: "This is merely an example of what can happen when I don't have your full and undivided attention—immediately." This was an example, he said, of "preemptive punishment," to get the boys' "unruly minds" properly focused and conducive to learning. To Father Rowley, it seemed that boys from the bog needed regular punishment as a civilizing action, to make them more respectful of higher authority and, therefore, more amenable to being educated. If Father Rowley had little respect for country lads, he seemed to have even less respect for the townies, and I felt better about this. I thought maybe that Father Rowley had come from the country himself and still carried unhappy memories of pastoral serenity, so he disliked everyone.

Father Lynch, bless him, believed that a young man's hair should not be trifled with and certainly not be removed by force from the side of his head. No, no; Father Lynch believes in the fine art of skin removal instead, at which he was the master. I knew because I was an early victim. It would have been bad enough had I been guilty of the offense charged—fighting in the classroom—but I was as innocent as the Baby Jesus. We were all seated at our desks—long bench desks that went across the classroom—waiting for Father Rowley, who was late for class again.

On my left was Joe Gavigan and on my right was Seamus Finn. We were seated alphabetically. These two townies didn't like each other very much—but then no one liked Joe Gavigan, including me. Joe was the class bully—big, fat, puffy face, small mean eyes, and always looking for trouble. Apart from calling him by various names such as Mountain and

Mohammed, the basic plan was to ignore him and avoid him as much as possible. As I had the misfortune of being seated beside him, this wasn't easy, but as few bulbs ever lit up in the lad's brain, he needed help with schoolwork, and I would give him a hand from time to time, to appease the brute.

On this sorry day while we were waiting for Father Rowley to show up, Gavigan began to pick a fight with Finn, and soon they were swinging at each other. Stuck in the middle with no way out, I tried to separate them. Holding the smallish Finn back with my right arm was easier than holding Mohammed back, who was all over me, trying to get at Finn. In the next classroom, Father Lynch was teaching a class in elocution to the second-year students. The two classrooms were divided by a wooden partition, except for a small "peeping" glass window up near the front of the room. Father Lynch, hearing the commotion in our classroom, looked through the little window and saw a fight in the third row. Sadly for me he didn't take the time to see what was actually happening: me trying to keep two townies apart. He saw Gavigan and Gallagher engaged in a thuggish brawl in a college classroom. He knocked loudly on the window, and in a second all eyes were riveted on Father Lynch's outraged face. Looking directly at Mohammed and me, he raised his hand and with his index finger summoned us to his classroom. I mouthed a protest to him, shaking my head and holding out my hands as a gesture of one truly without sin. His face flushed with anger, he banged on the window again and conveyed his insistence that I accompany Mohammed next door.

Just the humiliation of having to stand in front of the second-year students was punishment enough, guilt or no guilt. I saw neighbors who had been a year ahead of me at Culmore and Corthoon schools hold their heads down, not wishing to increase my embarrassment by looking at me. Father Lynch, his face redder than mine, something I did not think possible, had Mohammed and me face the second-year class in shame. Most of them looked frightened, a few seemed to relish the moment, and my neighbors looked at the floor. I turned to Father Lynch and opened my mouth to protest my innocence. I thought he was going to belt me in the face.

He roared: "Silence! Boys, we have here two sorry specimens of Irish manhood—thugs, fighting like animals in a classroom, bringing dishonor to our college, shaming themselves and our race. Over in England, in London and Birmingham and Manchester, we are known as The Fighting Irish because of savages like these. But, by God, we will do what we can in this place of learning to civilize them, to make them worthy of our noble race. Now, Mr. Gallagher, hold out your right hand please."

I was mortified. Nothing like this had ever happened to me in my life. I was completely innocent, but it counted for nothing. I was more angry than scared. Father Lynch reached inside his black robe and slowly removed the belt from its hook. I held out my hand, just wanting this humiliation to end. With the loop of the belt firmly in his closed hand, Father Lynch practiced a couple of wallops, and I was immediately aware that the belt made a very different sound than Willie as it cut through the air—probably because it had more air to displace. This was going to be on a different level altogether. I noticed that Father Lynch was careful to stand a precise distance from me, repositioning his feet until he knew exactly how much of the belt would collide with my hand—and it didn't take a genius to know why he was doing this. He was like an executioner about to behead his victim with an axe. Standing in the precise spot was critical.

I stared at him as he raised the belt over his right shoulder and brought it down with more force than Brannigan could ever muster. The pain was searing, like a bolt of lightning going through my body. My eyes instantly watered. The force of the collision caused me to wobble on my feet, and for a moment I thought I was going to faint. The end of the belt curled around my hand and then with split-second timing Father Lynch jerked the belt backward toward his body. This flicking action peeled skin from my knuckles, the punishment being delivered to both sides of my hand. Old Brannigan couldn't get Willie to curl around your hand, but an expert with a pliable belt could accomplish this quite nicely. I got four wallops, two on each hand, but after the first two, the other two didn't seem to hurt much. My hands had already taken as much pain as I could feel.

In disgust, Father Lynch dismissed me. With both of my hands burning as though they were on fire, I returned to my classroom, wiping the shameful tears from my eyes before opening the door. Father Rowley still had not arrived but the class was quiet. No one was laughing, and there were no smart-aleck cracks—just silence. Everyone was looking at me wide eyed. I got into my seat; there were no cold steel legs on this bench to ease my pain. Seamus Finn didn't look at me. He was looking very determinedly at an invisible spot on the blackboard in front. I almost felt sorry for him. He didn't come forward to tell the truth. Mohammed fared worse than me, his soft, fleshy hands that never saw any work didn't hold up very well. He looked pathetic, tears rolling down uncontrollably, his hands blue and swollen. I never experienced the belt again. Before I left St. Patrick's College, I told Father Lynch about his mistake. I didn't expect any satisfaction, but he seemed genuinely sorry and apologized. I wanted to tell him that the belt had to go, that students couldn't be treated like intelligent adults one moment and beaten like animals the next.

I had expected him to lecture me about the weighty responsibility of teaching and educating smart-aleck townies and boys from the bogs of Mayo and Sligo and beyond so that, ultimately, it mattered little whether I had been involved in the classroom fight or not. I should be able to grasp the larger struggle of St. Patrick's College, its difficult but noble mission: to convert the ignorant into the learned, the uncivilized into young gentlemen, capable of going out into the world and bringing honor to themselves, their families, their race, and their country. But I got no lecture about the smallness of the mistake measured against the greatness of the challenge. Instead I got an apology, and I walked away not knowing if I had a moral victory in hand or not. I had been ready for an argument, and I would not have been silent. To me the mistake of walloping me instead of Seamus Finn was not the real mistake. The real mistake was in the walloping itself. Father Lynch had called us thugs for being violent in the classroom. Yet in front of another classroom of students, he used far more deliberate violence than the two townies were capable of—while shaming and humiliating us at the same time. But I said nothing. He had apologized, and I didn't expect that. It was done.

CHAPTER 13

✦

ONCE IN A while, when we sensed the mood was right, we would dare to ask the teacher for a "free class." We would decide before he arrived if we should go for it, and someone would be nominated to make the brazen request. First we'd look the teacher in the face to see if he appeared to be in a good mood. If his face showed a reasonably happy countenance, we'd look quickly at each other for agreement and then nod the okay to the nominee, who would raise his hand and ask politely and in great deference, "Father, do you think we might have a free class for this period?" Sometimes the free class came about without any planning at all, just a spontaneous outburst: "Free class, Mr. Mangan; free class please." Mr. Mangan always carried with him a sad and serious expression, but we knew that this meant nothing—it was neither positive nor negative. Mr. Mangan was such a mild-mannered man that we knew we had a fair chance of a free class request, delivered in unison. We might not get the free class, but we knew he wouldn't be angry about our asking for it.

We asked for a free class very rarely, and when we did we usually got it. We only did this with Father Jack, Father John, Mr. Mangan, and once in a great while, Father Leonard. A free class meant that we could close our schoolbooks, for we weren't going to need them for the next forty-five minutes. The next question was, what were we going to do for forty-five minutes? It was usually up to us, the scholars, to come up with a list of topics for discussion, and we never had any trouble using up the clock. Topics included sports, sometimes our own school football team—especially if it was doing well against other colleges—where my older cousins, Kevin and Brendan Groarke, were two of the top players. We might discuss Irish politics, international politics, the American and Russian space programs, or the new American president—and how he'd deal with Nikita Khrushchev, who was still raving mad over the American U-2 spy plane incident the previous May. Khrushchev, a professed atheist and an avowed communist, had no friends here.

Free classes in which we'd discuss and debate practically any topic were as delightful as they were enlightening. But two topics were never discussed during a free class: girls and religion. In a Catholic college, girls, as a subject of discussion, were taboo, and who wanted to discuss religion during a free class? On occasion we'd take up the entire period singing songs, mostly Irish rebel songs about heroic struggle and martyrdom. Mr. Mangan, in particular, loved rebel songs, and we all knew that he had a great sympathy for the IRA in its continuing fight to free Northern Ireland from the "Saxon invader."

On one occasion in Father Leonard's free class, Eamon O'Grady rose to his feet without invitation to begin the sing-song. He couldn't sing worth a tinker's damn, but he thought he could because, apparently, no one had told him otherwise. His head high and his eyes soon glistening, he belted out a song about a family put out on the road by the landlord during the famine. After this opener we were on our way. Seamus Heaney rose up to give us his own rendition of "Sean South of Garryowen":

T'was on a dreary New Year's eve
As the shades of night came down
A lorry load of volunteers
Approached a border town
There were men from Dublin and from Cork
Fermanagh and Tyrone

But their leader was a Limerick man
Sean South of Garryowen.

In this attack by Sean South and his companions on a police station across the border in Northern Ireland in 1956, Sean South and Firgal O'Hanlon were killed, due to an alert police sergeant who spotted their shadowy figures approaching in the dark. Ireland had fresh martyrs and a new song to join an endless list. O'Hanlon's name would later be central in the international hit, "The Patriot Game."

Then Brian Rooney rose to make his contribution to the happy sadness that filled the classroom with "Boolavogue," and we all had to listen in total silence to Ireland's unofficial national anthem:

At Boolavogue as the sun was setting
O'er the bright May meadows of Shelmalier
A rebel hand set the heather blazing
And brought the neighbors
From far and near

Then Father Murphy from old Kilcormac
Spurred up the rocks with a warning cry
Arm, arm, he cried, I've come to lead you
For Ireland's freedom, we'll fight or die.

And die they did in great numbers in 1798—and lose they did, Father Murphy being burned on the rack for his rebellion.

Then came Harry McDonnell, the one everyone was waiting for. Harry had won several Irish song contests all over the country. He rose out of his desk, managing with grace that great Irish talent of showing pride and humility at the same time. Without fuss or bother he launched into "The Boys of Wexford," President Kennedy's favorite Irish ballad, we're told—Wexford being the county of his great grandfather's birth:

Tom Gallagher

In comes the captain's daughter
The captain of the yeos
Saying brave United Irishmen
We'll ne'er again be foes
A thousand pounds I'll bring, if you
Will come and fly with me
And dress myself in man's attire
And fight for liberty

We are the boys of Wexford
Who fought with heart and hand
To burst in twain that galling chain
And free our native land.

Harry had a beautiful singing voice, reaching all the high notes with ease. Soon we were in an emotional swoon, I caught up in the passion of the moment as much as anyone else. And the rebel songs went on, all about defeat, dying, and martyrdom in the cause of Irish freedom. Then my turn came, and I had a choice in my own mind: should I sing "Shall My Soul Pass Through Ireland," about Terrence MacSwiney, the Lord mayor of Cork City who starved himself to death in an English prison in 1920 after being convicted of treason? (The English discovered to their great embarrassment that MacSwiney, in addition to his loyalist duties as lord mayor of a prominent Irish city, was also a senior officer in the IRA. The English have no sense of humor.)

I decided that it was time to be different, to break the spell—and got a stunned silence for my effort:

There you go and baby, here am I
Where you left me here
So I could sit and cry
Well golly gee, what have you done to me
Oh, well, I guess it doesn't matter anymore

Do you remember baby, last September
When I held you tight
Each and every night
Oh, well, oops-sa-daisy, how you drove me crazy
But I guess it doesn't matter anymore.

Buddy Holly was my favorite singer. I knew all of his songs, and my fantasy for a while was to be a successful singer and bandleader like him. It was only a fantasy, though, not even rising to the level of a dream. I didn't have Buddy Holly's voice, nor his rhythm—and the only guitar that I'd ever seen up close was one that John Sweeney had before he bailed out to England. Like us, the Sweeneys had a small farm in Madogue, less than a slingshot from ours. Our boreen leading out from Dad's farm to Madogue Road passed through the Sweeney farm, and they had been our friends and neighbors for many years. Sometimes in the summer, John would ride his bike down Madogue Road on a Sunday afternoon, his guitar across his back. When he reached the Main Road, he'd leave his bike by Stenson's gate and walk along the road playing the guitar and belting out songs by Elvis Presley, Buddy Holly, Tommy Steele, Cliff Richard, and many other singers that we'd hear on the radio.

When I saw him coming over the road, I'd run to join him and tag along behind, thrilled to be this close to a rock-'n'-roll singer. John dressed the part: blue jeans, black leather jacket, and a head of curly brown hair—just like Tommy Steele's, he told me. And boy, did he have rhythm—at least that's what I think it was. Practically every car coming by would slow down to listen, and some would stop so people could get out to be entertained. John loved the attention, telling his impromptu audience that he was going to be famous one day.

Alas, John's time did not come, but the talent was in the blood. A few years after John went to England, his younger sister, Peggy, followed, eventually settling in Manchester, where she married a fellow Irish immigrant and my namesake, Tom Gallagher. They had several children, including Noel and Liam, who would go on to form the world-famous British rock group, Oasis.

Irish rebel songs are about constant struggle and are inspiring up to a point, but the endless singing of tragic defeat and heroic death leaves me empty, the earlier inspiration seeping away under the weight of blood and failure and epic tragedy. An American love song with a great beat and sad lyrics was my answer to my classmates' patriotic offerings.

When I finished my Buddy Holly song, there was absolute silence. I looked around and everyone was staring back and forth from Father Leonard to me. Father Leonard was looking at me with a puzzled expression on his face. Then he raised his hands and began a slow clap. My classmates joined in, and the clapping grew louder. I sat down in embarrassment. I knew they weren't cheering my singing voice for I was no Harry McDonnell. It must be the song. When things had quieted down, Father Leonard said, "Thank you, Mr. Gallagher. I have no idea at all what that was about, but it was certainly different."

To me Buddy Holly *was* different. He created a musical style and sound that were unique. He and his band, The Crickets, had been one of the great joys in my life, thanks to Radio Eireann, Radio Luxembourg, and American Forces Network, which all played his songs regularly. I remember that awful day, February 3, 1959, when we heard on the radio that Buddy Holly had been killed in a plane crash near Clear Lake, Iowa, along with the Big Bopper and Ritchie Valens. This was one of the saddest days in my life. After his death I went to the bog and stayed there for ages, alone in my misery as usual. Upon return, the radio stations were playing his records over and over in remembrance, but for weeks I couldn't bear to listen. A light had gone out of my life. Soon after the plane crash there was a new song in tribute:

Look up in the sky
Up to one who knows
There are three new stars
Brightly shining bright

They're shining so bright
From Heaven above
Gee we're gonna miss you
Everybody sends their love.

I left St. Patrick's College before completing my first year. In the spring of 1961, I was needed on the land to help Eamon as the year's work began in earnest. Dad wasn't coming home this spring or any other spring. Mom said that he just wasn't up to the heavy work anymore. There had been no more babies since Christina was born in 1955. Eamon took Dad's place in cutting the turf and putting down the tillage—and I moved up a rung in the ladder. The incredible thing was that I didn't want to leave school. If anyone had told me when I began my last year of penance that I would be sorry to leave St. Patrick's, I would have thought them completely soft in the head.

Father Jack came out to the house to ask my mother if there was any way I could return to school. He told Mom that I was one of his best students. While I knew he was exaggerating more than a little, my mind was in turmoil. For most of my life, or at least as far back as I could remember, I wanted to be out of school and away from teachers who profoundly believed that teaching and punishment were indivisible and inseparable, akin to the natural laws of the universe. In Corthoon School learning was accomplished through the ever-present fear of punishment. Now after sitting in the classrooms of Father Jack O'Neill, Father John McNicholas, Father Leonard, and Mr. Mangan, I knew that learning could be a wonderful and exciting experience. Because of Mr. Mangan's genuine love of the Irish language, I had even begun to like it, for God's sake! From these teachers I learned more in a few months than Mr. Brannigan had ever been able to accomplish. It was far more than book work and memorization. Here we were encouraged to think for ourselves, to question, to challenge, to even disagree with the teacher. Incredible! Freedom from fear was an exhilarating experience. I was beginning to understand what education was all about.

What I had dreaded had become a happy time. I was learning, I was growing in self-confidence, and I was doing okay. Father Lynch and Father Rowley were hard to deal with, but I learned to deal with them while not taking them too seriously. With them physical pain and humiliation were an essential part of their method, but after my initial bad luck, I managed to avoid physical punishment. I used to think that one day a week at school was enough, but now that seemed ages ago. My mother told Father Jack that circumstances at home made it necessary for me to leave school. I knew how she felt. Only eight months earlier, she had decided that, despite the hardship, I would go to college. When Father Jack left, she looked at me and then looked away with tears in her eyes. She said that maybe I could return in September, but I knew that even if it were possible, I would have to start over, repeating my first year again, as I had left before completing the year-end exams.

I did return to school in the fall of 1961, but it was not to St. Patrick's. Simple reality suggested that it was highly unlikely that I would be able to complete five years at St. Patrick's, or even three—but maybe I could complete two years at the Tech. So I started as a first-year student at the vocational school in Swinford, which everyone called the Tech. The Tech was a state school, and mostly free of tuition. Here, although we had regular subjects like English and Irish, the focus was on learning a trade. The Tech didn't turn out teachers, or hopeful intellectuals, or civil servants, or graduates bound for universities and degrees in areas of competence that were just words or terms to most of us. Then they might go on to advanced studies or to careers in law and medicine and the church and business management and, of course, the civil service, where a lifetime of security, good pay, and status awaited.

Those who attended the Tech had no such aspirations. They would not be swaggering about in hospitals with stethoscopes around their necks, or in courtrooms or tending their flocks, or sitting behind desks in nice offices, looking important, immensely proud of the fact that they were making a very respectable living by using their brains rather than their physical labor. In Ireland the next best thing to having a son or daughter taking Holy Orders was to have a son or daughter employed through use of brain rather than brawn. Brain work was admired; brawn work was not. Farmers, even well-to-do ones, who might be highly respected locally, were still fairly low on the social order. The many thousands of aging bachelor farmers around the country was grim evidence that Irish girls, if given a choice, didn't grow up to marry farmers.

The objective of higher education was to rise above the humble occupation of farmer, which accounted for more than 80 percent of the Irish population. My birth certificate said that my father's occupation was farmer. My father's birth certificate said that his father's occupation was farmer. My grandfather's birth certificate said that his father's occupation was tenant farmer, not much more than a serf. We were farmers, so there would be no putting on airs and graces, except by escape to Holy Orders or to the noble professions—and, of course, Ireland's perpetual safety valve, emigration.

No, the Tech would turn out beginner carpenters and electricians and the rare school-trained farmer who chose to learn the art and science of proper farming methods. The girls would become shorthand-typists and office clerks, working in jobs that afforded little or no opportunity for advancement, where twenty years of experience would be regarded as one year's experience repeated with dull monotony twenty times. After graduation from the Tech, most of the boys would have long years of apprenticeship ahead of them before they would be fully certified. During this time they would work long hours and make little money. I wasn't overly excited at this prospect but, as it turned out, I didn't have to worry about slaving through years of apprenticeship. In March of 1962, as in March of 1961, I left school to help with the spring's work on the land. Eamon had gone to the beet factory in England in October 1961, returning in March 1962, but only for a few months.

Tom Gallagher

The beet factories of northern England desperately needed labor in the fall and winter of each year to harvest the beets and, over the winter, to convert them to sugar in the factories. Much of this labor came from Ireland—where there was always an excess of labor, especially in the winter months when Irish farmers had spare time on their hands. There was open passage between Ireland and England, in both directions. No immigration and customs to slow the constant flow of labor. When you got off the boat at Holyhead, you walked or ran straight to the waiting trains, their engines running, ready to begin the journey to Birmingham, London, Manchester, Liverpool, and many other destinations. The open borders benefit was the result of Ireland being England's first and last white colony. By English standards beet factory pay was good, but by Irish standards it was fantastic. Every couple of weeks Eamon sent his own blue registered envelope home. Thanks to him, we were able to pay down our debt at Mahon's and, over the winter, there were no shortages of the basics like bread, butter, sugar, milk, tea, Sunday bacon, sausages, and pudding.

The morning Eamon left for England, he and I rode our bicycles from Culmore to the railway station in Swinford, he on his bike, I on mine. His held his suitcase in his right hand, his left hand on the handlebars. It was an unpretentious departure, without fanfare yet, for both of us, momentous. An era was ending. For Eamon, a new life in a new country was beginning, where Irishmen, mostly laborers, were still largely regarded as second-class citizens, and for me a new life at home and a newfound freedom. We didn't talk at all on the way to town. There was nothing to say. Alone in our thoughts, we pedaled on, mile after mile, staring straight ahead. On the platform we waited for the train, a few words now and then to break the silence. "So this is where St. Patrick's is," said Eamon. "I never noticed it before." When you got to the dead end of Station Road you had only two ways to go: left across the iron grate into St. Patrick's College, or straight ahead into the train station.

Here was my big brother whom I admired and feared in equal measure. Eamon was fearless and, like Dad, he never looked for a fight, but if one came his way, he didn't waste time trying to reason his way out of it. I was reluctant to fight and would only do so when my only other option was to walk away in shame, which I couldn't do. I have had a few fights in my life and have acquitted myself fairly well, but I didn't have Eamon's natural confidence. One time coming home from school, Seamus Flanigan called Eamon snotter-nose. Seamus was bigger and heavier than Eamon, but that counted for nothing. Eamon blew his nose clean, then told Seamus to take back the insult and apologize. Seamus bravely but foolishly refused. Two seconds later he was on his knees gasping for breath, dropped by a right to the jaw and a left to the solar plexus. I didn't know whether it was Eamon's natural confidence that fueled his temper or his temper that fueled his confidence, but whichever it was, I wasn't always a beneficiary.

Now we were about to say good-bye. I looked down the tracks to beg the train on. After fifteen long minutes, it came in, brakes squealing, air hissing. There was a quick, awkward handshake, emotions held in check, and then he was gone. I couldn't see where he sat. I wanted to see him stick his head out of a half-opened window—like they do in the pictures—to wave a last good-bye, but there was nothing. If he had waved from an open window, I would have returned the wave and our four eyes would have remained dry, but I would have felt better. I waited for the train to pull out of the station, then picked up both bicycles, riding mine and holding Eamon's by the handlebars as it ran alongside. I was more than an hour late for school, but it was only the Tech, and, besides, I had an acceptable excuse.

Eamon was assigned to the beet factory at Newark in Nottinghamshire. For the next four and a half months he worked ten hours a day, five and a half days a week. His sleeping quarters were arranged by the beet factory, and judging from his description, they were basic, to say the least. When he left, my great fear was that I wouldn't be able to step into his shoes. While I had worked at his side for years, there were tasks like cutting turf, ploughing with borrowed mules, and mowing a field of oats, swing by swing with a scythe, that I had never tried. And I wouldn't have a Tommy at my side to be my helper. My younger sisters would be there to help, as always, but the heaviest work would be mine.

I don't know whether I was more disappointed or relieved when Eamon returned home in March 1962 for the spring's work. Wintertime on the land is no test of ability. Taking care of the cattle, repairing fences, and fixing cart trails into the bog is tiring but hardly challenging. The hard things, like cutting turf and oats and ploughing, required skill and strength, and above all, endurance.

There was one challenge I faced a couple of days before Christmas in December 1961. I was already a seasoned killer of chickens and ducks, but I knew that this experience would be of limited value when it came to killing the Christmas goose. Once a year at Christmastime, we indulged in a special dinner on Christmas Day and again on New Year's Day with the remains of our earlier feast. The main course was either a turkey or a goose that we had raised through spring, summer, and fall for this sole purpose, to be sacrificed in celebration of Jesus's birth, while also giving the family our biggest treat of the year. Our goose was practically a giant compared to a chicken or a duck, and when she wanted you to know that it was time to back off, she'd flutter her wings in a great display of anger and raise up her head on its long neck until it was dangerously close to your face. The children teased her sometimes, but, like Polly, she was mostly a pet. After watching Eamon carrying out the execution several times in past Christmases, I knew it was going to be a battle. A chicken or duck will struggle, but once you've got them firmly between your thighs, you can finish the job quickly.

The first thing I had to do was coax the goose into the barn by letting her see that I had a little food in a basin. The best time to do this was at feeding time, when she was expecting her daily meal. Otherwise she might be suspicious about going into the cow barn when she was accustomed to eating her food off the ground in the open. I needed to have her in the barn with the door closed because I couldn't let her escape when the battle began. I had the sharpened gully knife in my belt. Next, I had to corner her, then grab her by the neck and quickly pin her powerful wings. This was easier said than done. The goose seemed to instinctively know that she was in a death struggle and went wild with terror. Screaming bloody murder, she rushed around the barn, half on foot, half in flight. And I chased her around the barn until we were both exhausted. I still didn't have her where I needed her to be—clamped tightly between my thighs with her wings and legs under control. My face and arms were already bruised and sore from wing blows, and my legs were bloody from scratches that have torn right through my trousers. The goose had clearly won round one, but I was determined—for if I were to lose this battle, I might as well die in the attempt and have the goose emerge the victor in all her righteous, indignant glory.

Round two began and, mercifully, it was a short one, conceded by the goose, who was, I suspect, saving her remaining energy for round three. I now had her pinned between my legs. I lifted her up and positioned her body firmly between my thighs, surprised that she was so heavy—but then I'd never picked up a full-grown goose before. Then the silent bell rang for round three. I placed my left hand over her beak and bent her head down toward her neck. I would need to wrap my hand around her neck and her beak and hold both tightly so that the back of her head was now facing me.

Next, with my right hand I plucked the feathers from the small soft depression at the base of her skull and removed the gully knife from my belt. This was the worst part and the most dangerous, for the goose will struggle like a demon possessed. I must cut quickly through the soft spot, then down through bone to reach the jugular and windpipe, and then hold on for dear life, for in these final moments, she has the strength of a young bull, and if she breaks free now, her blood and my blood will be all over the walls, and it will be hard to tell who got the worst of it.

The blood poured out into a shallow concrete drain that ran the length of the barn—where the cows deposit their urine and manure. Eventually she gave up the struggle and slowly went limp. I could now relax my aching hips and thighs, arms and hands, and knees. I had done my part. The rest of the work was for Mom. My last task was to clean out the blood from the drain, wash it down with water, and air out the barn so that the cows would not be afraid to enter in the evening.

CHAPTER 14

ON THE THIRTEENTH of November 1961, shortly after my brother had left for the beet factory in England, I tried out for the FCA—the Local Defense Force. I wasn't yet fifteen and had grave doubts about whether my short, skinny frame would be able to hold up the uniform of the Irish Reserves in a "fitting" manner, as one might say. I rang the doorbell of the FCA office, almost directly across the street from my godparents' shop and pub, the Groarkes'. It was answered by Quartermaster Frank Callahan, who looked down at me in a kind of fatherly way and said, "What can I do for you lad?"

"I want to join up," I said, in a voice that didn't sound like mine at all.

"Arrah, son, sure you're joking me," he said. "You're looking for the Boy Scouts—we're looking for soldiers." I insisted in an even stronger voice that I was at the right place.

Quartermaster Callahan, with exaggerated politeness, asked me to step into the office. I could tell that he just wanted to go out the back door and burst into a fit of uncontrollable laughter. Instead, he muzzled the urge and called upstairs for Captain Hume. "Sir," he said, "can you come down for a minute? We have a lad here who is lost and in need of proper directions."

Captain Hume came down the stairs, all six feet two inches of him. Slim, ramrod erect, and looking magnificent in his crisp and polished regular army uniform, he was, in my mind, the perfect image of a soldier—and I was anything but. I had seen Captain Hume a few times before when he would come out to the house to see Eamon, who was then on the roster rolls of the FCA—or more accurately, to try to find Eamon, who rarely showed up for his reserve duties.

"I think I know you," Captain Hume said. "You're Gallagher from Culmore."

"I am indeed, sir," I said.

"Where's your brother, Eamon, these days?" he asked.

"He's at the beet factory in England, sir."

"Ah, well, I suppose there's no point in looking for him anymore then, is there?"

"No, sir," I said, "but I'm here to take his place."

Unlike Quartermaster Callahan, Captain Hume did not think that this was a laughing matter, and I liked him right away. He had a friendly, easy way about him and when he spoke to you, you had the feeling that he was genuinely interested in you.

"What's your name," he asked.

"Tommy," I said.

"How old are you, Tommy?"

"I'm eighteen," I said, blushing from the usual red to purple. Captain Hume didn't seem to notice, but he pressed a little.

"Hmm, and Eamon would now be..."

"Twenty two," I blurted out, without giving him time to finish the question.

"My Lord," said the captain, "time certainly flies." Turning to the quartermaster, he asked, "Frank, do we have a uniform that Mr. Gallagher might reasonably occupy?"

"Sir," said Quartermaster Callahan, "I think we're pushing it a bit—sure the lad could fit entirely into a single trouser leg."

"Well, Frank," said Captain Hume, "let's see what we can do."

The smallest uniform was still way too big for me, but I assured the quartermaster that my mother could take it in here and there, and if it needed more than that, she had a friend in Charlestown who was an excellent seamstress.

"That might work," said Frank Callahan, with a big grin. "You can be the company's drummer boy."

I didn't mind Callahan's teasing humor anymore. I was in. Captain Hume gave me the oath, witnessed by the quartermaster. I swore to be faithful to Ireland and loyal to the constitution. I was now a new recruit in Company C, Eighteenth Battalion, Western Command, serial number 737807. This was an infantry company. Our main weapon was the Lee Enfield 303 bolt-action rifle with a ten-round magazine. We also had a few Bren light machine guns, three Vickers medium machine guns, and a couple of Gustav submachine guns. The rifle, the Bren, and the Vickers all fired the same 303 round and all came from our ancient enemy, England, except for the Gustav, which was from Sweden. Unlike the others, which were intended for longer-range shooting, the Gustav was designed for close-in combat and fired a heavier but slower 9 mm round. I reckoned a heavier but slower bullet would kill you just as dead as a faster but lighter 303 bullet.

Although the FCA had its own officers, like Lieutenants Mickey McNeela and Paddy Gordon and Commandant Eddie Boland in C Company, all FCA units had regular army officers in overall command and regular NCOs like Gerry Tierney to oversee training. The quartermasters were also from the regular army—to make sure that the part-timers didn't make off with everything, I thought. Over the winter months of 1961 and 1962, I would attend FCA drill and train meetings every Monday night in the Swinford Town Hall, where our hobnail army boots were most unkind to the shiny wooden floors that were only supposed to make contact with Sunday going-to-Mass kind of shoes. Still, I didn't feel too bad about this. The new town hall in Charlestown, together with Walsh's Central Ballroom, had left the Swinford facility to cater to the wearers of hobnail boots and other occasional gatherings and even less occasional dances.

When we weren't drilling, we were learning how to break down, clean, oil, and reassemble the 303, the Bren Gun, and the Vickers.

The 303 and the Bren were dead easy, but the Vickers had a devilish locking mechanism, and I had great difficulty breaking it down into its many parts and then reassembling it. The lock of the Vickers was central to the firing operation of the gun. This was the mechanism that performed or controlled the essential tasks: removing the round from the canvas feeder belt, placing the round in the firing chamber, firing the round, and extracting and ejecting the spent shell—and repeating the process over and over at an astonishing speed, enabling the Vickers to fire up to six hundred rounds per minute, or ten per second. My friend, Martin Neary, who was a corporal, could break down and reassemble the lock blind. He insisted that, with more practice, I could too, but I was still struggling with my eyes wide open.

Before firing the Vickers in a live-fire exercise, we had to load the feeder belts, and this was a miserable task. The canvas belts were stiff and hard. Spaced about a quarter of an inch apart were the little slits into which you must push the individual rounds. This wasn't easy, and soon my fingers were numb. All 250 rounds per belt must be pushed into the slits the same precise distance so that their bases were all flush and even. An uneven belt would probably cause a stoppage when firing, and we all knew that this was an unacceptable reason for a stoppage, numb fingers or not. I heard one of the NCOs say that the British Army had an automatic belt loader for their Vickers machine guns, but I reckon they didn't want us to have an equal advantage on the battlefield—or maybe the Irish army thought it perfectly acceptable to have their Vickers squads do this painful job the old-fashioned way—or maybe the government was just trying to save the few extra pounds.

The FCA office in Swinford also had jurisdiction over the Charlestown area, from where Captain Hume was happy to accept recruits. The Charlestown unit didn't have the Vickers machine gun, which I believed was a good thing. They had the 82 mm mortar instead. They were a bit rough and, therefore, less dangerous firing dummy shells across empty fields from mortars than live ammunition from machine guns. We trained with them from time to time, practicing small-unit tactics, and also practiced with units from other towns. When those of us who were able to get away to Finner Camp in Donegal in the summer, and maybe Renmore Barracks in Galway in the fall, we'd train as part of larger formations, whole battalions.

I learned that the regular army is only about nine thousand strong, and that wouldn't hold back the Russians for much longer than a vodka break if they decided to swallow up all of Europe. Corporal Tierney said we shouldn't worry about this too much. Gerry said that if the Russians crossed the Elbe on their westward march, they'd have to contend with a lot of American, German, French, Dutch, and British troops before getting to dear old Ireland. And if they did make it to Ireland, fifty thousand well-trained and highly motivated FCA troops—or at least as many as could be rounded up—would be at the ready to stand shoulder to shoulder with the regulars, to push the Godless communists into the sea, just as Brian Boru pushed the savage Vikings into the sea at the Battle of Clontarf on Good Friday in 1014, breaking their power in Ireland.

The Bren gun required a team of two to operate in live fire but, if necessary, could be handled by just the gunner—until the barrel became too hot and had to be replaced or more ammunition was needed, the job of the No. 2. The Vickers machine gun required, at a minimum, a team of three: the gunner, the ammunition belt feeder, and the ammunition bearer, who must ensure a continuous supply of ammunition, and who may, if the gun team was undermanned, have to double as the water bearer to ensure that there was a steady supply of water available to the water jacket, which was a little water tank, holding about seven and a half pints of water, surrounding the gun barrel. The water kept the barrel from getting red-hot from continuous fire. This, too, could eventually cause a stoppage—not a serious problem in training, we were told, but deadly if you were about to be overrun in battle. This sobering thought kept us very serious for at least a minute.

Our Vickers gun training took place on the forlorn ballroom floor of the once-impressive Swinford Town Hall. Martin Neary handled most of the training. Driving the horseshoed heel of his right boot into the floor, he would order, "On your mark; get set; on this spot; action." The team was ready. The No. 1, the gunner, rushed forward to the spot of Corporal Neary's heel, carrying the fifty-pound iron tripod. He set it down heavily on the increasingly dulled and dented pinewood floor, loosened the clamps on the legs, brought it upright, tightened the clamps, then dropped to his arse on the floor behind the tripod to await the No. 2, the ammunition belt feeder, who then rushed forward with the thirty-pound gun, placed it in the receptacles on the tripod, slammed in the securing bolts, and dropped to the floor on his right side to await the No. 3, the ammunition bearer, who rushed forward with the ammunition container. The gunner raised the gun sight, quickly adjusted the elevating mechanism, which raised or lowered the gun muzzle, and found his imaginary target on the town hall wall.

Lying on the floor by the right side of the gun, the No. 2 fed the empty ammo belt through the feed block of the gun to the gunner's waiting left hand, which pulled it into position. The gunner then went through the motion of loading the first round by pulling back the crank handle, which would, if the belt were loaded, extract the first bullet from the belt and drive it into the firing chamber. In continuous live fire, the water in the jacket will quickly boil, and the steam will escape into a water condenser that No. 3—or No. 4 if it's still early in the battle—will have provided. The steam would run from the jacket surrounding the gun barrel through a rubber hose into a container where it would return again to its liquid state for reuse—but you couldn't count on having enough reconverted steam to fully replenish the depleted water in the jacket, which is why the responsible team member must make sure that there is enough water at hand or nearby, like in a lake or a well, or a river—which is a bit tricky if you're in the desert.

Corporal Tierney told the story of British soldiers in North Africa in World War II pissing away to their hearts' content—but more likely in desperation—into containers, saving the precious liquid to cool their Vickers machine guns. Without an ample supply of water, you had better have a lot of extra barrels or a quick retreat to safety—unless this option wasn't available to you, in which case you would die gloriously for Ireland and with a bit of luck be buried amongst the honored dead in Glasnevin. The action exercise is completed when the gunner has both hands firmly on the wooden firing grips, both thumbs meeting in between and touching the thumb-piece, which, when pressed forward in live action, will cause the gun to fire—and keep on firing as long as the thumb-piece is pressed forward, or until you run out of ammo.

Setting up the Vickers for action must be done in seconds, with all team members in place, ready on their metal-studded toes and waiting for the last word of the command. Corporal Neary would count off the seconds from start to finish. If we didn't do it in fifteen seconds, we would repeat the exercise over and over until we did. Martin told us that our goal must be to get this exercise down to twelve seconds or less, evidence of a highly trained team working together with the precision of a fine Swiss watch. I didn't know how we were going to shave off three more seconds, especially when it was my turn to lug the heavy, awkward tripod across the floor to Corporal Neary's boot heel. I wasn't complaining though; this was great fun.

By the end of February when the Monday night meetings stopped, I had my first star: I was no longer a recruit, I was now a one-star private. Through all of this, I had to put up with the taunts and insults about what the letters FCA really meant—Fat Country Asses or Free Clothing Association; take your pick. I knew for a fact that you wouldn't see any fat country asses in the FCA. Some of us may indeed have been country asses, but we certainly weren't fat. And some, like Commandant Boland, were indeed fat, but they weren't from the country. You didn't get fat working on the land. As for free clothing…well there was some truth to this taunt. The FCA gave you a single, all-weather, army-green, bull's-wool uniform, including a nice beret and one pair of reddish hobnail boots with leggings. The uniform came in two parts, the trousers and a tunic top. The tunic top was fastened at the waist and buttoned up the middle.

Tom Gallagher

All the buttons were brass and had the Irish harp stamped in the middle. On each side of the harp were the letters *I* and *V* for Irish Volunteers. On each side of the tunic collar was a brass infantry emblem of a target with concentric circles, zeroing in to the bull's-eye and crossed rifles in front. The beret came with a very smart-looking brass badge containing an eight-pointed star with the words *Oglaig na h-Eireann*, meaning Irish Defense Forces. Centered inside the points were two bold letters, *FF*, meaning, I assumed, Fianna Fail, although I didn't know how Ireland's biggest political party could manage to commandeer the most prominent emblem on the Irish military uniform. Maybe because President de Valera believes that he was Father Ireland in the flesh, and named his party Fianna Fail, meaning Soldiers of Destiny. The other main political party, Fine Gael, means Irish Tribes.

Although I wasn't exactly sure what Soldiers of Destiny meant, it sounded kind of mystical and was a lot more impressive than Irish Tribes. When you think of Irish tribes you think of the tinkers, like the Wards and the McDonaghs, who traveled the country in their carts and traps and caravans. They were tribes because they're so numerous, have no fixed abode, didn't go to school, and showed little regard for other people's property. The rest of us were families because we were not quite as prolific, did go to school, though reluctantly, mostly abide by the seventh commandment, and of course we're fixed abode and not "on the cart."

One thing's for sure: you had a lot of brass to polish and shine before going out in public in uniform. Captain Hume took a very dim view of unpolished brass or unshined boots, and he'd let you know too—with a look that made words unnecessary. I did not intend to warrant this silent rebuke. Neither did I like the task of polishing and shining brass buttons and insignia and boots and leggings, but I did like the result, and I liked the one red star cloth badge sewn on each upper sleeve by my mother. Bare sleeves, other than the Connacht emblem near your right shoulder, meant that you were at the bottom of the totem pole: no rank at all. After more training there would be another star and later the triangular three stars, meaning that I was a fully trained and qualified private. The next rank above that was corporal, the bottom of the NCO ranks. Who knows...

You drilled and trained in your one uniform. You went to Sunday Mass in it before a field day. You got to parade through Swinford in it on St. Patrick's Day, and you went to a two-week camp in it. It was up to the soldier to wash, dry and press it if it got mucked up in training. Sometimes the uniform got mucked up on the farm because the soldier-farmer forgetfully put it on before going out to plough a field or cut a bank of turf. Captain Hume was well aware of these forgetful episodes, deeply embarrassing to the FCA lad if the captain came out to the farm to see him and there he was spreading cow shit on a spring meadow, wearing his army trousers and boots. Captain Hume took it all in stride, saying, ruefully, at a meeting one night that the only time he sees some of his troops was when they came into the FCA office to ask Quartermaster Callahan for a new pair of trousers or boots. I would never do this to my uniform, and besides, if I got forgetful, I had some of Jimmy's and Eamon's old uniforms that still had some wear left in them.

Field Days were a special treat when, after Mass on a Sunday, we were given a tasty but townie-sized lunch at the Café Royal in Swinford, compliments of the Irish army. Then we were off for a few happy hours of live firing at a shooting range or practicing small-unit tactics in open country. Before firing the 303, all new recruits must first fire a .22-caliber rifle. Fortunately, we didn't have to learn much about this ancient-looking, practice rifle, other than how to hold it and how to aim and fire. For bolt-action, single-shot shooting, we used a firing range by the railway near Charlestown, called Ardraigh. This wasn't a real firing range, like the ones on army camps; it was just a hillside with lots of brush into which we happily blasted away, quite unaffected by the terrified protests of wildlife whose peaceful Sunday afternoon was ruined, or worse.

I didn't know who owned the hillside, but no one seemed to care if the Irish army commandeered it on the occasional Sunday for purposes of state security and the preservation of our hard-fought freedom. Hopefully, not at the expense of wildlife, I discovered that I was a good shot. We fired at paper targets with concentric circles and a bull's-eye center—at ranges from seventy-five to two hundred yards. The .22 was easy to shoot, no kick at all. The 303, firing a larger, more powerful round, did have a kick but not enough to discourage a serious soldier like me. I was especially good at grouping bullets on the target, clustering them close together near the center. I wasn't sure why grouping bullets on the target was considered very important—maybe because it showed that you had a steady hand and a good eye, like Daniel Boone, who could probably put five bullets through the same hole, making it look like he scored a bull's-eye with the first shot and completely missed the target with the other four. I'm wasn't that good.

Captain Hume needed to visit his part-time troops from time to time, especially if they didn't show up for meetings or field days, or didn't respond to the odd letter asking them to check in. He had to be able to report to headquarters the number of FCA troops he could muster if there was some kind of emergency, like an invasion from east of the Elbe or a natural disaster such as a strike at the Guinness Brewery in Dublin. Captain Hume would always inspect the soldier's rifle when he visited, to make sure that it was being cleaned and oiled and well cared for. He'd hold his thumb in the breech, licked thumbnail reflecting sunlight down the small rifled tunnel, while he looks down the muzzle end. He'd better be able to see a lot of light coming at him, which was evidence of a clean and oiled barrel.

If he had any reason to distrust the lad, he'd sniff the breech and bolt and magazine and muzzle like a bloodhound, seeking to detect the most infinitesimal whiff of gunpowder. If the whiff was there and it shouldn't be, the rifle would be taken away, for it meant that the weapon had been fired without authorization, which meant that a bullet has somehow managed to find its way into the soldier's pocket at the firing range. Frank Joyce, being the recipient of this minor miracle, poured whole kettles of boiling water into the breech and down the barrel of his 303 after shooting Carlow Kavanagh.

Captain Hume drove his Volkswagen around the country trying to find his reserve army, one by one. He was always so dignified and professional in appearance—until you saw him trying to get his tall frame in and out of his little car, and then it was hard not to laugh. Sometimes he'd find that the lad he's looking for has gone to England or America and, therefore, can be removed from the FCA rolls. This could become a bit dicey if the departed soldier had not turned in his rifle to Quartermaster Callahan. It must be found and secured immediately. A missing rifleman is one thing; a missing rifle is altogether another. We've never had a problem of missing or stolen rifles around here, but there are stories of such happenings in other parts of the country. In hushed and conspiratorial tones, the suspected perpetrator would be named without being named:

"Who?"

"You know who."

"No, I don't know. Who?"

"The boys."

"What boys?"

"You're a fecking eejit, y'are. The boys who are trying to free the North from John Bull."

"Oooh, them boys."

Most people don't talk openly about the IRA because to some they're heroes, continuing an ancient struggle to free all of Ireland from British control, but to others they are no better than criminals, robbing banks and killing people in the name of a long-lost and questionable cause. Still it seems that the occasional FCA rifle gets confiscated in the cause of a united Ireland.

Captain Hume and Corporal Tierney were both veterans of overseas duty with the United Nations in the Congo. The Belgian Congo gained its independence in 1960 and promptly descended into civil war, much like Ireland did in 1922. The United Nations called for member countries to provide troops to restore the peace and bring secessionist Katanga Province back into the fold. Ireland had been accepted into UN membership in 1955 when the Soviet Union finally dropped its veto, exercised repeatedly because of Ireland's neutrality in World War II. The Irish government quickly volunteered a couple of battalions. Only a few months after their arrival in the middle of Africa, tragedy struck on November 8, 1960, when a small unit of eleven Irish soldiers was ambushed by a large number of Baluba tribesmen near the village of Niemba in Katanga Province. They had gone out to rebuild a small bridge over a river. The Irish troops regarded the Baluba as a friendly, pro-UN tribe, having encountered them before, and did not expect trouble.

But these tribesmen were not farmers; they were warriors, heavily but primitively armed with spears, machetes, bows with poison arrows, and clubs. Lieutenant Kevin Gleeson, the Irish unit's commander, quickly realized what was about to happen and yelled at his men to take cover. Several, including Lieutenant Gleeson, who had gone out in front to greet the Baluba, were cut down immediately in a hail of arrows and spears. The survivors of the initial barrage fought a ferocious and grim battle at close quarters, using their Lee Enfield rifles, a couple of Bren Guns, and a Gustav. As their ammunition dwindled, two Irish soldiers made their escape into the bush and were picked up in a rescue operation the following day. Nine soldiers died, including Trooper Anthony Browne—whose mutilated body would be found two years later. The happy-go-lucky, guitar-playing, twenty-year-old private died a terrible death. He would later be posthumously awarded Ireland's highest military honor for valor. The citation said that he gave his life to save a comrade.

The Baluba lost many more of their number—their chief later insisting that the Irish attacked first. Another report said that the Baluba mistook the Irish for the hated Belgian troops. And still another story suggested that the Baluba attacked because they were the ones who had destroyed the bridge to prevent secessionist Katanga troops from crossing into their territory—the Baluba were loyal to the new central government, which the United Nations was supporting. The Baluba, according to this version, were angry to see the bridge about to be repaired by troops they thought were on their side. Later, there was talk that there's more to this tragedy than meets the eye, that the public was not being told the whole truth.

What we did know for sure was that nine Irish soldiers died bravely far from home, in a steamy tropical climate. They wore heavy bull's wool uniforms and hobnail boots, suitable for northern climates. None could speak French—spoken by many Congolese—or the local language. On patrol they had no interpreters with them and could only communicate using hand gestures and signals. Their electronic communications equipment was almost as primitive. Operating in mostly jungle or bush terrain over a wide area, individual Irish patrols could not talk to each other or their base if they were separated by more than a few miles and often much less. Tragically, support was close at hand, but not close enough. In order for help to reach a unit in trouble, that help had to be practically within earshot range.

In fact, the two Irish battalions in the Congo could not communicate with army HQ at the Curragh in Ireland, except by telex. Ironically, on the very day of the Baluba ambush, the commanding general of the Irish Defense Forces, Lieutenant General Sean McKeown, had left his headquarters to visit a priest's residence in a Dublin suburb so that he could listen to a live broadcast on a ham radio from his troops in the Congo. This was going to be a real treat for the general, but it turned out to be the complete opposite. General McKeown listened in horror to a junior officer reporting the Niemba ambush. The ham radio set-up was engineered by an Irishman working in a neighboring African country who happened upon an Irish army officer and was understandably appalled that these guys had no radio/telephone capability to communicate with HQ in Ireland.

The whole country was in mourning when the bodies of the slain were returned to Dublin for burial with full military honors at Glasnevin Cemetery, a centuries-old resting place for Ireland's heroes and martyrs. Thousands lined O'Connell Street as the sad procession consisting of a gun carriage bearing the body of Lieutenant Gleeson and open army lorries bearing the bodies of his small platoon, slowly bore the flag-draped coffins to Glasnevin, where military pallbearers completed the journey. The nation wept for its lost sons and the citizens of Dublin shed volumes of salty tears on Ireland's broadest and most famous street. For a while the army basked in newfound affection and goodwill. For a while the uniform and those occupying it were treated with a new respect, even a little deference. For a while the FCA didn't mean Fat Country Asses.

But only for a while. It didn't last. Perhaps we Irish didn't quite know how we felt about our army. We loved parades and martial music and rebel songs and endless displays of our defiant past, but there would be very few mothers or fathers proud to have a son join the regular army. It's just not considered a respectable career for anyone—unless you were an officer. That made a big difference. Captain Hume ranked up there with teachers and priests and bank managers and other professionals. Corporal Tierney and Quartermaster Callahan were not commissioned officers like Captain Hume, but they were liked because they were respectful and courteous to the townspeople—and at least they were employed, which is more than could be said for many others. Since the FCA is only part-time—and therefore not a career—we are spared any permanent disdain, but still must take our share of insults.

A final accounting of what happened at Niemba remains to be written. The question: could this tragedy, whether accidentally triggered or not, have been avoided? The tentative answer is yes. The first armed Irish troops to be sent on a UN mission overseas were woefully unprepared. The first battalion to depart was pulled together from different commands in a few days and dispatched to equatorial Africa almost immediately. There was no time for special training and no trainers if there had been time—for no one had any experience in overseas peace enforcement. The Irish troops lacked essentials, from proper clothing to equipment to necessary supplies—even borrowing at times from the Swedish contingent, welcomed in the Congo because, like Ireland, Sweden was a neutral. When they arrived there was no time for orientation, seemingly no time to learn even the elementary words and phrases to aid communication that might help save their lives. A civil war was raging around them, and the Irish went into the breach as soon as they arrived.

In an utterly alien land, they hit the ground running, brave, good-natured and clueless. The Niemba Ambush was the still-young Irish army's baptism of fire and a bitter lesson for the government that so generously volunteered its soldiers with virtually no notice and no preparation. Ireland, remaining neutral in World War II, was eager to prove its commitment to the United Nations, but its membership had been vetoed by the Soviet Union since the United Nations' founding. Ireland desperately wanted into the New World Order, and in so doing, committed its virgin troops with no experience either in battle or in peacekeeping—and few had ever been out of Ireland.

It was also a valuable lesson for the United Nations, forcing a reevaluation of its military role in international conflicts—the more aggressive peace enforcement policy evolving into a less confrontational peacekeeping strategy. More than fifty years on from Niemba, the wisdom of that decision has been sorely tested around the world with the rise of militant extremism and the horrific, indiscriminate, and often deliberate slaughter of civilians. Moving on from tragedy, the Irish learned quickly. There would be more UN missteps in the Congo and more Irish deaths, but no more Niembas. Their deficiencies were corrected and they would, in time, become one of the United Nations' most experienced, professional, and requested troop contingents, keeping—and perhaps now leaning once more toward enforcing—the peace in some of the world's most dangerous places

---

*Grateful acknowledgement is given to David O'Donoghue, Irish author and historian, for his excellent analysis of the Irish army's tour in the Congo, *The Irish Army in the Congo 1960-1964: The Far Battalions*

Corporal Tom Gallagher, C Company, 18th Battalion,
Western Command, FCA, 1964

CHAPTER 15

I WASN'T SURE that Eamon would return from England in the spring of 1962. He had often said that after the beet factory work was over, he would just go south to Birmingham where Dad and other members of the family were. But he did come home, I think maybe because Mom asked him to in a letter, because she was afraid that I might not be up to the task on my own, or maybe because she hoped that I could stay in school. He didn't stay long. By mid-May he was gone again, this time for good. At fifteen, I was now finally in charge of the farm, still largely untried but exhilarated at the prospect of managing without my brother. Summer was upon us, and there was much to do and little time to worry whether I could do it or not. It was there in front of me, and there was no way around it.

When I left the vocational school in Swinford in March 1962, a few months before completing my first year, I knew for sure that now my schooling was over and, as I had feared for some time, there was no joy in this reality. I faced the work on the farm with a ferocious determination to be as good as or better than Eamon had been, but behind it was a feeling of loss, a sense that a great opportunity had passed me by. I wanted an education. Without even being aware of it, I had acquired this thirst for knowledge, and St. Patrick's only whetted my appetite. The Tech was hardly inspirational—for that was not its purpose—but it did provide an environment where I was with fellow students. Here, at least, I was a participant in the educational process.

Like Father Jack a year earlier, Mr. Reagan, headmaster at the Tech, came out to our home to ask my mother if it might be possible for me to return to school—and again my mother explained our situation. From now on I would be a spectator, watching secondary school scholars cycling by on the Main Road near our house, waving to them, former classmates and others, and envying them because they were doing what I could no longer do. I felt like I was being left behind, that the world I wanted to be part of was moving on without me.

But the summer's work was ahead, and I had to focus on this, the biggest challenge of my life. I was both scared and excited. Even though Eamon and I had put down the spring's tillage, it was now my responsibility to bring it all to fruition. Eamon would not be back, nor would Dad. And I had Mom and my younger sisters, who would now be counting on me to step into Eamon's shoes.

Our first task was to stand up into *groigins* all the year's supply of turf that Eamon had cut in the bog. Mom and my sisters and I did this, *groig* by *groig*, bank by bank, and it was done. We saved the hay, as we had always done, and I built the haystacks—hundreds of forkfuls of hay hoisted up to me by my mother, hour upon hour, and me, with a short-handled fork, taking each forkful from my mother, and Mom showing me how to place each forkful of hay, to bind the one before, circle by circle, from center to outside. I learned quickly and soon needed no help in making haystacks tall and straight so they would withstand the wind and rain.

After the hay there was the oats. This, too, was the first time in my life that I must mow down a field of oats, swing by swing, with that ancient implement, the scythe—as Eamon and my father and grandfather and great grandfather had done. I had practiced many times with the scythe in preparation for this task, cutting little patches of grass here and there and corners of meadows that Mick Burns could not get to with his tractor. Getting the swing and the rhythm just right takes time to perfect; even a few degrees off meant that you wouldn't cut evenly or at the right level. Then what you've got is a field of stubbles, the part of the stalk still in the ground, with no uniformity of height—*monched*. All stalk stubbles should be about an inch high, showing that the bloke with the scythe knew what he was doing. If your field was by a public road and it's cut poorly, it's an embarrassment. Not only that, but you've also wasted precious fodder by cutting too high off the ground.

After threshing, when the grain is removed from the stalk, what's left is fodder. Fodder can be used for lots of things, like bedding in the cow barn or for thatching a house roof, but it can also be used as cattle feed in the winter. Cattle didn't like oat fodder and would give you that cross look when you gave it to them, as if to say, *You expect me to eat this shit?* But hungry cows will eat it, especially when it's mixed with the sweeter hay. It makes the hay last longer—and may be necessary if the winter was long and cold, meaning a shorter growing season.

At first, the hardest thing for me to master was to edge the three-foot-long cutting blade of the scythe so that the oat stalks would fall easily before the blade. For this I used a bluestone sharpener, a piece of bluestone about twelve inches long and two inches thick at the center and narrowing to an inch at each end. It required practiced skill to slide the bluestone up and down the blade edge at a steady rhythm and precise angle, one outward stroke on the inside edge, one inward stroke on the outside edge, about twenty or so on each side. Next you had to sharpen the tip of the blade, focusing the stone on the last six inches. This was the trickiest part. You could get a deep wound or even slice a fingertip off if your mind wandered. After a fair amount of practice, I could sharpen the blade from end to end that would make old Gillette himself proud. And I was proud, and relieved too. The joy of seeing that blade slice easily through the swath of oats before me was a great confidence builder, for you could never hope to cut down a field of oats if you couldn't sharpen the scythe. With a sharp blade, a measured swing, a steady rhythm—and endurance—I knew that whole fields of grain wouldn't have a chance before me and my scythe. Fortunately, I had just one field to worry about.

Not yet sixteen, Patricia left the Marist Convent in her second year and crossed the pond to England, which meant one less mouth to feed but also one less to help at home—and I had lost my best pal. Not many Irish farm girls finished secondary school, or even got as far as their Inter

Certs. And not many farm lads did either. One reason was that not many attended to secondary school in the first place. Another was that five years of secondary school was a long commitment, and life on the land was demanding as well as unpredictable. Circumstances changed and with them plans...and dreams. People who lived in town just seemed to have a steadier and easier life, though sometimes I wondered where they got their money. If someone had a shop or a pub, or was a chemist, a teacher, or a doctor, I could understand where the money was coming from, but many people in town didn't seem to have any visible means of support at all, yet strolled around in suits and ties, at any hour of the day, tipping their hats to women and priests and stopping to chat with other townspeople.

The towns of Swinford and Charlestown were less than four miles in opposite directions from our farm in Culmore, but sometimes they might as well have been in a different time zone. Townies for sure had a far better chance of finishing at St. Patrick's or St. Mary's or the Marist Convent, unless they were real dunces and had no business being there in the first place. I saw no pupils from Swinford or Charlestown at the Tech. The Tech was beneath them, fit only for country people. Still, you had a better chance of finishing if you went to the Tech because it was only a two year commitment instead of five.

Soon after Eamon returned to England, Patricia came home—to begin preparations to emigrate to America. This brief seven-month period was a happy time for me. Patricia and I always had been close. As my older sister by two years, she was my defender in family squabbles—and there was rarely a shortage of those. In a large family, with scarcity fairly common, and want never too far away, life was competitive. Alliances were rare and fleeting, intended to serve immediate goals, then dissolve until the next crisis required the same or a new pairing. But I could always count on Patricia. She was on my side no matter what. When Mom was doubtful about me going to Finner Camp with the FCA in August 1962, it was Patricia who talked to Mom and convinced her that I could go, that the farm could wait—and that I needed this time away from the land and family, "to get the feel of being on his own," she said. I was fifteen, and this would be my first time away from home—and Patricia, too, had felt her own way in Birmingham at fifteen. It was great to have her home again, but I didn't look forward to the time when she would leave for New York, thanks to Mom's sister, Aunt Jo Gunter, who lived there and was sponsoring my sister.

The two-hour journey by special CIE bus to Finner Camp in County Donegal turned out to be the most enjoyable part of my two-week holiday. We were all singing and shouting and carrying on, all eager with antici-pation. There were lots of tales being told about Donegal girls. Seamus Halligan, sitting beside me and maybe a couple of years older, had been to Finner last year and assured me with a knowing wink that the girls of Bundoran were "fabulous and dead easy," which meant I think that they didn't mind kissing back. I immediately thought of Maura Kenny and her beautiful laughing eyes and teasing smile and, boy, I just wanted this bus to speed up. Halfway to Finner someone yelled out, "Stop the bus; I have to piss." Suddenly everyone is shouting, "Me too; me too." Without fuss, the bus driver pulled over to the side of the road and forty uniformed soldiers poured out with determination.

Unfortunately, we had stopped in an area as flat as a pancake with no concealment at all—not that anyone seemed concerned about the obvi-ous lack of privacy. We all lined up, military like, on the side of the high-way and emptied our bloated bladders to the usual refrain heard in men's lavatories throughout Ireland, "This is where the long wans hang out." Some motorists sped up to pass this pissing exhibit, looking disgusted, as though they never had to piss. Other cars slowed down, occupants gawking, girls giggling and laughing. Some of the lads responded to this encouragement in very uncivilized ways, but soon we were all happily relieved and on our way again.

We got to Finner Camp and promptly fell victim to a highly conta-gious viral infection, known to everyone at Finner Camp as "the shits."

For much of the two weeks, the entire camp was infected and, effectively, quarantined. Our painful and embarrassing condition at Finner made the national news. All of Finner Camp, by the many hundreds, were defecating wherever they could or couldn't when the uncontrollable urge struck—in lavatories if they were still working and had no lines outside, or out of lavatories, if they weren't working or were working but had long lines of desperate males waiting for merciful relief, arses puckered and legs crossed tighter than a well-raised country girl on her wedding night. Long streams of hot diarrhea were exiting bodies at practically the speed of light between two of Ireland's loveliest resort towns, Bundoran and Ballyshannon, both nearby on the coast. Whole torrents of steamy, semiliquid fertilizer lent a distinctly unpleasant and sickly smell wherever the winds carried it—and carry it they did to these two picture-postcard towns in their peak tourist season, having a somewhat depressing effect on business. Yes, we were definitely Fat Country Asses again.

Apart from the shits plague, my two weeks' holiday at Finner Camp was tolerable, if barely. Alas, most of us, as far as I could tell, including me, didn't get to see just how easy the fabulous girls of Donegal really were. While most of us did make it into Bundoran before returning home, we must have been carrying with us a lingering whiff of infection, for the bonnie lassies we encountered quickly distanced themselves from us. Of course it's possible that they had heard of our misfortune on the news—and maybe smelled it too—and were not moved by the Christian spirit to be friendly and sympathetic. There was no hiding the fact that we were FCA lads, because several were wearing full uniforms, hobnail boots and all. I had been looking forward to trying my luck with a willing young lady just waiting to be kissed by a shy, red-faced but earnest young lad from County Mayo. Well, maybe next time. I'm still young.

The good news is that my friend, Martin Neary, was promoted to sergeant, and despite the insistent needs of Mother Nature, I earned my second star. Equally important was that *I got paid* for the two weeks. Two weeks' reserve army pay didn't amount to much, but on top of that I received what the paymaster called a gratuity. The gratuity was compensation for all the Monday-night meetings and the field days, and it was by far the biggest portion. I came home with more than ten pounds in my pocket. On the bus home, I looked a lot at the crisp, brand-new ten-pound note. I had rarely seen banknotes of this amount and had never earned this kind of money in my life. I might earn ten bob for helping a neighbor bring a bullock to the fair or maybe a pound for two hard days of digging a neighbor's spuds—but this was *real* money.

I was careful though not to look at it in the open too much—another lad, Jackie Connor, wasn't as careful and somewhere between Finner Camp and Swinford, Jackie was relieved of his money. I felt sorry for him because he was a neighbor, and I knew how badly his family needed that money. Now he had nothing to show for his two weeks except an empty pocket and a sore arse. As for my ten pounds and change, most of it went to Mom, but I kept a couple of pounds for myself and felt quite rich.

The field of oats was waiting for me when I got home, just as Patricia had promised Mom. My only worry was whether I had the endurance to stay with the job until it was finished. It would take thousands of swings with the scythe, and I knew that my arms would grow tired, and my legs too. Leisurely breaks were never an option when saving hay or harvesting. When God gave you good weather, there was no time at all to waste, and you stayed at it even if it meant missing a meal or working until there was no light left. After a few hours, I was aching everywhere: my legs, my arms, my back, my neck, and my blistered hands. Mom, her back bent low gathering the oats, kept asking if I was okay, and I kept telling her that I was in fine form. And when I thought I would fall down because my arms and legs were going numb, the miracle happened. The pain suddenly began to ease, and I got my second wind. Into the afternoon I was going strong and by day's end, I was two-thirds home.

I think what happened was that in the morning hours I had not developed the rhythm. Eamon had told me about the importance of rhythm when using a scythe but didn't try to explain it, just saying, "You'll know it when you have it, and when you don't you'll know that too." Eamon liked to state the obvious, but the truism, without demonstration, was of little value. I thought I understood what rhythm was, but understanding it was one thing; having it was quite another. I think maybe it was like dancing—some people had a natural grace on the dance floor, their bodies moving effortlessly to a rhythm or beat, while others, like me, had to listen real hard to feel the beat. I was putting too much energy into every swing. As stiff and straight as an ESB pole, I was forcing my arms to do the work.

Eventually, I got my rhythm, not as a result of clear-headed thinking, but because my primal brain and tired, aching body figured out what needed to be done, and having no choice in the matter, I went along. Out of sheer weariness, I began to take a more relaxed stance, leaned forward a little, and, without being consciously aware of it, began to turn into the swing at my waist, letting my upper body do most of the work.

In only minutes I was feeling a new energy. I could feel the pain leaving my body and the life coming back into my sore arms. With stiff legs and straight back, I had been fighting the oat stalks and fighting the scythe, refusing to bend and wearing myself out in the process. Then, when I was near exhaustion, rhythm was forced upon me. Suddenly, and in less time than you could swat a blood-sucking crower, I discovered the *art* of mowing with a scythe. Cutting turf and ploughing and sharpening a blade are learned skills, but using the scythe the way God intended was an art. Once the rhythm was in your head, your body follows along, the scythe becomes part of your body, and it was like music. Mom noticed the difference, saying, with a great big smile, that now I was mowing with the same ease and style as Eamon and Dad.

The weather remained good, and in a day and a half, the field of oats was mown. Behind me, my mother had gathered the felled oats into sheaves, and behind her, my sisters had tied the sheaves with thin bands of oat stalks and then stood them upright, four sheaves to a stook. Another band secured the stook near the top, and then we hoped for a week of good drying weather to season the oats. Like hay, oats must be seasoned properly for storage, whether in a stack or in a sack. If there was any moisture left in either, they would begin to heat under the pressure of their own weight—and then begin to rot. We are mindful, however, of the delicate palates of the crows and blackbirds and jackdaws and magpies and numerous other winged thieves that prefer the grain to be softer, meaning less seasoned. It's easier on the beak and the gullet, you see. Perhaps, being God's creatures, if they could speak they would tell us that they appreciate our thoughtfulness in giving them our grain just the way they like it. And if they could understand me, I would tell them of my most fervent desire to see them all suffering the agonies of broken beak and ruptured gullet.

Some farmers used scarecrows in a desperate hope that they would keep the birds away, or at least reduce the loss from this stomach-churning daylight robbery. I didn't know why they bothered—we stopped doing this long ago because scarecrows were a waste of time, about as useful as tits on a bull for all the good they do. They were helpful, however, to the birds. After a bellyful of precious grain, as many as could fit would tarry awhile, resting on the outstretched arms of the scarecrows—for it was easier to fly their increased bulk from a four-foot-high stook of oats to a five-foot-high scarecrow than it was to lift their stuffed bodies up to the electric wires overhead or to nearby trees. The scarecrows gave them time to let the stolen food settle a bit, and maybe even allow them to top off again before calling it a day. Still, Mom reminds me that God is good, and He will not let these shameless gluttons leave us only chaff.

Before I left for Finner Camp, I had gathered the turf out of the bog and stacked it into two unfried reeks the other side of the railway. Because the weather was always unpredictable, the objective was to get the turf out of the soft bog and onto more solid ground as soon as it was dry enough to be gathered. A wet summer could be a disaster, for everything was at risk, from the hay to feed our cattle through the winter; to oats that we would have crushed into meal to feed chickens and turkeys and dogs and cattle and a pig if we had one—and the occasional treat for our ass, Coco; to our vegetables in the garden; to our vital potatoes, the core of our diet, that will not grow, except for banners, if the ground is too wet; to our turf in the bog, the only fuel we have for heat in the winter and for cooking year 'round.

I think that farmers all over the world, whether they have great big farms, like in America and Australia, or small holdings like ours, are at the mercy of the weather, and the worry never leaves them. Even in winter we worry that it might be long and cold—which means rationing for man and beast alike. The first words of greeting from a farmer's mouth are always about the weather:

"It's great weather we're having, Sean, thank God."
"It is that, Pat, an' I pray we'll have a lot more of it, please God."
"It's a mucky oul day, Mickey, ishn't it?"
"Aye, good for nothin but the ducks—but with God's help tomorra will be an improvement."

And then to show that the farmer is not too demanding of God, there's:

"By God, Paddy, that was a great day we had last Tuesday, washn't it?"
There are no rosaries said in Ireland for more rain.

Late June and into July, was haymaking time, and if the weather was good the second half of July was for gathering the turf with ass and cart. Because asses are much lighter than mules and horses—and pound for pound stronger—they were far better suited for work in the bog. We couldn't modify the weight of the cart very much, though, and the huge, heavy spoked wheels with their three-inch-wide and half-inch-thick iron tires were definitely not ideal for hauling cartloads of turf through soft, spongy earth. Even a single day of steady rain could make the bog a treacherous place. If the cartwheels break through the soft surface, they could quickly sink to the axle, and you had no choice but to empty the load and dig your way out. Sometimes poor Coco would sink, too, and then I might have to unhitch the cart and free him first. If he has sunk to his knees, I'd have to take the tacklings off—collar, hams, straddle, and britch—and put my right shoulder under Coco's shoulders and lift him up. Then, if he was not able to plunge forward and free his hind legs, I'd get behind his arse end and do the same.

Gathering turf and hauling it home was a miserable job. In windy weather turf-moul from the sods was constantly blowing in your face, mouth, nostrils, ears, and eyes, and it was hard on your hands too. The rough, dry edges of the sods, especially the hard, black turf, left my hands scratched, sore, and swollen. But that was to be expected. What I dreaded most of all was having both ass and cart sink in the bog or, worse, a capsize. It wasn't just the time it took to get going again; it was the risk of damage or injury to this critical transport system. I'd seen a couple of bogeys around and I wished we could afford to modify our cart into a bogey. This meant replacing the big wheels and axle with the wheels and axle of a trailer. These wheels were like the wheels of a car. They were small and had pumped-up tires—and were great for the bog, or anywhere else. They made the cart much lighter and easier to pull, and were a god-send in soft ground.

The only thing I could change about our cart was whether I used the fifteen-inch tall boards, which surround the cart bed, or the thirty-six-inch high crib, which sloped out in all directions. The great advantage of the crib was that you could haul double the load and finish the job faster. The great disadvantage was that you might not get out of the bog with a crib-load of turf because the cart was now heavier and more likely to sink, and Coco, too, would sink more quickly under the strain of pulling a bigger load. So, unless God and nature had been unusually generous with the weather, it was just too risky to use the crib. In olden times when there were no bogies and few carts, people gathered their turf in creels. Homemade from the sally rods of willow trees, creels were baskets about two feet by two and two feet deep. A set of two would straddle a donkey's back, each hung on a peg attached to a padded wooden straddle. You filled each creel and off you went. Creels were fairly easy to make and easy to repair—and were a lot safer and kinder on the pocket than a big-wheeled cart. The problem was that creels took forever to gather the turf out of the bog. It was hard to imagine how people back then had time to do big jobs with such old-fashioned means.

Mom told me that when she was a young girl, she remembered seeing neighbors, bent over, cutting down fields of oats with the sickle, still in use then, though replaced generations earlier by the scythe. Old ways die hard. She remembers farmers turning whole fields, sod by sod, with the *loi*. The loi was a spade, for God's sake, a hand tool. It was even harder to imagine a farmer having the time and the endurance to turn a field by hand for his potato or oat crop—and yet there were those, like Jim Goldrick in Corthoon, who still turned a small hillside field for potatoes, too steep for the tractor—or even the horse. I could see him on the steep slope on my way to school, and all I knew then was that I never wanted to have to do that. Turning the headlands at both ends of each tractor-ploughed potato ridge is more than enough for me. The headlands are those final few yards to the fence or the end of the field that a tractor cannot plough because there wasn't enough room.

Some of our neighbors didn't bring their turf out of the bog to a temporary safer location a couple of hundred yards above the railway as we did. The Kavanaghs, for example, hauled it all the way from the bog to their house in one go. As that trip was more than twice as far, it took much longer per trip, but if the bog was not too wet and the weather held, they saved time in the long run by not splitting the job into two separate pieces and having to reek the turf twice. Their risk was that if the weather broke halfway though the job, they could be in a bad way with half their turf still in the bog—while we would have all of ours at least on better ground. If the turf could not be brought out of the bog, you had no choice but to either clamp it or reek it on the driest ground available, mostly on the higher uncut turf banks rather than the lower, ever-extending cut-aways, which can be partially under water in the wintertime.

A clamp of turf was a circular mound sloping upward to a point. It was about five or six feet high and, looking at it vertically, the shape was triangular. A clamp would contain a few cartloads of turf and must be fryed all the way around and up because, like the much larger, rectangular reek, it must withstand wind and hail and rain and snow. Unfortunately, clamps and reeks of turf in the lonely bog, no matter how well fortified against the weather, are defenseless against a thief in the dead of night, another risk of having to leave turf in the bog over the winter.

Thieves could be tinkers or gypsies or others of no fixed abode, like the odd beggerman, and sometimes maybe a neighbor, near or distant, whose own supply is low or gone and had no money to buy from someone with plenty. Tinkers were skilled at making amazing tin cans with simple crude tools, which they'd sell to farmers for a half a crown. We used the cans for bringing water from the well and sometimes when milking the cows, but they were not as strong as the buckets we bought in town, and after a few months they'd begin to leak. They were also opportunistic thieves who would steal hay for their ponies and donkeys and straw for bedding in their tents, which they set up in sheltered areas along byroads, like Madogue Road, which is close to us.

But not all tinkers were thieves, and Mom would often invite an old tinker-woman in for a cup of tea when she'd come by to ask for a few coppers. Sometimes Mom would have her fortune told for a half a crown and swear afterward that the old woman "had the gift." We knew the ones who could be trusted. The ones we didn't know, we had to be on our guard until they moved on. We knew that they lived a hard life, traveling the roads of Ireland, often being run from place to place by the gardie—but we must measure our kindness, because our lives were hard too.

Gypsies were a different class of people. Like the tinkers they were of no fixed abode, but they were mostly horse traders and often seemed to make a better living than many of us who were permanently attached to a piece of ground. Beggermen were mostly harmless, but in the wintertime they needed a warm fire too. At Mass one Sunday, the priest explained when a sin was not a sin. He said that the teachings of Jesus told us that when you were hungry and had no food, it was no sin to steal, and when you were freezing cold and had no fire, it was no sin to steal. That may be so, but when we were stolen from when we had barely enough for ourselves, this meant that we may go hungry or freeze our arses off on cold wintry nights when even water and milk inside the house froze solid. And since we rarely had extra money, did this mean that we, too, could go out and steal? What if that first sinless theft resulted in countless other thefts? Were these also sinless? Did Jesus mean that in cases of dire need, it was not a sin to break the seventh commandment, "Thou shalt not steal," or the tenth commandant, "Thou shalt not covet thy neighbor's goods"? Could we just steal and covet away until the need was satisfied? I didn't think so. I reckoned we'd be well on our way to bloody murder before the stealing and coveting got very far.

After saving the field of oats into two stacks in the garden by the barns, to await thrashing in October, the next pressing task was to haul the turf from its temporary site above the railway to the house for reeking and frying near the west gable. With Coco, cart, and crib, this task took a little more than two weeks of nonstop work, except to eat and sleep and go to Mass on Sunday. When done, Coco and I had made more than one hundred round trips. We were both tired of this dirty job, but Coco was willing to go on, I'm convinced, until he fell down dead. It was mostly uphill on the way to the house, and grueling on poor Coco, pulling a heavy crib-load of turf. By the time we got through the long Field of Rushes and reached the bottom of the Field of the Fairy Bush, we both rested, for ahead was the steepest part of the journey, Heartbreak Hill, as Eamon named it. Only a few feet from where we rested, on the other side of the *maren* fence, was Drennan's spring well. I kept a bucket and a cup by our resting spot so that I could get a welcome drink for both of us. Coco was always anxious to reach this spot, anticipating the cool water. He would stop at the exact same spot, to the inch, every time, and would not move another inch until he got his drink. I'd have a couple of cupfuls, and Coco would guzzle the rest. He knew that he wouldn't drink again, nor would I, until we reached the same spot with the next load.

The hill before us rose steadily for two field lengths, finally leveling out as we approached the cow barns. As strong as Coco was, he needed help on this leg. When Eamon was here, he and I would grab the front crossbar on each side of the cart, one hand on the shaft for balance, the other gripping the crossbar, and we'd pull along with Coco and not stop until we crested the hill—and then only to let Coco's labored breathing return to normal. Without Eamon on the other side of the cart, it was better for me to push from behind so that I could push evenly. My big fear was that this long hill would prove to be too much for Coco and that sooner or later his wind would break. When a donkey was wind broken you knew it right away. His breathing was fast and heavily labored, like a dog panting, only much louder and deeper, and without his tongue hanging out. A wind-broken ass had no spirit left in him; his strength was sapped, broken by work too hard for even a strong donkey; and he would never be the same again.

As it turned out, my worry about Coco's wind was all for naught but he did acquire another condition that brought me at least as much grief as a broken-down ass would have wrought. Coco acquired an uncontrollable desire to propagate his own kind, to the point where it became almost impossible for me to keep him confined within the boundaries of our land. It started when a neighbor several farms over got a female ass, a bess, and put her in a lower field near the railway. When Coco wasn't working, he spent his lonely hours, mostly by himself, also near the railway. If he couldn't see the bess across several fields, he could certainly hear her, and when she came around, she definitely wanted to be heard. On hearing her mating call, Coco would rush to the maren trench between us and the Kennys, head skyward, and bray himself for all he was worth. There was no secret about what Coco had in mind. It was there between his hind legs, ready to go. He'd stamp his forefeet on the ground and back up a little as if about to jump the trench—but he wouldn't jump, at least in the beginning, not until overcome by final, fatal desperation. Until that time I had little peace of mind and often little sleep.

CHAPTER 16

❧

IN THE SUMMER of 1962, one of the biggest hit songs on the radio was "I Can't Stop Loving You" by Ray Charles and the Ray Charles Singers. Everyone in the house was looney over it. I never thought anyone could compete with Buddy Holly, but Ray Charles and his singers were on a different level altogether, at least with this song. The heartbreaking sadness and despair in the lyrics, the hopeless longing for a lost love, gone forever, was deeply moving. I still thought about my lost love, Maura Kenny, but not as much as I used to. If this song had come on the radio right after Maura mangled my heart on a public road, I wouldn't have been able to bear it. I'd have had to leave the house to be alone in my misery. But I was beginning to notice that there were other fine-looking girls around. I could understand, though, why someone might be so heartbroken that, as Ray Charles sings, to live in memory of a happier time was all they could manage for a while.

I didn't know why I looked at girls' figures, but I did. Sometimes a girl's face might be so lovely but the rest of her wasn't, and I knew that the decent thing was to see the loveliness in her face and the beauty in her eyes and forget the rest, but I couldn't. I was confused and ashamed of this and sometimes asked God to forgive me for my animal instincts and help me to be better than Coco, who made no effort at all to curb his desires. I didn't think Coco gave a shit what a bess's face looked like—or her figure. All he knew was what nature told him to do when a bess came around. I didn't know why girls and women didn't come around the same way as cows and donkeys and sheep and horses do, but they don't—at least I didn't think so. I'd never seen a girl going crazy like a young heifer. I think it would be easier on both sexes if they did. At least you'd know when they weren't interested at all. More importantly, you'd know when they were—not that it would matter much anyway because I had no doubt that there would be a law on the books saying that all girls and unmarried wome had to be locked up during this time—so maybe it was better the way it is.

Basically, my initial attraction to a girl had more to do with her face and especially her eyes. A girl's eyes were magical. They could be cold and distant or warm and inviting, like asking you to come closer. They might be blue or green or brown, but all you had to do was look into them to see whether you were welcome or not. When going into town with the ass and cart, it was easy to tell whether a girl found me interesting or not—even if she was not impressed with my ass and cart. Of course the only way I could know for sure was if I actually looked at her—and, mostly, I didn't do this. Why? Because an ass and cart, even with powerful Coco, still screams out silently to the lovely young girls of County Mayo that you were a young man of modest means, which was another way of saying that you were poor. So I couldn't really tell if I was a young Errol Flynn or not, but I seriously doubt it—unless red-faced young men suddenly become all the rage. If they were looking at you with total disinterest, like you weren't even there, or worse, pointing at you because you had the reddest face they'd ever seen…well, these were the times when you wished you had a flour sack over your head with small holes for your eyes.

I knew that a girl's personality, often reflected in her face and eyes, should be most important because they spoke to you of the heart within, and maybe a future life of wedded bliss, but I needed to look at the full prospect. My friends felt the same way. When we talked about girls, we seldom mentioned their beautiful eyes or lovely smiles or how intelligent they were—that was considered sissy talk. We talked about their figures, broken down into the various anatomical parts. I knew that a girl's character, whether she was kind and friendly and saw you as another human being instead of the animal you probably were, was very important, but if God, in His goodness, also put her together in that particular way, I couldn't help but notice. God forgive me!

Maybe one sorry day I'll be called to account for these unholy attitudes and feelings I had, but that's what I thought and how I felt. If it was wrong, it was wrong and maybe I'll be damned for it, but if I am I'll probably have plenty of company. I also knew that sometimes the loveliest faces and loveliest figures didn't have the loveliest personalities to complete the picture. I thought it was diabolical that some girls had everything I liked and yet had no interest in me, while other girls that I had no feelings for weren't at all put off by my red face and embarrassing shyness. Then there were girls who were more interested in the latest fashion or hairstyle and behaved like they were on display for viewing purposes only. I was sure that God was well aware of this riddle down here on earth because He was responsible for the whole thing. But sometimes I had the feeling that He was just playing a game, never making it easy, always forcing us to make choices, to compromise, to use the good sense He gave us to settle for the possible rather than the simple perfection I preferred.

Until a few years ago, the most common dances, at least around here, were ceilis. These were traditional Irish dances, danced to traditional Irish music. Irish music was either slow and sad or fast and lively. It was played mostly on accordions, flutes, fiddles, Irish pipes, melodeons, tin whistles, and drums. Ceili dances, like "The Siege of Ennis" and "The Stack of Barley" and "The Haymaker's Jig," often involve interacting with other couples, dancing in circles, changing partners, and other antics, none of which I had the slightest interest in. Ceilis, it seemed to me, were for old people who just liked to mingle and be sociable on the dance floor, meet friends and neighbors, chat about the weather or a relative home from beyond, and had no interest in a slow, face-to-face waltz, which was of considerable interest to me. Not that I could do very much about it anyway. I'd been to a couple of house dances, but never to a real dance in a real dance hall. The Higgins family used to live down Hull Road but emigrated to England years ago. They kept the home place so that they could return from time to time on holiday. All the neighbors looked forward to the Higgins' holidays because they always threw a party, a house dance, and all were welcome, no invitations necessary. The chair dance was popular because when the fiddle and flute and accordion players stopped the music suddenly, everyone must quickly find a seat, but there had to be one chair short so that one person would be without a seat. This person then had to choose a partner to go outside into the dark with for a little while, like a fifteen or twenty-minute date.

One time Katie Mac was left standing, and she chose me, red face and all. I liked Katie Mac. She was very pretty, and we knew each other but not very well. Out we went into the night and back we came in less than five minutes. I didn't have a clue what to say or do—and she didn't either—so we did the sensible thing: we said nothing and we did nothing and rejoined the party inside, and that was that. My weekly night out on the town was to the pictures at Mulligan's cinema on Sunday night. The pictures cost a shilling and the ceili costs two shillings and sixpence, two and a half times the price of a visit to the cinema. Need I say more?

When I turned sixteen, I went to an occasional ceili but thought it wiser to just observe and not risk wounding my delicate sensibilities too early in the game. My plan was to confine myself to old-time waltzes where I could improve my sadly lacking conversational abilities with girls at close range. Truthfully speaking, I was not much interested in improving my dancing skills, which caused me some concern because Mom, my old-time waltz and two-step teacher, had often said that a good dancer would always turn a girl's heart. I'd just have to find another way—but I knew that she had a point. I had heard from my older sisters that Sean O'Neill, a neighbor who lived down Hull Road, was an outstanding dancer, not just with Irish dances but also rock 'n' roll and jive. I had seen him at house dances in Culmore, and I could honestly say that no one rocked and jived like Sean. He was so good it was disgusting, and the girls practically lined up waiting their turn to be asked by the master.

Tom Gallagher

Sean O'Neill was the only one in the whole country who wore a three-piece suit to a dance—even a house dance. The only people I'd ever seen wearing three-piece suits were in American gangster movies or maybe the odd old-age pensioner who'd been wearing the same Sunday suit for thirty or forty years – back when three-piece suits were popular. Sean probably wasn't trying to restore their popularity but did want to stand apart – and it worked. To complete the picture, he had a watch tucked into a vest pocket and a chain coming from the watch across his chest to another vest pocket on the other side. I didn't know if the watch and chain were real or not, but they looked real enough to me. Sean was handsome and a big hit with the girls, but his older brother, Owen, was the one our family would remember fondly.

Often in the wintertime, we kept our cattle close to home because the swampy hollows in Madogue were more treacherous when there was more rain than there was drying. The problem was that the long Field of the Rushes in Culmore was little better—except, at least it was flat, and closer to home. We named our cows by their color. There was the gray cow, the red cow, the soon-to-be black cow who's still a heifer, and the white cow. Our white cow was snow white and had a face that was so gentle and calm in appearance that she looked almost saintly. She deserved a real name, so we named her Joan after St. Joan of Arc, the French girl who was burned at the stake for trying to free her country from the English, who were up to their usual tricks, trying to steal other peoples' countries. That time, three years ago, in late winter, when Eamon went to bring the cows up from the Field of the Rushes, he couldn't find Joan. As there was no place for a cow to hide, Eamon was fearful that Joan, now heavily in-calf, might have slipped into one of the long maren trenches that separates our land from the Drennans on one side and the Kennys on the other.

Walking the trenches, Eamon soon found Joan—and heard her at about the same time. She was lowing weakly for help and in desperate straits. Wedged deep down in the trench between the Kennys and us and almost completely buried, she had blocked the passage of water beneath her. Now it had risen up and was about to flow over her head, insistent on completing its journey to Phoill Bui, then on to the Sonnagh River, which flowed into the West's biggest river, the Moy, but not before a couple more name changes. As it flowed through Madogue, it was called the Madogue River. On entering the village of Corthoon, it became the Corthoon River, and near the Sonnagh Bridge, it became the Sonnagh River. Eventually, the water that was threatening Joan's life and our livelihood would flow into the Atlantic Ocean on Mayo's north coast many miles away.

Frantic, Eamon began shouting in all directions for neighbors, knowing that Joan would soon sink below the mucky water. Across the fields, to the west, Owen O'Neill heard Eamon's cries and, dropping his work, ran toward my brother for all he was worth. Owen arrived breathless but ready. Together with Eamon they kept Joan alive by keeping her head above water—but by themselves could do little more until more help arrived.

Soon, Mike Horan, alerted by his young daughters, who had heard Eamon yelling for help, arrived on the scene from the other direction. Mike, had just come home from Swinford, and was still in his Sunday going-to-Mass clothes. He didn't wait to change. He grabbed a rope and a shovel from the barn and ran for the bog where Joan was shivering uncontrollably from the cold and slowly giving up the struggle to live. Mike, much older than Eamon and Owen, quickly took charge. He threw the shovel to Eamon and told him to widen the other side of the trench to give himself and Owen more room. Eamon pared away the side of the trench like crazy. With the rope in his hand, Mike dropped down between Joan and the narrow side of the trench on his side, squeezing himself impossibly into the cold muck, almost up to his neck. Several years older than Eamon, Owen O'Neill slid down the other side of Joan. Barely holding their heads above the water and muck, Mike reached under Joan's bloated belly and pushed the rope to Owen's outstretched hand. They had the first critical connection. By now there were other neighbors on hand. Another rope was looped under Joan's udder and slowly the men began to pull her out of her would-be grave.

Once safe, Joan was washed down and cloaked in blankets and coats brought from the house. She cocked her ears and looked around at these strange people about her. I knew for sure that she was grateful to be alive and I think she knew that Eamon and these men saved her life. Mike Horan's Sunday going-to-Mass suit would never go to Mass again. Owen O'Neill's and the other men's clothes must be washed at home in a tub of hot water and scrubbed clean on a washing board—by a wife if they had one, by themselves if they didn't. But no one was thinking about this now. There was no thought about the fact that they were cold and wet and mucky. Instead there was joy and handshakes and back-slapping all-around, for a cow's life had been saved and a family spared a heavy loss. This was sweet victory. Eamon slowly walked Joan back to the barn—and that night we said a long thanksgiving rosary. Two weeks later Joan gave birth to twins. Instead of the loss of one, there was a gain of two. Praise the Lord!

As for me, without my three-piece suit, dancing skills, wit, or charm, the first impediment that I had to overcome was my great fear of approaching a girl to ask her to dance. I couldn't imagine what I'd do if she refused. My sister Kathleen told me that she had no problem saying, "No, thank you" to a man old enough to be her grandfather, or to a lad who wobbled in after the pubs closed and could barely stand up. She told me that before the dance began all the girls lined up, about four or five deep on one side of the dancehall, and all the young men and old men did likewise on the other side. When the band started up, every proud but fearful male waited for some other proud but slightly less fearful male to cross that vast expanse of floor between the two sexes to ask a girl to dance. Once the first couple was dancing, other males, suddenly brave as lions, moved toward the waiting but wary females.

The first fellow to cross must be very courageous, or very confident, or very stupid, for if the girl cruelly refused after his lonely pilgrimage across no-man's-land, the distance back across the great divide had just tripled, becoming the longest walk a mortally embarrassed lad could take. A real brazen or drunk fellow might take the refusal in stride and immediately ask another girl, often the one next to the one who'd just refused, and maybe a third—but this was almost always a bad idea, for no self-respecting girl would accept being second choice, and third choice almost demanded a slap across the face, or a cutting insult at the very least, like "I wouldn't dance with you if you were going to die heroically for Ireland at midnight, you ugly oul thing." Kathleen explained that at every dance she had obligations, same as many other girls. They couldn't refuse a neighbor, a family friend, or a cousin, for that would be a serious breach of custom and good manners. She said that often the first brave lad to cross the floor is just that, a neighbor or friend, who wasn't so brave after all, for he knew he was going for a sure thing. I asked her if good manners might extend to brothers, just to get a shy, red-faced lad started. She said I'd better warn her first or she might forget her manners and tell me to buzz off.

My sisters Kathleen and Patricia were gorgeous. When they dressed up for a dance, boy, they were something to see! I didn't understand though why they backcombed their hair for ages until it was all puffed up and rounded like an upside-down pot and required a gallon of hair-spray to keep it in place, but I was told that this is the height of fashion, as all smart young men know, but apparently not a younger, not-so-smart brother. I was smart enough though to know when something was going on in the steamed-up cars that I could see from time to time parked up on the Main Road by our boreen late at night after a dance. My sisters were very popular, and they had no shortage of dates. They did have one condition, however: their dates must have a car. There was nothing at all fashionable about having to ride a bicycle miles into town to meet some-one outside the dance hall—or worse, to meet him inside after a girl had had to pay her own way in. This was the height of bad manners, but some lads did it, maybe because they didn't have much money, God love them, or maybe because they didn't have enough money left over for two dance tickets after a few pints of Guinness or Harp in the pub.

After the dance the dates-with-cars took my sisters home—well, not quite home but close enough for me to carry out my responsibility to see that these smart young men behaved like the good Catholics I'm sure they're weren't. Now, I want to make it very clear that I'm no Peeping Tom prowling the roads at night looking for steamed-up cars. I only did this when I was asked to by my sisters or Mom—and this only happened when it was a new date and my sisters were not quite sure what to expect when they were alone in a car with a big lad on a dark, lonely road—or maybe an old date that they were willing to chance again provided I was there in the darkness. Brothers do come in handy sometimes. On these occasions it was my job to see that things didn't go too far.

With some experience in my lonely work, I knew that a little steam on the windshield and windows is okay—windows rolled up on a cold night and my sister enjoying a few quiet moments with her date and in no immediate danger. When the car quickly fogged up, that was another story, evidence of more heat than normal being generated, and worse if the car began to rock back and forth. As I was reasonably certain that my sisters were not a willing or too-willing participant in this steam and rocking commotion, it was time for me to emerge from the darkness. Fortunately, it was not a question of me having to challenge the guy in the car—because he was always bigger and older than me. All I needed to do was let him know that there was a most unwelcome presence outside his car, a thing that he could not see. Usually, a couple of heavy thumps on the boot of his car was enough to calm the lad down.

Mostly, my decisions to intervene, in the heat of battle, so to speak, were the right ones, like with Pat O'Donnell: tall, blessed with Hollywood good looks and dark curls falling down his forehead, who absolutely believed that he was God's special gift to females. The notion that a mere young girl should resist his advances was unthinkable—and unacceptable. A sudden blow across the rear window of his rocking Ford Zephyr with a blackthorn stick helped cure him of his delusion, at least for a while. And then there was Jack Carn, a proud member of the county football team. Jack, whose family owned multiple businesses around Castlebar, as well as land in the country stocked with bullocks, was of the considered opinion, like many of the town fellows, that country girls were easy because they just weren't very smart and would, therefore, be suitably deferential to a young man of means from the town, especially one who was also on the county football team. Jack's hands had never seen a day's work and were only soiled a little on the pitch where he excelled in the art and skill of Gaelic football.

Shortly after Patricia returned from England in early June 1962, she and I went to a football match at Father O'Hara's park in Charlestown to watch a game between County Mayo and County Sligo. Although we were well acquainted with the long rivalry between Mayo and next-door neighbor Sligo, neither of us was a great fan of Irish football—I much preferred soccer, probably because I was good at soccer and worthless at Gaelic football—but it was something to do on a Sunday afternoon. In the first half, it was all Mayo's game with Sligo hanging on in grim defiance. Just before the half ended, Patricia and I left our seats to go outside to buy ice cream from a vendor. Moments later a football came soaring between the goal posts, over the stands, and out of the park to land right on top of my sister's head, almost knocking her out. Another point for Mayo just as the half ended. Unsteady on her feet, Patricia sat on the grass as a crowd gathered around, gawking. There was a growing bruise on her head and she looked like she was about to faint.

As both teams were leaving the field for their half-time break, Jack Carn learned that a young lady had been injured by his team's last first-half point. Soon he was at my sister's side. With him were several other Mayo players, all extending their apologies—and, in truth, all of them seemingly sincere. Jack, in fact, was feeling so bad about the football attack that he insisted on making it up to Patricia by offering to take her to a dance that very night. She declined and Jack quickly recovered from a momentary flash of embarrassment. Next on the scene was Eamon Walsh, captain of the Mayo team and a Charlestown native. He offered his apologies to my sister and then turned to his teammates to deliver a brief pep talk, and brief it was because Mayo had the game well in hand. "They're finished, lads. We've beaten the piss outta them. Now all we have to do is convince them of this fact."

Alas for Mayo, Sligo wasn't at all convinced that they were beaten. Undeterred by the odds, they came back from miles behind and in the second half, with remarkable determination, leveled the game and ended the match in a draw: Mayo one goal, thirteen points; Sligo three goals, seven points. As a goal is equal to three points, both teams scored a total of sixteen points each. Two weeks later in the replay at Markievicz Park in Sligo Town, Sligo beat Mayo, ending Mayo's hopes of winning the Connacht Championship.

Patricia and I did not wait to see Mayo's reversal of fortune in Charlestown. We got our bikes and went home. Jack Carn was persistent in his attempts to date my sister, and eventually Patricia went out with him. It was a romance of short duration. Jack believed that a young man of his stature and breeding could have his way with a naïve young girl from the country, even if that young girl had grown up fast, earning a living in England's second largest city. My sister, with a little help from her brother, helped him to understand that he could not.

Good Mass-going Catholics or not, most of my sisters' dates were the gentlemen that Irish sensibilities and tradition demanded, meaning that they were polite and gentle and often, like me, shy to a frustrating fault. My sisters would often tell Mom of sitting in a parked car up on the Main Road, hoping that their date would show some sign of life, like reaching over to hold a hand, put an arm across a shoulder, or, God forbid, attempt a kiss. It was news to me to learn that both Patricia and Kathleen had whiled away hours on many a night in a parked car in stone-cold silence, to be broken only when they tried, as they would repeatedly, to start a conversation with a fellow who had nothing to say and nothing to do or even attempt. Equally disappointing was the up-and-coming manager at the creamery in Sligo who talked nonstop into the wee hours about the complexity and demands of his work converting milk cream into butter, which we do at home all summer long in an old-fashioned churn; or the ambitious lad who had happily escaped farm life and was now, proud as a peacock, driving a bread van for a bakery, suit and tie not altogether hiding behind a white apron.

Excluding the steam-makers, my sisters' date stories were hilarious, and I was all ears while Mom was frequently in stitches. Importantly, I found these debriefings very enlightening and very encouraging—for it meant that girls may not be quite as different from boys as I had thought. I got the impression that it has much to do with the way a lad approaches the serious but promising business of romance. I also got the feeling that, while approaching the matter the wrong way can be entirely unwelcome—and why I needed to be lying in wait in the darkness sometimes—not approaching it at all was almost as bad. I was beginning to understand, too, that dating, from a girl's point of view, was fraught with risk, to reputation as well as to mind and body, while the worst thing that a fellow may have to endure was a bruised ego. If a young lady liked the lad she was with and kissed him in a way that let him know this, he might think this was a come-on for more, and if she then resisted—and he was of low degree—she's a prick-teaser. If she didn't resist, she's of questionable virtue, and if he had his way with her, with or without her consent, she's a hoor.

A girl's reputation could be easily destroyed by a deliberate lie or even a rumor—and there'd be little she could do about it but head for Dublin or England where she'd be lonely but faceless. Listening one day to my sisters talk about a friend of theirs whose reputation was trashed not for what she did but for what she refused to do made me feel ashamed. I had been a willing participant in conversations about girls in which all kinds of rumors were happily shared. I didn't do the sharing, but I had been willing to listen and that was just as bad. At least, when I didn't believe a rumor was true, which was much of the time, I had no problem saying so. Patricia and Kathleen lectured me regularly about how to treat a girl and reminded me often that I was lucky to have sisters who were willing to educate me on the fine art of courting a girl.

Nevertheless, Mom loved to hear about my sisters' dates and alternated between concern or outrage over would-be rapists, to being very sympathetic over a date that was as dull as a priest's sermon. Mom, too, was once a young girl, and she remembers. She cautioned and counseled and worried. She pleaded with them not to think only of good looks but also about a young man's prospects. She often told them that it was just as easy to fall in love with a man of means as it was to fall in love with a man of no means. She prayed nightly that they would be lucky in love—and delighted in hearing about their romances.

Kathleen and Patricia, at this point in their lives, had little concern about marriage or settling down. They were enjoying their time together, their girlfriends—and sometimes competitors—their popularity with the boys, and being taken to dances near and far. They danced to the music of many of Ireland's best show bands that traveled the entire country, and were not infrequently asked out on a date by band members. I was both envious of them and happy for them, as I listened to their endless tales. They both knew, and Mom knew and we all knew, that all too soon it would come to an end. Patricia would go to America in a few months and would likely make her home there, like so many of our relatives. I couldn't bear the thought that I may never see her again, even knowing that this was not like olden times when emigration and wakes had much in common. Still, New York was three thousand miles away, ten times farther away than England. After Patricia it would be Kathleen's turn. She would go to nursing school in Stoke-on-Trent in England, and I would become the oldest still at home. But not yet—these sweet times still had a way to go.

CHAPTER 17

❧

HANDBALL WAS ANOTHER very popular game in Ireland. There were regular handball alleys in many towns but they were mostly used by the town lads. It's not that country lads couldn't play in the town alley; it's just that we weren't welcome. Maybe a few times a year, after last Mass on Sunday, a few of us would head over to the Charlestown ball alley to see if we could play a game or two. Games were either one against one or two against two—although you might have one good player take on two not-so-good players. The game was won by the player or team that reached twenty-one points first. Basically, a point was scored when your opponent fails to return your serve or your return. If there was no one at the ball alley, it was ours. If a bunch of townies showed up when we were midway through a game, the unspoken rule was that we finished our game and left—there was only the one alley, meaning that only one game could be played at a time. The town boys know that they were on their own turf and to us it wasn't worth a fight on a Sunday afternoon.

I learned earlier that the Charlestown lads were also very possessive about their Father O'Hara Park, where they regularly practice Gaelic football. In my final year at Corthoon National School, some genius came up with the bright idea that our school should challenge the Charlestown National School to a football game in Father O'Hara's park. Incredulous, if not stupefied, at our audacity, Charlestown accepted the challenge. We had only a few lads who knew anything at all about Gaelic football, and I certainly wasn't one of them. Nevertheless, I was named to the team, as was every other lad available—just to complete the team. We had no substitutes, no one to replace an injured player or a team member who fell down dead of fright or just ran off the field. Our opponents had many times our number to choose from, and they practiced in the park several times a week. The Corthoon School team practiced together at least once or twice before the match, as I recall, and I did not join them in this futile exercise. I had no football boots, no togs, no jersey, no nothing, so I said to myself, why bother?

I did, however, write an urgent letter to my father in Birmingham, asking him to buy me a pair of proper football boots with accompanying knee-high socks, togs, and a jersey. I had never asked Dad for anything before, and I wasn't at all sure that he would take my letter seriously, but he did. About two weeks later our postman, Jim McNicholas, delivered a parcel from England, addressed to me. I could hardly believe it. Everything was perfect: the boots, the socks, the whole outfit—everything. I may know nothing about the game, but by God, I would look the part. Now that I was properly attired for the game, I decided that I would go practice with the town lads on their turf in Father O'Hara's park. There was no time to be lost, as the game was less than a week away, and I needed at least one practice with real footballers to see how the game was played up close, as one might say. I rode my bike into town wearing my brand-new football uniform and boots. I was pleased with the attention I drew from passing motorists.

The town boys were on the field when I arrived, and I asked Pakey Hennigan, who seemed to be in charge, if I could join in the practice. Pakey and I knew each other by sight; his parents owned a shop, and my mother was an occasional customer. Quickly I was surrounded by Pakey's pals, gawking at me like I had just parachuted in from a passing plane. One of them said, "Who in the feck do you think you are, Pairig Carney?" I thought that was kind of funny. Pairig Carney was one of Mayo's greatest footballers ever, and in Irish sports his name was known throughout the country. Even when he became a medical doctor in America, the Mayo team would fly him back to Ireland to play for the team in important matches. Because of these trips he was known as the Flying Doctor. He and I were closely related, though not by blood. Jimmy Groarke in Swinford was my uncle and godfather, and he served in the same capacity to Pairig Carney. Uncle Jimmy's sister was Pairig Carney's mother.

More to the point, Pakey Hennigan wanted to know if I could play football. I told him the truth: I said I was doubtful but I was there to learn. Pakey was probably the only one who believed me. "All right," he said, "you're going to play full forward, so your job is to score, okay? I won't mark you, so you'll have the goal all to yourself."

"No problem," I said.

Practice began and I was passed the ball with some regularity, and with no defender around, except for the goalie, I had little difficulty kicking point after point from directly in front of the goalposts. After a while Pakey halted the practice and demanded to know why I wasn't going for goals. I told him the truth again. I said, "Because there's a goalkeeper in the goal, and I don't see any obstruction at all up there on the crossbar." Pakey said that he thought I should move to the sidelines and be a sub for the rest of the practice, or I could leave the park if I wanted to. Wisely, I didn't object. Shortly after I retired to the sidelines to gain further insights into the game, a tinker came up the field and started yelling that he wanted to play too. Pakey Hennigan had had enough of these unwanted intrusions. He walked up to the tinker, and said, "Tinkers are not allowed in our park"—and then flattened him with a vicious blow to the jaw. When the luckless tinker recovered sufficiently to get to his feet, he ran away sobbing "Da, me jaw is broken; me jaw is broken." I expected to see "Da" coming at a gallop with a tree limb in his hand, but Da was nowhere in sight. The townies resumed their practice, and I headed home, knowing that under controlled circumstances I could score.

On the following Sunday afternoon, the infamous mismatch was played in Father O'Hara's park with mercifully few spectators in attendance. I was the best-dressed player on the field, for all the good it did me or my demoralized teammates. I did not touch or kick the ball during the entire game, but I'm almost certain I saw it blur past me on a couple of occasions. For Charlestown the match did not even approach the level of a casual practice. For Corthoon it was the longest hour since the beginning of time. The final score was Charlestown twelve goals and ten points, Corthoon nil, zero, no score. I later learned that my impressive outfit had nothing at all to do with Gaelic football. The boots, socks, togs, jersey—the lot—comprised the complete uniform of a Birmingham boy's school soccer team. Not surprisingly Dad couldn't find a Gaelic football uniform in the industrial heart of England, so, with the help of a kindly neighbor, he was directed to a shop that made soccer outfits for local schools. With little soul searching, I came to the conclusion that Gaelic football was not my game, and I lost no sleep over it. I liked soccer and was fairly good at the game. I liked handball more and was better at it.

Playing in a real ball alley was a great treat because it was enclosed within four walls, not just a front wall like most country alleys. Regulation alleys were thirty feet wide and sixty feet long. The front wall was about thirty feet high and the rear wall about ten feet tall. The side walls slope in a straight line from the front to the rear. The floor, like the walls, was made of concrete. A regulation handball was about two inches in diameter and was called a "half-solid," meaning that its hollow core was surrounded by an extremely thick, hard rubber. If you were playing with a half-solid, you had to wear a padded handball glove if you didn't want to end up with a very sore and swollen hand that won't be much use Sunday evening milking cows. The great benefit of playing in a regulation alley is that you learned all the skills necessary to become a very good player. I could play in a country alley forever and become very good, but an accomplished one-wall player could never compete in a four-wall alley with an accomplished four-wall player. Learning to play the ball off of four walls in a naturally fast game required a lot more skill than just playing it off a single wall.

Apart from the one in Bushfield, as far as I knew, most of the country handball alleys had just the one wall because most of them were part of a road bridge over a river. When the river was flowing through a narrow valley or a hollow, the bridge had to be built up to a higher elevation to carry the road so that all manner of traffic could pass over without having the worry of being washed away by a river swollen with flood waters. These bridges always seemed to be constructed of huge blocks of cut limestone. The important thing was that at least one of the huge walls elevating the road could be easily used as a one-wall handball alley. All you had to do was carve out a rectangular floor at the bottom, extending out at right angles. Bridge handball alleys had no pretensions and never complied with regulation measurements. From bridge to bridge, the one wall always varied in height and length, as did the size of the floor beneath. We made do with what we had. And, as the saying goes, it was sound enough for a country job.

There were two Sonnagh bridges, about a half a mile apart. One carried the Main Road over the river, and the other carried the railway over the same river. Sonnagh Bridge was the place where I learned to play the country version of handball. We didn't use a half-solid ball because it would be far too lively, and with no side or rear walls to confine it, we'd be losing balls all the time. Instead we used a regular sponge ball about three inches in diameter. It was less lively than a half-solid and, therefore, less inclined to get lost—and it could be hit all day long without a glove. Still, we did manage to lose a ball from time to time and always in the same direction, when someone accidentally hit it over the top of the wall, across the Main Road, and down into the "graveyard of balls," so called because finding a *skyed* ball in that dense growth was difficult, at best, and time consuming.

We gathered at the Sonnagh Bridge on Sunday afternoons in the summertime—unless we were haymaking or harvesting. There were about ten regular or mostly regular players, the ones who could be counted on to show up, barring bad weather or other priorities. The regulars came from various villages, like Culmore, Corthoon, Sonnagh—and Madogue—which contributeed a single player, my friend, Martin Neary. Joe Murtagh, from Sonnagh, was, by far, the best handballer. He could play equally well with either hand and hit the ball with a beautiful underhand swing, meaning that he would swing his arm up over his head in a complete arc, making contact with the ball at the bottom of the swing. I could do this only if I had the time and only with my right hand. Like most players, my left hand is a poor partner.

Martin Neary had the most curious and effective serve anyone had ever seen. It would easily be banned by majority vote if it wasn't so funny to watch. Martin began his serve, like Joe Murtagh, with a full arc swing, but as his arm came down behind him he raised his right leg and hurls the ball toward the wall from under his leg. The result was that no one ever knew how the ball was going to come off the wall. All we knew was that it was going to come off the wall fast and its path would be as unpredictable as the roulette wheel. Martin had perfected this to the point that the ball was rarely out of bounds, yet unless you had the sheer luck to be in the precise spot to return his crazy serve, forget it. Joe Murtagh claimed that Martin was putting a wicked spin on the ball. I thought it was a combination of spin and the uneven wall. Cut limestone blocks will last forever, but they weren't nearly as smooth as a plastered wall. The surface of a limestone block was a little bumpy, meaning that even the most gentle of serves could surprise you. But combine an unkindly wall with Martin's serve, and you just didn't want to be on the receiving end.

One Sunday, after Mass, I rented a camera from Colleran's Chemist in Charlestown so that I could capture forever scenes and images of this happy pastime we shared. It cost almost nothing to rent it for a few hours, and I knew that long years into the future these pictures would bring back a flood of memories. I would label each one on the back, naming the people and the date, like "Joe Murtagh and Tony Moran after winning 21–17 over Jimmy Foley and Garrett Horkan—15 July 1962." I would have a picture of Martin Neary midway through his unique serve, and I would just label that picture, "Martin Neary: The Serve," for there was nothing else to add. As I had never taken a picture before and knew nothing about cameras, Luke Colleran loaded the film into the Kodak for me and showed me how to take the picture, advance the film, and rewind the roll when no more pictures were left. It seemed simple enough.

I was ready to capture posterity. I framed the perfect picture of Martin Neary in action and pushed down on the button, but nothing happened. Luke had said that I would hear the shutter opening and closing in a fraction of a second, but I heard nothing. I tried again and again—nothing. Then I tried to advance the film to get to the next picture, but the knob wouldn't turn. I didn't want to ride my bike back into town and have Luke Colleran laugh at me because I hadn't done some simple little thing. Maybe there was an on-off switch or something that needed to be turned so that the shutter would open.

If there was an on-off switch, I certainly couldn't find it, nor could a couple of other geniuses who were trying to help. Since the film wouldn't advance either, we concluded that the film was probably stuck. Taking control of the situation, I opened the back of the camera and there was the shiny blackish film extending out from its tube on one side and back across to the empty spool on the other side, which was operated by a round knob on top of the camera. I tried to turn the knob but it wouldn't budge. Indeed it did look like the film was stuck—that was why the spool couldn't turn.

The solution was now at hand and not a moment too soon, for Martin was getting wild applause below me. I removed the film from the camera and began to slowly and carefully pull the film from its container, looking for the slightest snag that would confirm my diagnosis. Sure enough, near the end of the unwinding there was a clearly detectable snag, which gave way with a slight tug on the film. Now with the problem fixed, I carefully rewound the film back into its container, carefully reloaded the camera, closed the back, and...it worked! Holy Mary, it worked! The button went down, the shutter clicked, the film advanced, and all was well. I was very proud of myself. Through the application of pure cerebral power and deductive reasoning, I had proven that I could fix unfamiliar and complex devices. I got twelve pictures, including two of Martin Neary's ferocious serves.

That evening, on my way to Mulligan's cinema, I returned the camera to Collerans, entering through the private door on the side, as the chemist shop was closed. I wanted my pictures as soon as possible and didn't want to make a special trip the next day. A week later I did make a special trip into town just for my pictures. They were all perfectly and identically black. So much for posterity; so much for memories. I learned a rather fundamental lesson about picture taking: don't expose the film, except by…well, by taking pictures. Why something so obvious had escaped me I can only put down to a massive brain malfunction brought on by the exhilaration of taking my first pictures. I did not throw away these black memories. As they represented my first experience at photography, they established a baseline from which I had only one way to go: up. In fact, I had a special affection for these marvels of incompetence. I gave each one a name. There's "Midnight in Moscow," "A Bad Dream," "Outer Space," "A Dark Beauty," "Culmore at Night," and—well, you get the idea.

While our humble ball alley would never be mistaken for the professionally built ones in the towns, it did have its own little secrets, like small areas in the wall where the limestone bumps were a bit more angular than average. It took practiced skill to bounce a serve from that spot and a great deal of skill to return a ball in play to that spot. In both instances the ball would come off at an angle, but only a lad with an eagle's eye and the memory of an elephant could tell which way it was going to angle. Another secret of Sonnagh Bridge Handball Alley was the hidden "jungle."

The jungle was a spot where one of the two western pillars anchoring the bridge stands. Extending from this pillar three quarters of the way to the next one was that portion of the wall that we had made our own. But the pillar was not flush with the wall. It stood slightly in front of the wall and mostly westward of where the wall began. The pillar and the wall were joined by interspersed curved limestones. In between pillar and wall was a small recess, a trap that ran the full height of the wall, from bottom to top.

A well-placed shot into the jungle always resulted in a point won or a serve lost—for the ball could not come out. In more sedate circles, it would be called a "dead ball," which wouldn't count, but our rules said it counted because it took considerable skill to place it there. Apart from a "reeler," it's our only guaranteed kill shot. When the ball hits the wall about an inch above the floor of the alley, you've got a reeler.

Sonnagh Bridge was more than a place to play handball, and often players were outnumbered by others just there for the craic. They'd come to watch the games, sometimes betting a little money on the more competitive matches but mostly just sitting around gabbing on a small rise on one side of the alley. Others would hang around on the edge of the roadway above looking down at the game below—or maybe completely ignoring the sport but still happily feeling part of the gathering.

The summer of 1962 brought us more than Ray Charles; it also brought us the portable radio. I mean a practical portable radio, smaller than any radio I'd ever seen and way, way lighter than our Bush radio at home. Even before we got electricity, there were a few battery-powered radios around, but these were big, heavy things, more like pieces of furniture. Our neighbors, the Kennys, had one, but I'd only seen it a couple of times—we didn't visit the Kennys much because they were older people and had no kids—and I'd never heard it because, I figured, they only turned it on for the news. Every now and then, Sean Kenny took the battery in to P. Duffy's in Charlestown to have it recharged. Even the battery was a big, clunky thing with a carrying handle on top.

Sean Rowley's brother brought him a portable radio from London, and Sean, an occasional attendee and not much of a handballer, brought it to Sonnagh Bridge sometimes, probably just to show off. We couldn't get over it: a small, thin, light radio with a great sound that came to life the moment you turned it on—no waiting until it warmed up like our radio at home. You could strap it over your shoulder and walk around with it, listening to the news on Radio Eireann or BBC, or rock 'n' roll on Radio Luxembourg. Before this, apart from making our own music or singing songs, the only music that you could take with you to a house dance or a bonfire at the crossroads was a gramophone. Bretts in Corthoon used to have one, and I remember Mom borrowing it once when I was very young. The music or songs came from records that were placed, one at a time, on a kind of disc that went around and around at a steady speed. You had to wind it up first, using a crank handle on the side to get the disc rotating, and the sound came out of a horn-like speaker above the record. You certainly couldn't listen to Charles Mitchell reading the news on a gramophone.

There was no doubt about it: a transistor radio made a young fellow look very fashionable and smart. Sean was already acting the part, suddenly becoming an expert on electronics, explaining to us why his transistor didn't have to be plugged into the wall in order to work—as if I didn't know. I knew that when I pushed down the short-wave button on our radio and slowly turned the station dial I could sometimes bring in New York. I knew it was New York because even though the languages were foreign to me, once in a while I would hear a voice say in English, "This is United Nations Radio in New York broadcasting to Africa." Since last I heard, Ireland was nowhere near Africa, I reckoned that New York didn't much care if their broadcast was received in County Mayo or London or even Moscow. I knew too that Sean's radio had to have a battery inside just like Kenny's, except it must be much smaller and lighter than the one I saw Sean Kenny bringing into P. Duffy's.

Sean Rowley and I got into a bit of an argument when I asked him where he got this incredible radio and he said that, while he could understand my ignorance—not using these words exactly—this was not a radio; it was a transistor. I told him that he could call it whatever he wanted, but it was still a radio. He was very upset and insisted with the certainty of the pope that it wasn't a radio, that radios were, as of the moment he came into possession of his transistor, as old fashioned and backward as creels on an ass. Radio or transistor, or both, it began to change our perception of the world, the notion that you could carry around with you, wherever you went, on foot or on bike, the means to keep in touch with the world, was wondrous indeed.

Sonnagh Bridge was well known for something else quite unrelated to handball and Sunday afternoon gatherings. It claimed more than its fair share of lives in horrific car accidents. The accidents didn't actually occur on the bridge but on the western approach to it. Like many bridges that I have seen, the road didn't meet the bridge head on. Instead, it came at the bridge from an angle, meaning that the road banked before crossing the bridge. With Sonnagh Bridge the Main Road banked on both sides of the bridge, from east and west. The bend on the east side was back far enough that the road had time to straighten out before the crossing. Not so on the west side. Not only does it not straighten out until you're practically on the bridge, there was also a fairly steep decline, accompanied by a sharp bank to the right just before the crossing.

The accidents always happened the same way and always at night. According to the gardie, the three major reasons were speed, unfamiliarity with the road, and drink. Going too fast, the driver didn't quite complete the turn and either smashed into the left pillar of the bridge or went sailing off into the air just before reaching the bridge, and landed in our graveyard of balls, or in the river itself or, on occasion, the east side of the river if the lad was in a real hurry.

While the county council was not very good at sign-posting dangerous bends, it was very sympathetic to grieving families that wanted to place a white cross on the spot where the tragedy occurred. Sometimes there would be more than one cross at the crash site or the point of departure if the car takes flight. This could mean more than one fatality in a crash or more than one crash. Then another lad comes along and goes airborne, removing in his helpless haste the memorial crosses that were already there—and we were back to one cross again—and more to come with the help of the county council.

The summer of Ray Charles's smash hit passed to autumn and life went on in County Mayo with unrelenting regularity. Happily, Patricia and Kathleen were off to dances almost every week, bringing home news, gossip, and stories galore of their ups and downs with dates and boyfriends. Patricia has had a steady boyfriend now for a while, and we knew she liked him a lot, but she will soon be leaving for America and he will not. On the land things are beginning to slow down a little as the days surrender more daylight and the nights win back more darkness in a devil's trade. The workload in the fall wasn't great, but then you didn't want it to be because the days were getting shorter by the minute and all too soon the frost would come. What had to be done had to be done quickly. There was the threshing of the oats, at which time we learned just how generous we had been to the crows and the blackbirds and their thieving brethren who rule the skies and, like the tax man, take their share off the top.

I dug the potatoes out of their ridges with a short-handled, four-pronged fork. A good crop would yield ten to fifteen potatoes per seedling sown. Three seedlings were sown crosswise on the ridge and the rows were about twelve to fourteen inches apart. An Irish acre of potatoes yielding a good crop meant no scarcity—but Irish weather teaches one thing: never get your hopes up too high. But at least this year we saw little or no blight, and we offered up a few rosaries for this blessing. When digging the potatoes out, you had to be careful to avoid spearing them. An experienced hand would rarely do this—not that a pronged potato is ruined; it's still okay, but too many of these mishaps suggested a careless digger and a lot of unhappy spuds. Some people prefer to use a spade to dig the potatoes. Spade users usually stand on top of the ridge, and the longer-handled spade may be easier on the back, but this method looked a bit odd and inefficient to me.

Standing in the seoch, the shallow ditch between the ridges, I could, with my short-handled, four-pronged grape, alternate between the ridges on my left and right, leveling out two-thirds of one and one-third of the other, while leaving a trail of potatoes in my wake. A spade was also harder on the potatoes. While a grape may spear a potato, it almost always remains intact. Not so with a spade. A spade cuts a potato in two, often making the smaller part useless. Digging a field of potatoes was more than just harvesting the spuds. When the job is done, you should have a perfectly flattened black field, the ridges all leveled out into the seochs whence they came and the potatoes secured into well-sealed pits to last out the winter. In the following spring, the remaining potatoes will be removed for storage close to the house, and the field will be ploughed over for a grain crop, and for us that's oats.

Picking the freshly dug potatoes was the job of my younger sisters when they came home from school around 3:30 in the afternoon. They'd eat a hurried dinner, and then out to the potato field where I would, by this time, have dug almost two ridges the length of the field. Using buckets, the girls must pick quickly while there was light, concentrating only on the larger potatoes. The *poreens* would be picked afterward and placed in a different pit. The poreens may be small but, when boiled and mashed up with a little bran or pollard, they are greedily devoured by our four-legged animals as well as our chickens and maybe a turkey or goose that we're trying to fatten up for Christmas.

Sometimes we couldn't wait until the girls came from school. If it looked like rain or if our winged tormentors were circling overhead in battalion strength, Mom would come out to pick as I dug. Wet potatoes couldn't be put into a pit because they would rot, so if they got wet, they must lay bare in the field until they dry. While they were out there naked, they were food for all of God's creatures in the neighborhood that had beaks or teeth. Even our own chickens and turkeys, or a loose calf, happily joined in this gluttonous feast. It seemed that no matter what we did on the land, no matter how much we worked or how hard we worked or how fervently we prayed, nature's forces were mostly working against us. We had to offer up a portion of our work and bounty to the heartless gods of rain and wind and frost and snow, to rats and mice and birds and beetles, to foxes and rabbits and hares and snails, to millions of insects of all manner and kind, to tinkers and gypsies and beggars and blight. And still we lived and the battle went on—with God's unwavering help, as Mom would say.

A few international events captured our attention in 1962: John Glenn, one of America's first astronauts, orbited the earth in Friendship 7 on February 20. After falling behind the Russians, who beat the Americans with the first satellite in space, Sputnik, in 1957 and the first earth orbit in April with Yuri Gagarin, there was fresh hope that the Yanks were back in the race—at least that's what the radio was saying. There was—and still is—real concern that Russia would win the space race, but I hadn't heard what exactly that meant, except that it wouldn't be good for America or Europe—and that meant probably not good for Ireland either—although we were reassured from time to time that we were a neutral country like Switzerland, which is supposed to be a good thing. Spain and Portugal were also neutral. They were run by dictators and, like Ireland, are among the poorest in Europe. Ireland was run by Fianna Fail. Tom Horkan told us one night that the reason Ireland and Portugal and Spain were so poor was because they remained neutral in World War II, even quietly sympathetic to Nazi Germany. They paid a heavy price for that, Tom said, by not being allowed to participate in America's Marshall Plan, which rebuilt Europe after the war.

Adolf Eichmann was hanged in Israel on May 31 for crimes against humanity, and there were few living souls on the face of the earth that shed a tear for him. Well maybe a few—those who believed that law and order and obedience to higher authority trumped everything else. I had followed his trial closely in the newspapers and got an education on the Nazi's Final Solution, which Eichmann implemented with terrifying efficiency. Adolf pleaded that he was practically as innocent as a newborn babe, that as a soldier he was merely obeying the orders of superiors, as all honorable and loyal soldiers must do. The papers said that there were some who believed that Eichmann should never have been brought to trial at all because of this absolute requirement by governments and military organizations the world over. It could be that the politicians and generals were concerned that if soldiers were permitted to question orders from above, or worse, disobey them, it could lead to a total breakdown of order and discipline within the ranks and maybe even wars having to be called off as a result—and then where would we be?

The biggest event for the whole world began on October 22. President Kennedy addressed the American people on radio and television from the White House. Ireland and much of the world heard the address on radio. The Cuban Missile Crisis was upon us. The president's words and tone were as serious as a heart attack. We all knew about the atom bombs that had destroyed two Japanese cities in World War II. We knew well that America and Russia had huge numbers of nuclear weapons that could destroy the world many times over. We *knew* it, but until this moment in time we didn't, or at least I didn't, grasp the inexpressible horror of it. The Russians had placed offensive nuclear missiles in Cuba, eighty miles from the United States, and President Kennedy made it clear that these missiles had to be dismantled and removed.

To make sure that Khrushchev knew he was serious, Kennedy had ordered the US Navy to quarantine Cuba, an act of war in itself. What if Khrushchev wouldn't back down? Everyone knew that he was proud, pig-headed, and a bully. The crisis for America began on October 15, when the missiles were positively identified, but it was another week before the president went public—after a response had been agreed upon. The crisis would last another heart-stopping week, but by October 28 Khrushchev announced over Radio Moscow that the missiles would be removed. Not so long ago, I would have regarded this whole drama as just about the biggest thrill of my life. But I realized now that my life and the lives of everyone I knew and loved could have ended in a blinding flash, and that if nuclear weapons were unleashed, Ireland's vaunted neutrality wouldn't be worth a fistful of ashes, for that's about all that would be left.

In November things were quiet enough at home, and I was able to go off to Renmore Barracks in County Galway for two weeks of training with the FCA. Renmore Barracks was a former British fortification a mile or so outside Galway City. Just about everything, including the huge wall that enclosed the facility, was built of limestone...yes, Ireland had lots and lots of limestone. As a result of the Cuban Missile Crisis, our training program at Renmore was modified to include a crash course on what nuclear war and nuclear winter might look like. During the crisis we had heard terms like nuclear winter on the radio, and I was able to grasp one essential truth: the lucky ones would be those who did not survive the initial blasts—what one might call nuclear summer—and, therefore, would not have to see nuclear winter, the aftermath. It was fairly clear to all of us in the classroom that the regular army captain teaching the course was about as inexperienced on the subject as his students were. Yet how could it be otherwise?

Basically, the assumption was that the Republic of Ireland would not take a direct hit because it would be an unconscionable violation of the Geneva Conventions to launch a nuclear strike against a neutral country—and one without nuclear weapons at that. It would be much more serious than, say, being unsportsmanlike, like "Oh shit, I just incinerated Ireland. Do I get a red card or a yellow card?" I'm sure the Swiss, too, felt very comforted by their neutrality, snuggled up close to Germany and France as they were.

As a direct nuclear strike against Ireland was considered highly unlikely, we would be spared the terror of instant oblivion, without time to prepare for St. Peter. Instead, we were told that our nightmare would come, as usual, from England. In a nuclear war, Britain, being part of NATO, would most assuredly take multiple direct missile hits, and these monster explosions would obliterate everything and scatter radioactive fallout over thousands of square miles. This fallout would reach Ireland in a matter of hours or, if we were really unlucky, days. When it did we were all finished—but not right away. We would die slowly and in agony, and there would be no one who could help: no doctors, no nurses, no ambulances, no hospitals—just us, each one becoming increasingly radioactive, glowing in the dark and praying for death to come. So much for neutrality.

We all voted for instant oblivion, including the captain. We agreed that the sensible thing would be to ask the Soviet Union to detonate a nuclear missile about five thousand feet above the Bog of Allen and that should take care of dear 'oul Ireland. The course ended when we were shown a small sliver of radioactive material. It was removed from a small but heavy lead box. The captain used a Geiger counter to show us that this was the real McCoy. It was hard to believe that this tiny metallic disc that you could place on your fingertip was deadly—and would continue to emit radioactive poison for hundreds of thousands of years.

CHAPTER 18

***

THE WINTER OF 1962–63, Radio Eireann reported, was one of the coldest on record, with hard, black frost for seven long weeks. The earth was rock solid, and I was terrified that the potatoes and turnips in their soil-covered pits were doomed. It was too late to put more soil on the pits because the earth was already frozen too deep. We hoped and prayed that our potatoes, especially, were safe. Turnips we could live without; potatoes we couldn't. If the frost had gotten to them, we'd have to buy new seed potatoes for the spring planting, and after a brutal winter, the cost of seed would be sky high—and, of course, it would be a lean spring.

In early January our dog, Rover, went missing. At first we weren't overly concerned. Rover loved to wander, to find willing bitches and make little Rovers. Without fail he would return in a day or two, sometimes cut and bloody from fights with other dogs, but he'd always come home when he was hungry enough. Food for Rover were boiled potatoes and milk if we have it to spare. If not it was potatoes and water. If no potatoes it was bread and milk or bread and water. Rover never complained. He wolfed down whatever we gave him.

Flower had died a couple of years ago. We didn't know why. We just found her dead one morning, not a mark on her. She was only about twelve years old, too young to die. Maybe she had picked up poison somewhere. Rat poison was often laid down by farmers in the never-ending struggle to control rats and other pests. We had stopped doing that years ago after our own cat became the victim. Or maybe it was the final result of all the times she had the fits. We never knew what caused the fits—we couldn't take Flower to the vet even if we had the money, for no self-respecting vet would waste time on a dog or a cat. Vets were for horses and cattle. When Flower got the fits, it was a terrible thing to see. She would go completely wild, foaming at the mouth and howling like a banshee, and she'd race around in ever-widening circles. If the fits came on her in the kitchen, she'd run directly into the fire, scattering red-hot coals all over the place.

If the door was closed, you had to open it quickly to get her out of the house. The fits would only last a few minutes, and eventually Flower would collapse in exhaustion, panting loudly. She never seriously injured herself—even the scattered coals in the kitchen didn't have time to do any permanent damage—and Flower always seemed to recover quickly after the attack. Maybe whatever this thing was shortened her life, or maybe it was just her time. When she died we grieved for another member of the family gone, and our occasional rabbit meal from Madogue came to an end.

Rover did not return in a day or two or three—and I began to fear the worst. It was time to start looking for him. I cycled the Main Road and the byroads into other villages, asking neighbors and strangers if they had seen our dog. As the days passed, I forced myself to accept the reality that my dog may not be coming home this time. Rover was the family dog, but he was mostly my dog. Over the years the bond had grown. In the fields and in the bog, in Madogue and Culmore, he was my pal, my faithful friend, and now the thought of losing him was more than painful. He was big and lovable and all heart, but not very bright.

On January 14, a neighbor came to our house to tell us that he had seen a large black dog dead by the Main Road near Culmore School. I got on my bike and rode toward Culmore School, praying to God to not let this be Rover, but in my heart there was a terrible fear. I found my dead dog at the intersection of the Main Road and the byroad that led up to the Devaneys', the Lynskys', the MacNicholases', and other families up the school road. I knew instinctively that it was Rover. His eyes were open and glassy frozen. A blood stream from his mouth to the ground was also frozen. He was frozen stiff—my poor dog.

I struggled to pick up his heavy, dead weight and hugged his frozen face and talked to him, scraped away the hardened blood, begged his frozen corpse back to life. Rover was dead, hit by a motorist who probably didn't even care to stop. I scolded him for his carelessness—he knew the road as well as I did, had been on it thousands of times. How could this happen? I placed him on the carrier of my bike, behind the saddle and, holding him in place with my right hand, I rode back home. Cars slowed down to get a closer look at the scene: a frozen dog across the carrier of a bicycle, front paws stretched out. There were a few horn honks and a few shouts, but I continued on to the far end of Culmore, my dead dog and me.

At home there was grief, the whole family gently stroking our frozen pet. They were expecting this. Rover lived up to his name, and maybe it was always just a question of time. Goodbyes were said, and then I carried him to the Sloe Garden for burial. This was my job. The Sloe Garden was beside our barns, my mother's home in olden times. It was a peaceful, sheltered place, encircled by tall blackthorn and hawthorn bushes and a couple of oaks—and under its soil, treasures of old. Here, as children, we would dig into the ground, finding all manner of household things, from clay pipes to crockery to old pots and pans—the broken or damaged throwaways from an earlier time. One thing was clear: the things we found showed that the Morans and the McHughs before them had lived better lives than we were living. Now, in this ground, we would put down our own used and broken things, our own memories, our own contributions to the past.

In this ground I would bury my loyal friend, who would have, without hesitation, died to protect me—or anyone else in the family. The problem was that the ground was frozen. I knew that the surrounding tree cover would have reduced the depth of frost, but I would still need a pickaxe—and I didn't have one. So I borrowed one from the Joyces and went to work on digging a grave for Rover. I chose a spot close by Flower's grave. It was exhausting work. I slammed the pickaxe into the ground a hundred times, until my arms were numb and sore. I eventually dug through a foot of rock-solid frozen ground and then went deep so scavengers—or neighboring dogs—would not dig him up. Five feet down I placed my old friend, enclosed in a flour bag that Mom would otherwise have used to become part of a sheet for one of our beds. I closed up his grave and put a cross on top—and said the Act of Contrition just in case God was looking out for dogs too.

In a few months, we got another dog from a farmer the other side of Swinford. It was another male, not full grown yet but no longer a pup, handsome and wearing the shiniest coat of black fur you ever saw. I named him Rusty. Rusty, like Coco, our ass, started out with great potential—and even though he would never replace Rover, we were happy to have him. Sadly for us, and more sadly for Rusty, he seemed to have a bit of the wolf in him, and soon I began to suspect that it was this attribute of Rusty's that sparked the generosity in our friend above the town.

On January 19, 1963, my sister, Patricia, left Ireland for good. For me it was one of those days that I'd never forget, the splitting of memory and time into before and after. A couple of fields over, Mary Joyce was leaving with us. We left together, all of us in Horkan's hackney car, packed in like sardines: Mary and Patricia, my mother and Mary's mother, Kathleen and me, and Mary's brother, P.J. It was a sad day for everyone, the combined sardine families making the three-hour journey to Shannon Airport, the discombobulated remainder behind in two lonely homes. For me, just leaving the house to get into the car was like getting into a coffin. I wanted to run away to the bog, my lifelong escape. Only a week before, I had buried Rover, and now my best friend at home was going to America. I knew—we all knew—that we would see Patricia again. We just didn't have a clue when that would be, and that's what made it so hard. And even when we did see her, probably years from now, it wouldn't be the same; it could never be the same again. This chapter was closing forever.

There were lots of long silences on the way to Shannon. We looked at the passing scenery. We pointed out differences between scenes we passed and home. Mom said the land in Galway was a big improvement over Mayo, but County Clare not so much. Mostly we stayed quiet. We stopped once to get out and stretch for a few minutes, then resumed our unhappy journey. I thought about times long ago when sons and daughters and brothers and sisters left, when heartbroken good-byes were said by the door or by the end of the boreen, for then there was a fair chance you'd never see them again. I knew in my brain that this was different, but in my heart there was little difference. As we neared Shannon, more than a hundred miles from home, we saw huge jet planes coming in and going out. There was momentary excitement in the car. At home we had seen many jets high above, small silvery objects silhouetted against a blue sky, heading to or returning from North America, streaming their long jet trails—magical. Now they were thundering away just above us, gigantic and loud, magnificent but not magical anymore.

At Shannon Airport, Patricia and Mary checked in at the Aer Lingus counter, checked their baggage to New York for my sister and Chicago for Mary. We then gathered to have coffee and sandwiches at the airport res-taurant. We had Irel Coffee that tasted awful and sandwiches that had no taste at all. Worse, we tried to make conversation—two families, forever close in proximity and necessity, and friendship, my mother and Mary's mother, parting with two daughters; and for us, sisters, both of whom had worked so hard on the land, who made hay, stooked oats, picked potatoes, spread and groiged turf, and cleaned house—and who washed and hair-sprayed and perfumed up, had been so popular at the dances, had given us so many stories to remember and relish. And now they were leaving our lives.

At this moment it was hard for me to see how this was a good thing. I wondered how my sister could say good-bye forever to her boyfriend of several months, one of the nicest and best-liked guys in the county. I could see why Eamon wanted to bail out—endless work with little or no reward—but Patricia, no, she was one of the most popular girls. So was

Tara's Halls

Mary Joyce; they were both knockouts. Why did they have to leave? Why could they not see a future at home?

Of course I knew the answer. Being a farmer's wife, or the wife of an ever-struggling husband with another child always on the way, in an impoverished land, was not for them. They left because they did not see any future with their boyfriends, or the kind of futures they dreamed of—relationships that when they did exist were temporary and bitter-sweet, for the ending was already known. Hardship at home wounded spirits, but emigration broke hearts. In the scenically beautiful West of Ireland, where postcards showed idyllic views, smiling garsuns, and beguiling colleens, widespread depression and despair lurked just beneath the deceptive surface. With the faith of children, and the wisdom of ancients, emigrants took to the boats and the planes in search of a better life, regardless of the risks—and there were risks—for we knew, and they knew, the dangers of life in cities like New York and Chicago and Birmingham and London and beyond.

My sister settled in New York, working sometimes in department stores and sometimes as a housekeeper and cook for famous people, such as the Arlens. She worked long hours for Harold Arlen, music writer of the hits "That Old Black Magic" and "Over the Rainbow" from the movie *The Wizard of Oz*. Patricia somehow managed to meet the exacting standards of the Arlens, of whom she grew fond, and they of her. But to us she was gone now, living in another world, far away. As for me, I was still at home, without my champion and with my own challenges…and dreams. Soon after Patricia left for New York, Kathleen left for Stoke-on-Trent in England to begin nursing school. With each departure there was one less mouth to feed, but also one less to help on the land. The reality was that the farm didn't get any smaller when one left. Even if we could get by on fewer potatoes and fewer turnips and fewer vegetables, all of the land must still be worked—for you couldn't just let it go to ruin. Unworked land would quickly return to its natural and happy state of freedom and chaos. This meant that those remaining must do more.

Tom Gallagher

For me, in the spring 1963, I faced another challenge, a task that I had never done before. I had to cut the year's supply of turf. I had done everything with turf, spreading it, groiging it, gathering it, clamping it, hauling it home, and reeking it—everything but cutting it out of the bog with the slean. This task was daunting. My fear was that I wouldn't have the required skill or the endurance. I had to cut seven banks of turf, the same seven banks that Dad used to cut and then Eamon. The previous year, my fear was that I might not be able to mow down a field of oats, swath by swath, with the scythe—or even be able to properly sharpen the scythe blade. But I managed both tasks, and once I got into the rhythm, mowing oats was like dancing a waltz, but with a lot more sweat.

To my great relief, cutting turf was not quite the challenge I had feared. It was hard work and brutal on the back but once I had mastered the knack of giving the slean a quick sharp twist to the right or left or both, to break the sod free of the spit, the rest just required old-fashioned elbow greese, throwing the sod either on top of the bank for the upper spits or the cutaway below for the lower spits. From these seven banks, over fourteen days, I cut more turf than my brother had cut the previous year and repeated this in the following years—before I bailed out myself. It was important to me to be as good as Eamon at this physically demanding task because he would sometimes say that I was not much help when working alongside him. We both knew better. He was my big brother, whom I had always looked up to, and now I was matching him and more.

As ever, my sisters and my mother did most of the spreading and the groiging. Eamon came home from England for a brief holiday later that summer. Coco and I had just finished bringing the turf out of the bog to its usual temporary place above the railway. It occupied the same two tracks that we had used for years except that this time the second track was extended. Eamon asked who had helped me cut this much turf. He would not believe that I could have done it myself. He asked Mom and she confirmed it. My brother still pretended to be in disbelief, but I knew and he knew that he and I were now on equal terms.

The rest of the spring's work went ahead on schedule. Taking out cartloads of cow muck, accumulated in the *dunkle* near the cow barn since the previous spring, to bare meadows was a dirty, smelly job. This was the best kind of fertilizer you could use to encourage growth—and also the cheapest—but spreading it out evenly and sparingly over several fields with nothing but a hand tool was another test of endurance and, like cutting turf, a back-breaking task. The tool we used for this was the grape, the same one I used to dig the potatoes and flatten the ridges. The grape was handy for all kinds of farm jobs, not just digging spuds and spreading cow muck.

When we could afford it—or when cow muck was more scarce than usual and we had no other choice, we'd buy a few hundred-weight bags of "special," a heavy, powdery chemical fertilizer that smelled worse than shit and burned the hands and face and eyes and any other unprotected body part. There were no clean jobs on a farm, and few nastier than shaking chemical fertilizer by the bucketful with a bare hand, walking up and down the length of a one-acre field and trying to ensure that when the bag was empty, the field was done. When finished you had to wash yourself clean and sooner rather than later, or you'd have blisters and sores to keep company with a scratchy throat.

Mick Burns, with tractor and double mouldboard plough, turned last year's oat field into this year's potato field and last year's potato field into this year's oat field. Crop rotation in County Mayo was a fairly short two-year plan. A longer rest for the soil would have been more beneficial for both soil and crop, but on small farms you didn't have that luxury. Sowing oats on a freshly ploughed field is similar to shaking special but without the unpleasant side effects. With a bucket of oat seed in one hand you walked up and down the field, shaking out seed to your left and right as evenly as possible—and always, always keeping in mind the amount of seed you had and the amount of ground to cover.

To run out of seed before you run out of field was not only a great embarrassment to the young farmer, it also presented a problem as to what you'd do with that precious piece of ploughed but unseeded field. You might see some cabbages or turnips growing in strange places far from the vegetable garden. Fortunately, that wasn't a problem I faced in my first sowing of the oats in the spring of 1963. Immediately after the oats were sown, the field had to be harrowed to break up the soil and conceal the seed. Speed here was critical, for the winged tormentors of the sky were most definitely not going on holiday during the planting season and would, without doubt, reduce God's bounty, taking their share both before and after the seed took root.

The harrow was a flat, heavy wooden contraption, about four feet by four, studded underneath with six-inch iron prongs that break up and even out the soil—and, mercifully, concealed most of the seed. Coco, despite his willingness and heart, was not strong enough to pull the harrow, so I borrowed the Joyces' mule, Dolly, for this cover-up. Next task was to "roll the field," that is, to flatten out and compact the soil, further concealing the seed and giving the field an overall smooth appearance. A roller was a five-foot-long round hunk of concrete, like a round pillar laying flat, with hook-up attachments on each end. I also used Dolly to pull the roller up and down the field. Now I was finished with the oats until harvest time, and we prayed for fine weather, meaning enough sunshine—we never had to worry about enough rain—and a good harvest.

The potato field this year was the Hill Field just below the barns, and it also had to be prepared for planting. Mick Burns ploughed the ridges beautifully, each ridge composed of four furrows, two facing two and leaving a two foot wide seoch between them. At both ends of each ridge I completed the "headlands" by hand with a spade. This was one of those nuisance jobs that must be done, but when I thought of earlier generations turning this entire field with a spade, I was humbled and didn't complain. Turning headlands was not necessary when ploughing for oats or barley because, without the necessity of having to create seochs, the tractor could plough crossways at both ends of the field. The seochs were needed later for moul. Mom and I had already prepared the seed potatoes needed for this year's crop. Smaller potatoes are used intact, with no splitting.

Larger potatoes could be cut into two or even three parts, but we must ensure that each part had at least one eye, which would bud in the ground and produce the stalk, which would grow a cluster of new potatoes under the soil. Using the *stibhin* I made the holes in the ridge, and Mom placed the seed in each hole. In the afternoon when my sisters came home from school, they took over from Mom. You didn't want to get too far ahead of yourself when dibbling potatoes. Overhead the enemy was circling: crows and blackbirds and jackdaws and other pitiless scoundrels. If the holes weren't quickly covered in with soil, these mocking marauders would swoop down and quickly devour the seed. Even when the seed was covered, a more determined or hungrier thief would search for and sometimes find the concealed seed and remorselessly rob the nest.

Next, more cow muck had to be hauled from the dwindling supply in the dunkle out to the potato ridges where it was spread evenly and sparingly, but adding a little extra on those ridges that had the more pedigreed seed. Then I went over to the Joyces to borrow Dolly again, but this time must wait because the Joyces were using their mule to harrow and roll their own mixed oat and barley field. While I was waiting I removed those parts of the plough that I would not need, like the mouldboard and coulter. My task was not to make furrows but to break up the hard-packed soil in the seoch and create loose moul, which would be placed on top of the ridges. Each seoch required three trips, once down to break up the left side of the seoch, then back to break up the other side, then once down the center. Poor Dolly got a night's rest, and I fetched her in the morning. I harnessed Dolly to our English-made Pierce plough and, in this spring of 1963, found out if I had what it took to plough the seochs, just me and Dolly.

Thank God for this gentle, steady mule, for she knew a lot more about ploughing seochs than I did, and her long experience made my job easier than I thought it would be. The most difficult part for me was to lift up the heavy plough at the end of the seoch and turn it around. Dolly knew that she too had to turn around and, watching me, the novice ploughman, instinctively turned slowly, her big eyeballs looking down at my feet and giving me time to turn the plough around and not create a tangled mess.

Alas, now it was mouling time, and this was probably the most physically demanding job on the land. It was not new to me. I had mouled spuds in the next seoch side by side with Eamon before, but now I was on my own and there were just as many ridges to moul. This was one of the jobs that Mom and my sisters could not do because the work was physically too hard. The hand tool of choice for this job was the shovel. The basic idea was to completely cover the cow manure on the ridge and speed up its decomposition in the soil. The task was to shovel all of the loose soil in the seoch evenly on the ridge to the left and the right, covering half of each ridge as you slowly moved forward down the length of the field, leaving a clean, smooth seoch in your wake. When you got to the end of the seoch, you moved to the next one and repeated the task, seoch by seoch until the field was done.

A month later, the whole process had to be repeated. Both mouls were necessary to help growth and provide more anchor to the fresh stalks as they began to break the surface and climb upward. Then we hoped – and prayed – that the blight wouldn't come, or if it did come, that it wouldn't be too bad and could be held at bay with a couple of crop sprayings.

June and July were haymaking time, and everyone pitched in because when God gave you good weather, you had to seize every minute of it. Mass on Sunday was the only acceptable reason for not being in the hayfield. In the bog, we hoped that the groiged turf were drying nicely and would soon be ready for gathering up by the cartload and removed to a safer, more solid location above the railway, ideally accomplished in late July and early August.

On June 3 we heard the sad news that Pope John the XXIII had died. Mom was very sad. I believed all the country people in Ireland were sad, and if not all the country people then certainly all of the poor people of

Ireland were sad. Pope John was loved for his simplicity and humility. He had no airs and graces. Mom often said that if ever there was a living saint on this earth, it was Pope John. The new pope is Paul VI but I didn't think we'd be taking Pope John's picture down from the mantelpiece for a while.

If June started out with sad news, it ended with a huge dose of the best tonic Ireland could have hoped for: a presidential visit. President Kennedy arrived in Ireland on June 26 for four wonderful, blissful days of sunshine and happiness. Well, three days to be truthful, but since he arrived late in the day on the twenty-sixth, being the generous people that we are, we gave him credit for the full day and ourselves too. The entire population went completely mad, and our ever-decreasing family happily and proudly took part, insofar as we could, that is. We didn't have television, but every chance we got, we tuned in to Radio Eireann, which was broadcasting the visit almost nonstop.

Air Force One flew in to the Dublin Airport from Berlin a little after 8:00 p.m., where that morning the president drove almost half a million Berliners delirious with his "Ich bin ein Berliner" speech. He said, "Two thousand years ago, the proudest boast was Civis Romanus Sum, I am a Roman citizen. Today, in the world of freedom the proudest boast is Ich bin ein Berliner, I am a Berliner." According to the radio, the president visited Berlin to do two things: (1) give heart to Berliners, who were now completely surrounded within East Germany by Soviet and East German troops and tanks, cut off from relatives, neighbors, and friends since the communists erected the Berlin Wall two years before, splitting the city in two; and (2) put the Soviet Union on notice that the United States would defend West Berlin and West Germany. Radio Eireann said that JFK's visit to Berlin was a spectacular success: Berliners wept, and for us bringing people to tears was the highest praise a speaker could get.

The only slight tinge of disappointment was that when the president left Ireland on the twenty-ninth, he would go to England, the ancient enemy, for a private meeting with Prime Minister Harold Macmillan, like they were old friends or something. We may not be a world power, but we are a proud people and we would have felt better if Air Force One, carrying *our* president—for we had a rightful claim to him, too—headed west instead of east on Saturday evening. Still, President de Valera, all members of Dail Eireann, and just about everyone else magnanimously put aside any begrudgement and welcomed JFK with an ecstatic embrace, heretofore reserved only for the Second Coming of Jesus Christ.

President de Valera and members of the government met President Kennedy at Dublin Airport on his arrival from Berlin. Dev offered JFK a heartfelt, emotional welcome, the first few words in Irish—for the benefit of the 1,963 people living in the Gaeltachts whose primary language was Irish—the rest in English. He spoke generously of America, of the "great republic of the west, upon whose enlightened, wise, and firm leadership hang the hope of the world." Dev spoke of an America where so many Irish people sought refuge away from their motherland, driven from our shores by "England's tyrant laws." I laughed when I heard Dev mention England's tyrant laws. I knew he just couldn't pass up this wonderful opportunity to kick old John Bull in the arse in a broadcast heard far beyond Ireland. The old warrior would never forget or forgive.

In his warm response, President Kennedy did not refer to England's tyrant laws but did refer to the devastating years of the Great Famine that decimated the population and forced a million more, including his great-grandfather, Patrick Kennedy, to leave Ireland in 1848 on a ship bound for Boston.

The second day of President Kennedy's visit began with a helicopter trip to County Wexford and the ancestral home at Dunganstown. It was a grand affair altogether. Dunganstown never saw so many people shouting, cheering, laughing, and crying, all thrilled at this most magical moment: the president of the greatest, most powerful country on earth and he, this brilliant, wonderful, handsome man, had come here to visit his Irish relatives. His cousin, Mary Kennedy Ryan, current owner of the ancestral home, kissed him on the cheek by a banner that said

"Welcome Home Mr. President." This epic scene opened the floodgates of the proudest tears ever shed in Dunganstown or in Ireland, or in our house in Culmore. In that moment, if only a moment, almost eight hundred years of English occupation might be forgiven, for that occupation, in part, led to this moment of unqualified triumph: a son of Erin—in spirit if not in fact—visiting the home place, who just happened to be the president of the United States of America. Mrs. Ryan served her cousin the traditional Irish treat: tea and cake. The president said, "I want to drink a cup of tea to all those Kennedys who went and all those Kennedys who stayed." In Wexford Town a boys' choir sang the president's favorite Irish ballad about the Uprising of 1798, "The Boys of Wexford," so moving the president that he left the cordon of secret service and gardai and joined the choir to sing the chorus,

> We are the Boys of Wexford
> Who fought with heart and hand
> To burst in twain the galling chain
> And free our native land.

The next day the president addressed a joint session of the Irish parliament, Dail Eireann and Seanad Eireann, at Leinster House, seat of the Irish government. He joked that if his great-grandfather had not emigrated from County Wexford to the United States in the 1840s and President de Valera had not emigrated from the United States to Ireland in the 1880s, their situations on this day, June 28, 1963, might be reversed. He assured his adoring audience that he, a FitzGerald on his mother's side, was not going to lay claim to Leinster House, the majestic, historic home of the FitzGerald Earls—and which later inspired the design of the White House by Irishman James Hoban.

> Ye Geraldines, ye Geraldines
> How royally ye reigned

O'er Desmond broad
And rich Kildare
And English arts disdained

Your swords made knights
Your banners waved
Free was your bugle call
From Gleann's green slopes
And Dingle's tide
From Barrows banks to Youghall.

I hung on his every word. I loved him—we all loved him. We loved his humor and easy wit. He didn't look much like any of us, but he was one of us. He was ours, and tomorrow we would shed more tears of pride and loss when we gave him back. He spoke of the famous Irish Brigade in the American Civil War and their heroic but doomed charge at the ferocious Battle of Fredericksburg in December 1862.

Irish born and raised, and a leader of the failed Young Ireland Rebellion of the late 1840s, Union General Thomas Francis Meagher commanded the twelve hundred Irishmen, mostly Irish immigrants recruited in Boston, New York, and Philadelphia, that charged up the hill at Marye's Heights outside Fredericksburg, Virginia, on December 13, 1862. By day's end 545 lay dead or wounded. Defending the heights behind a stone wall was the Confederate Twenty-Fourth Georgia Regiment. The Irish Brigade came on, green flags waving, all emblazoned with harps and shamrocks and the Irish words, Fag An Bealac: clear the way.

The Twenty-Fourth Georgia paused and sent up a cheer in marked respect for the men they would soon decimate. Robert E. Lee, Confederate commanding general at the Battle of Fredericksburg, received an assurance from his No. 2, General James Longstreet, that not even a chicken could live on the field in front. But the Irish Brigade came on anyway. The Twenty-Fourth Georgia poured volley after volley into the charging men. Lee, looking at the scene of carnage, turned away. Still, the Irish came on, leaning into the hail of fire as one would lean into a strong wind. The Twenty-Fourth Georgia continued its grim task but without jubilation, for they had reason to feel a kinship with the Irish Brigade. The Twenty-Fourth Georgia was mostly Irish or of Irish stock, and they were mowing down their own blood. Later Lee would say: "The gallant stand that this bold brigade made on the heights of Fredericksburg is well known. Never were men so brave. They ennobled their race by their splendid gallantry on that desperate occasion. Their brilliant, though hopeless, assaults on our lines excited the hearty applause of our officers and soldiers."

President Kennedy continued his remarks at Leinster House: "Today, in recognition of these gallant Irishmen and what millions of other Irish have done for my country, and through the generosity of the Fighting Sixty-Ninth, [the New York regiment and one of the three regiments that comprised the Irish Brigade], I would like to present one of these flags to the people of Ireland." The flag that JFK presented bore the names of the battles that the Irish Brigade had fought in during the Civil War. There were many names, but the one that stood out for me was Gettysburg.

Gettysburg was the turning point in the war, an epic battle fought on Northern soil in Pennsylvania, a battle that the Union had to win—or lose the war. After three desperate days in July 1863 and fifty thousand casualties, it was won, and Lee was in retreat, never again to regain momentum. Later that year President Lincoln would come to Gettysburg to deliver his brief but timeless Gettysburg Address. Speaking of the sacrifices made, and the work that remained, Lincoln concluded: "It is rather for us to be here dedicated to the great task remaining before us...that from these honored dead we take increased devotion to that cause for which they gave the last full measure of devotion...that we here highly resolve that these dead shall not have died in vain...that this nation under God, shall have a new birth of freedom...and that government of the people, by the people, for the people, shall not perish from the earth."

Tom Gallagher

President Lincoln is one of my great heroes. He ended slavery and saved the American Union, and his words—his beautiful, perfect words—were so carefully chosen to express the emotions and sentiments of a shattered country and his conviction that right would triumph. I memorized the Gettysburg Address and often recite it to myself. It inspires me and renews my faith in mankind.

President Kennedy's last day was spent in Galway and Limerick, with more people gathered in one place than these cities had ever seen before. Galway was the closest that JFK came to our farm outside Swinford in County Mayo, about sixty miles away. I felt a sadness now creeping over me. Soon he would be gone, leaving an adoring country at his feet. At Shannon Airport the president bid an emotional farewell to the people of Ireland and promised to return, a promise he would not keep. The band of the Irish army's Southern Command played "Come Back to Erin," and he was gone. I did not meet him or shake his hand, and he didn't get within three score miles of me. He could not have known that I existed, yet I missed him as you would miss someone you cared about and who had just walked out of your life.

CHAPTER 19

❧

WHILE PRESIDENT KENNEDY's historic visit to the land of his ancestors was a source of immense pride and joy for the people of Ireland, an altogether different kind of history was being made in the spring and summer of 1963 across the Irish Sea in England. The Profumo Affair was first made public in 1962 but with few details, such that it looked like just another pro forma sex scandal involving people in high places, which the English reveled in—and we in Ireland too, because it proved once again, if indeed proof was needed, that England was a latter-day Sodom and Gomorrah where unspeakable things went on between consenting adults all the time. The man at the center of the growing scandal was John Profumo, secretary of state for war and a close personal friend of Harold Macmillan, leader of the Conservative Party and prime minister of Great Britain and Northern Ireland. In March 1963, Profumo decided that it was time to nip this thing in the bud, that his sterling reputation had been impugned by unnamed persons of low degree. He stated before the House of Commons that there was "no impropriety whatsoever" in his relationship with Christine Keeler, a beautiful and fashionable lady of easy but expensive virtue. Further, the happily married Profumo warned that he would issue writs for libel and slander if these preposterous allegations continued.

They did. On Radio Eireann and in the newspapers, as the scandal grew and other names were added, we learned words and terms that would excite our imaginations and expand our vocabulary, even if they were unutterable in most company. Words like call girl, prostitute,

243

whore, pimp, sexual intercourse, fornication, carnal knowledge, immoral purposes, and immoral earnings. The ever-expressionless newsreader, Charles Mitchel, the man who never laughed or smiled or altered his gaze, was seen to awkwardly clear his throat to allow the unmentionable words to escape over the airwaves. In country homes children were shooed out of the kitchen when the news came on—or the radio was turned off until the fifteen-minute broadcast had ended. Over in his mansion, John Charles McQuaid, archbishop of Dublin and primate of Ireland, was, no doubt, holding his hands over his ears to block out the dreadful details of Satan run amok in Godless England.

Or maybe not. This unholy scandal could serve the archbishop's purpose—that is to say, God's purpose. It was time to draw a clear distinction between morality and immorality. Ireland: pious, God-fearing, Mass-going, virtuous, and obedient under His guiding hand; and England: unholy, immoral, and Godless, save for the faithful Irish living there. The contrast was self-evident to all but the blind and the dumb and those without faith or conscience.

Other names in the Profumo Affair surfaced: Dr. Stephen Ward, an osteopath who had introduced Profumo to Keeler; Mandy Rice-Davies, another call girl; Lord Astor, a member of the House of Lords; and Yevgeni Ivanov, a naval attaché at the Soviet embassy in London. On June 5, Secretary of War Profumo resigned, accepting that his earlier statements to the House of Commons were, in effect, no longer operative. He was, apparently, having sexual intercourse with Christine Keeler. Unfortunately for Prime Minister Macmillan and his government, Miss Keeler was also having a similar relationship with Yevgeni Ivanov, believed by British Intelligence to be a Soviet spy. What sensitive secrets passed between Profumo and Keeler while between the sheets and later between Keeler and Ivanov while between perhaps these same sheets? Oh, the very thought of it!

Three days after Profumo's resignation, Dr. Ward was arrested and charged with living off the earnings of prostitution, his employees being

Christine Keeler and her friend, Mandy Rice-Davies. Osteopathy was good but pimping was better. Dr. Ward had lots of friends in high places, including Lord Astor, whom he had introduced to Mandy Rice-Davies. At Dr. Ward's trial at the Old Bailey, the prosecuting counsel, attempting to protect the impeccable reputation of Lord Astor, who was already under some suspicion of indulging in this carnal contraband, challenged Miss Rice-Davies's credibility, stating that the good Lord Astor, from whose lips no lie could pass, had denied having sexual relations with her or having ever met her. To this question, Mandy Rice-Davies thoughtfully opined, "Well, he would, wouldn't he," eliciting a howl of laughter in the courtroom.

On July 31, Dr. Stephen Ward was found guilty of living on the immoral earnings of Keeler and Rice-Davies but not of procuring, a.k.a. pimping. It hardly mattered. Dr. Ward had taken an overdose of sleeping pills and was in a coma when the verdict was reached. He died on August 3, and two days later the trial was closed with no sentence pronounced, for to pronounce sentence on a dead man would have been considered unsporting, if not in poor taste. The scandal gravely wounded the Conservative Party and Prime Minister Macmillan. Citing health reasons, he resigned in October, a little more than a month before that terrible day in Dallas when the man he had come to admire and regard as a friend was no more. The following year the Conservatives were swept from power.

I returned to Finner Camp in Donegal in the summer of 1963 as I had the year before. I had a purpose: I needed to earn my third star in order to be a fully qualified three-star private in C Company, Eighteenth Battalion, FCA. That was the easy part. A more challenging task was at the local ceili at a dancehall in nearby Bundoran, where I and a few friends ventured one night after duty. We were all in our regular clothes—for only a lad who had fallen hard on his head when he was a wee babby would wear his FCA uniform to a dance—and a few did but they weren't our friends and we studiously ignored them. But, alas, the girls seemed to smell us out anyway and knew that we were country mugs. We all immediately picked out the prettiest girl there, and then there followed a truly dispiriting chain of events. Sean Shields, a bright and good-natured lad with a face as wild and rugged as the West of Ireland, volunteered to be the first to cross no-man's-land to ask Miss Ireland to dance. It was mercifully brief.

"Thank you, but I don't feel like dancing at the moment," said Miss Ireland.

"Well why are you here then?" said brave Sean.

"That's none of your business, now, is it?" replied Miss Ireland.

We welcomed Sean back to our ranks and complimented him for his courage—and then the rest of us, in turn, repeated the process, each going across the floor and each receiving an unsmiling and firm "No, thank you."

I was the last to make the hopeless but brave charge, "once more unto the breach," in the immortal words of Shakespeare and possibly Henry V. I desperately willed my burning face to cool down before spontaneous combustion. Miss Ireland was now sitting down with some friends along the wall on the far side of the hall. I approached her, feeling strangely exhilarated, yet terrified—evidence, I think, of the duality of sheer stupidity and blind optimism at play. As she was sitting I got down on one knee and politely said, "I would like to have the pleasure of this dance with you, but I know you're going to refuse and that's okay—but I'd like you to look directly into my eyes when you break my heart."

Miss Ireland stared at me, her lovely face tranquil and unmoved, her beautiful eyes as cold and distant as a hard black frost atop Croagh Patrick. She said, "No, thank you," and even though it was expected, it was still like getting punched in the face. While I had considered how to best frame my request, I hadn't planned a response to Miss Ireland's certain refusal, so I just arose with as much dignity as I could manage and turned to walk the lonely walk.

Then came a voice from behind: "Wait." I turned to face her, my heart at a dead standstill. She burst out laughing, as did a couple of other girls on each side of her. It was a wonderful laugh, warm and friendly, her eyes not distant now, but welcoming. I was stunned and confused and embarrassed and must have looked like a complete jackass. She said, "I accept your gracious invitation." I couldn't believe my good fortune. I was about to dance with the best-looking girl in the dance hall, and the band was playing an old-time waltz, my kind of dance, slow and close.

There is a God; I knew it all along! We talked a lot. Her name was Eileen. I told her I was from around Swinford and at Finner Camp for my summer holidays with the FCA. She was a local girl from Bundoran, about my age, and said that she could tell I and my pals were all temporary escapees from the camp. She said she was very choosy about whom she danced with and never danced with soldiers, whether they were FCA or regular army, for reasons that I should know, but she was making an exception for me because I looked harmless enough and she didn't want to break my heart. And besides, she said, wasn't it the neighborly and Christian thing to do for a lad away from home, and especially for a *culchie* like me. We were having fun, and I was having the time of my life—and I didn't step on her feet even once—*thanks, Mom*. It was just the one dance, but I must say I was completely satisfied with myself. On our bidding each other good night, she even promised a repeat if I returned to Finner the following year.

At the end of my first week at Finner, early on Saturday morning, I came home to mow the field of oats. Lieutenant Mickey McNeela needed to go home too, so I and a couple of other lads got a ride with him, all of us on a weekend pass for agricultural purposes. We were all farmers, and when there was work to be done and the weather was behaving, you couldn't afford to miss the opportunity. For me the oat field was ready for the scythe. The best part of a car trip with Mickey behind the wheel was when the trip ended and you exited the vehicle alive but not before enduring multiple near-death experiences. He thought he was Stirling Moss at the Grand Prix. Mickey completed the usual two-hour drive in a little over an hour—which, in a way, was helpful for me because it gave me an extra hour in which to mow oats. The weather held up, and by late afternoon on Sunday, I was done; the oats were mowed and stooked and ready for the devil's playmates squawking noisily overhead. A couple of hours later, Mickey picked me up on the Main Road, and we all returned to Finner to complete our second week of training—but, in truth, for us it was a holiday on the government's pound. At holiday's end I had my third star and money in my pocket, and it was time to gather the oats into the garden.

While bad things happening in a country with no moral bearing, like England, were to be expected, we in Ireland rightly felt a certain smugness in the simple, undeniable truth that truly bad things do not happen here, at least not since the Civil War. The horrors that accompanied our birth as a nation were no longer talked about in polite company. And then, on August 17, that smugness was blown to smithereens when we learned of a murder in Dublin so horrible that it numbed the senses. Hazel Mullen was sixteen years old, pretty, happy, outgoing—and daring. Originally from County Mayo, she and her family had moved to Dublin when she was a child. She worked in a bank and dated a twenty-two-year-old medical student from South Africa who was studying medicine at the Royal College of Surgeons in Dublin. Shan Mohangi came from a respectable family and, like many Negroes from former British colonies in Africa who wished to study abroad—and had the means to—preferred to study in Ireland rather than England. Ireland, also a former British colony—indeed its first and last white colony—had fine schools, based on the English model, like Trinity College and the Royal College of Surgeons. These students wanted a fine pedigreed English education but obtained in Ireland rather than the mother country, from which, I imagine, they wished to maintain a prideful distance.

Mohangi had a small flat on Harcourt Street, over the Green Tureen Restaurant, where he also worked part time. In a violent confrontation with his girlfriend over the delicate matter of fidelity, Mohangi, in a rage, strangled Hazel. That, in itself, would have been enough to convulse the country, where violent murders are virtually unheard of. The horror afterward was the numbing part. After strangling Hazel, Mohangi's terrible dilemma, hand-wringing at least, was what to do...with the body, of course. To escape justice he had to conceal the crime and concluded that he could not remove poor Hazel without being noticed. So he dismembered her body. Using a meat cleaver from the restaurant kitchen, and, as was said sarcastically by some, using the fine medical training he was receiving in Ireland, he chopped Hazel Mullen into many pieces. Then he proceeded to burn the body parts in a stove in the basement of the building.

His plan was to incinerate the body completely, at which point he could more easily get rid of the ashes, but the smell was so strong and so awful, and wafted its way through the building, that his crime was discovered. He confessed immediately. He said that it was all the result of a terrible misunderstanding, and her death a tragic accident. The trial was not expected to begin until early the next year. The whole country was expectant, waiting.

As the summer turned to fall, other events took the collective national mind off of Mohangi's upcoming trial. Around the corner was one of the most tragic days in American history and equally in the history of Ireland. And in the same month as that terrible day in Dallas another event occurred far from both countries—in the Republic of South Vietnam. On November the 1, 1963, a military coup removed President Ngo Dinh Diem from power. The following day, Diem and his brother, Nhu, were murdered by army officers. President Kennedy was, by all accounts, horrified, but perhaps not completely blameless. When John F. Kennedy took the oath of office on January 20, 1961, Diem was president of South Vietnam. He already had powerful friends in Washington and across the United States. Diem, a Catholic in a predominantly Taoist and Buddhist country, was born into a wealthy family. His father had made a fortune working for the French Colonial Administration in Vietnam, and Diem followed his father's footsteps into government.

By the late 1940s, he had his sights set on becoming prime minister of an independent Vietnam, but the French weren't quite ready to let go, and it wasn't until 1954, following France's ignominious defeat at Dien Bien Phu, that Diem, with US support, was made premier of a partitioned South Vietnam. Four years earlier, Diem had traveled to the United States to make important friends, court political and financial support, and meditate at the Maryknoll Seminary in Lakewood, New Jersey. In no time at all, he was the darling of the American Catholic elite, with friends like US Senator Mike Mansfield, Congressman John F. Kennedy, and Francis Cardinal Spellman.

Back home in Vietnam, Diem was, by nature, an autocrat. He would probably have risen high in the Catholic Church had he decided to become a priest. Instead, he set his sights on ruling South Vietnam. The problem was that he had little time for the give and take of democratic politics and, in effect, ruled as a dictator. Mindful of his benefactor, Diem catered to his American ally by surrounding himself with the trappings of democracy, such as the virtually powerless legislative assembly. Tragically, Diem was never popular with his people, to whom he simply could not relate, and they, in turn, regarded him with suspicion and contempt. To most Vietnamese he was a dubious character, a friend, admirer, and beneficiary of the hated French and their harsh, repressive administration, a man cloaked in the religion of their oppressor, purporting to be one of them. And for all the wrong reasons, the Americans bet on this horse.

By early 1963, President Kennedy realized that Diem was the wrong man in the wrong place at the wrong time—that he would never be able to deal effectively with the increasing communist insurgency throughout the country, no matter how much American aid was provided. The problem for JFK was how to persuade Diem to go. He wasn't quite the puppet. Diem had his own agenda and used the Americans as much as they used him.

On November 1, 1963, a military coup solved the president's problem, but the murder of both Diem and his brother the following day placed Kennedy in a terrible position. American complicity in both events was immediately suspected. JFK wanted Diem out. His disenchantment with Diem was well known to the senior military staff of ARVN (Army of South Vietnam). Kennedy's ambassador to South Vietnam, Henry Cabot Lodge, was in close contact with top ARVN general Duong Van Minh. Minh was a leader of the coup and Ambassador Lodge was almost certainly aware that the coup was imminent—and may have deliberately kept his boss in the dark in order to give him cover, or "plausible deniability," in the arcane world of politics.

While JFK may well have quietly approved the coup, it is highly improbable that he sanctioned the murder of Diem and his brother, but he should have known that this was likely in the brutal world of Vietnamese politics. A deposed but ambitious and ruthless man like Diem, with powerful friends in America and France, could not be allowed to live. Three weeks later President Kennedy himself, my hero, would fall to an assassin's bullet. November 1963 was a terrible month for America, and for Ireland that grieved as much as America, and for Vietnam.

In November 1963, with the potatoes dug and sealed in their pits for the winter, I was able to go off with the FCA to Renmore in Galway for another two weeks of training and good times—but this time my luck ran out and I, a now fully trained three-star private, was picked at random for two weeks of kitchen duty, the dreaded chore of working in the Mess Hall, peeling hundreds of potatoes and slicing thousands of carrots, washing by hand piles upon piles of dishes and cutlery, cleaning floors and setting tables, and doing all the other things, except the cooking, to ensure that our lads were well fed, morning, noon, and evening.

On Friday, November 22, I finished my work in the Mess Hall around 7:30 p.m. and returned to my barracks, tired after a long day of nonstop work since 6:00 a.m. I had just changed out of my work fatigues and was about to go wash up when a wide-eyed soldier rushed in yelling, "President Kennedy was shot in Dallas!" My immediate response, forever seared in my memory was "Boy, the Secret Service will catch Hell for this." I knew the president would be okay. My hero could not die, could not be killed—this was a superficial wound inflicted by a crackpot. The thought of him being killed was utterly beyond my capacity to comprehend. I quickly washed up, changed into my civvies, and headed for the canteen, where the only television at Renmore available to the troops was located. I needed to know what happened, needed reassurance that the president's wound was superficial, that he would make a full recovery.

The canteen was the place where many of us went after a day's training for a cup of tea, even coffee, and for me, always, a thick slice of rich Irish fruitcake with a glass of milk. The canteen was completely packed; I could hardly get past the door—but I could see the television on a high shelf inside. Charles Mitchel, trying hard to keep his composure, was making it official: John Fitzgerald Kennedy, thirty-fifth president of the United States, was dead, assassinated in Dallas, Texas. I was completely stunned, and all around me there were shell-shocked faces, mouths open, complete silence, disbelief, horror. I waited awhile and there were more details of the nightmare in Dallas: the frantic race to Parkland Memorial Hospital and Jackie's ashen face and blood-stained clothes.

When there was no more at the moment to add to the horror, Telefis Eireann began a replay of the president's unforgettable visit to Ireland only a few months earlier. I couldn't bear to watch anymore. Had I been at home, I would have headed for the bog and stayed there a long time. Here at Renmore, I returned to the barracks to commiserate with a few fellow soldiers about a hero dead and a world gone mad.

Michael O'Hehir was Ireland's most famous broadcaster and commentator. His specialty was Irish football and hurling games at Croke Park in Dublin, but he was so good that he was paid handsomely to provide live commentary on major horse-racing events in Britain as well as in Ireland. On radio O'Hehir could make the dullest game exciting, calling the action as fast as an auctioneer. When television came along, he had to curb his natural instincts to excite and maybe exaggerate a little—but only slightly. He was holidaying in New York with his wife, Molly, on

November 22 when he received an urgent request from Radio/Telefis Eireann to go to Washington to broadcast to Ireland the tragic events there. Listening to his live coverage of JFK's funeral was gut wrenching. O'Hehir's famous, unmistakable voice, his boundless, rapid-fire commentary now breaking repeatedly, unable to conceal his own grief.

The pictures, the images of those few days, were never to be forgotten: the desperate, chaotic scenes in Dallas; Mrs. Kennedy and little Caroline approaching the flag-draped casket in the Capitol Rotunda; Mrs. Kennedy kneeling down to kiss the American flag and Caroline reaching under the flag to touch her father's coffin; John-John saluting on the steps of St. Matthew's Cathedral on his third birthday; the magnificent white horses pulling the caisson on the president's final journey to Arlington National Cemetery; Black Jack, the saddled but riderless horse, riding boots turned backward in the stirrups, symbolizing the fallen president; the heads of state of many countries walking, *walking* in silent respect behind the Kennedy family, which decided to walk behind a fallen son, husband, brother, uncle, friend, president, rather than enclose themselves in darkened limousines; the heartbreaking scene at the burial site—and, altogether, the monumental majesty and solemnity as a great nation laid to rest a beloved president.

Grief-stricken Ireland was honored that the president's widow asked for a special Irish army guard of honor to be present at the president's burial ceremony at Arlington, where they executed a flawless funeral drill. On his visit to Ireland, the president had been deeply moved when viewing the officer cadets perform this silent, slow-motion drill in remembrance of the dead at Arbor Hill Cemetery. For the cadets this was the proudest and saddest day of their young lives. But in Ireland we all knew that our time in the sun was over.

I was thirteen years old in the fall of 1960 and in my first year at St. Patrick's College in Swinford when I became aware of this Irish-American Catholic guy running for president of the United States. Even then I thought it was improbable, but our teacher priests were wildly optimistic—and encouraged us to pray for his election to the highest, most powerful office in the world. Father O'Neill told us how important his election would be for Ireland and for Catholics all over the world. I didn't care much about Catholics all over the world, but I did care about an Irish-American president of the United States.

In November all of our hopes were realized. Following that glorious day, all of our classes were free, meaning that we could close our books and just revel in the joy of the moment. He was ours and we had given him to America to save the world from communism, and now he was in a position to do that and so much more. Suddenly, I could hold my head higher, nod that knowing nod to neighbors that the world was now changed and that, yes, an Irishman was in charge. With the exception of Michael Collins, I had always been lukewarm to Irish hero warriors, who seemed to prefer to die for Ireland rather than live for it. Now, here was an authentic white knight, and nothing seemed impossible. A common sentiment around northeast Mayo following JFK's election went something like "By God, we're on the map now." And we were.

JFK's death affected me in ways I could not understand. I had seen death up close before. I had been to several wakes in families' homes when a neighbor would die of old age. These were not times for mourning. A wake was a fun, all-night long doo—well maybe not exactly a doo, for family members of the departed soul would be sad and crying and mourning their loss, but the rest of us would be having the craic, sending the soul to Heaven in an almost jolly manner, as who should say. Wakes, like doos, were great places for free whiskey, beer, food, and cigarettes, and the bereaved family had little choice but to meet the time-honored requirement of ensuring that all neighbors in attendance were solemnly welcomed and catered to.

A wake was the only time you could enter a neighbor's home without knocking on the door—you just opened the door and walked in, so as not to disturb the dead. Your only obligation was to first make straight for the coffin, almost always in the kitchen and on a stand provided by the undertaker. You promptly dropped to your knees—or one knee if you were an older man—by the coffin, and said a few prayers for the occupant, asking God to mercifully accept the soul into Heaven, following the shortest possible stopover in Purgatory. Then you had to meet the family members of the man or woman laid out in the coffin, extend your hand for a handshake, and mumble the words "I'm sorry for your troubles" repeatedly until you had extended your sympathy to all adults of the family.

Now, with your duty done, you would find a place to sit or stand and look around to see who was there and, equally important, who wasn't there. Soon, you would be offered a glass of whiskey or bottle of stout or beer. I wasn't yet brave enough to accept or ask for a beer, but the fags were plentiful, usually removed from the box and lying on a dinner plate in a convenient location, like on top of the corpse, signifying his/her personal contribution to the occasion. I had a keen interest in the fags as did other young lads and as often as possible would pocket the extra fag or two, trying not to be too obvious about it. Cigarettes were very expensive in Ireland, and the poor people could only afford Woodbines. You wouldn't see Woodbines at wakes, just the better brands—Sweet Aftons and Players—and maybe the in-between brand, Goldflakes.

The more I could pocket, the less I would have to buy—nothing complicated about that. President Kennedy's death was a different matter altogether. On November 22, 1963, I felt an overwhelming sense of personal loss, an emptiness inside, a profound feeling that the whole world had been turned upside down and would never be the same. I felt diminished and, like my country, brought down to size again.

The last few days at Renmore were a blur, with sliced potatoes and bleeding fingers and bad jokes to lessen the pain. My friend Pat O'Toole from Toormakeady became Pat no Tool from Hoormakeady. I became Tommy Yankabout because I had told anyone who cared to listen that America was where I wanted to be, not England—and even though there would be no Irishman in the White House, there was already hopeful talk about Bobby and Teddy. What had started out as another welcome respite from the doldrums of home ended in an overwhelming sadness. I collected my pay and said good-bye to a few friends who were going in other directions. I threw my suitcase into the back of an Irish army English Bedford lorry and climbed in with my English 303 Lee Enfield rifle, and bade farewell to the English-built Renmore Barracks. I was going home.

It was sixty miles to Culmore, with many stops along the way as we dropped off other FCA lads at or near their homes. When we approached the far end of Culmore, a place called Farrageen, I tapped on the floor of the lorry with the butt of my rifle, and the regular army driver slowed down and stopped, and I got out with my rifle and suitcase. To save time I jumped the fence at the Main Road and walked diagonally across this year's now bare oat field. Mom came out to meet me, looking like the life had gone out of her and said, "Oh, Tommy, Tommy, we're in a different world now."

"Yeah" was all I could say. I could not bear to look at the mantelpiece over the fireplace where President Kennedy's handsome, tanned, smiling face still looked out with a quiet confidence. Anchoring the other end of the mantelpiece was Pope John XXII, still there, his gentle smile maybe saying that this too shall pass.

November passed and life returned to a new normal. JFK was dead and buried, and we Irish were no longer quite as special as we were before. Our hero was gone. Lyndon Baines Johnson (LBJ) promised to continue President Kennedy's policies, especially on civil rights for Negroes, but LBJ was a Texan, without a hint of Irish heritage in his lanky frame. And, besides, he was already suspect to some of us—there were rumors that he may have been involved in JFK's assassination. But there were many rumors. One thing everyone seemed to agree on was that Oswald could not have acted alone, that there was a monster conspiracy behind President Kennedy's assassination, involving important people in high places. It was said that the Kennedys had little regard for the vice president and that JFK went out of his way to keep Johnson out of his way—and LBJ was getting even for years of insult. The Kremlin was also suspect because Oswald had lived in Russia and married a Russian woman. Was he a trained assassin, like the *Manchurian Candidate*, returned to the United States by the KGB to lay low until the opportunity presented itself?

Fidel Castro was high on the list too, having suffered a humiliating loss of face the previous year during the Cuban Missile Crisis when Khrushchev caved in to Kennedy and withdrew his missiles, leaving Comrade Castro to accept the bitter truth that to the old men in the Kremlin, he wasn't worth a nuclear war with the United States that might end life on earth. There were rumors about CIA involvement, or even the FBI and Secret Service. And the ugliest rumor of all was that Robert Kennedy, the president's own brother, was behind the murder—because, went this sick rumor, Bobby and Jacqueline were in love and having an affair. No rumor was too loony. What most people in America and Ireland and everywhere else found so hard to accept was that a complete nobody could, by his own hand, with a mail-order $12.78 rifle, kill the most important person on the planet. But Oswald—a reasonably good marksman with a depraved mind—could and did.

And so ended 1963, by any standard an unforgettable year. It began with the death of our beloved dog, Rover, and less than a week later we bade good-bye to Patricia at Shannon Airport. Then came the sad news of Pope John's death, followed by the excitement and joy of President Kennedy's visit, later bookended with the unbearable sadness of his death in Dallas. In between we took great pleasure in the sex scandal across the pond, which broadened my education and my vocabulary. On the other side of the world, in Vietnam, a coup and brutal murder foretold of things to come, and at home the country reeled in horror at a murder in Dublin, so gruesome that we could not imagine it happening in Ireland. In England, yes, but not in Ireland.

CHAPTER 20

NINETEEN SIXTY-FOUR BEGAN with more than half of the family gone; Jimmy, Maureen, Eamon, and Eveline all in Birmingham, where Dad had worked for so many years; Kathleen in Stoke-on-Trent; and Patricia in New York. At home were Mom, Anne, Angela, Christina, and me. Financially, times were easier now, fewer mouths to feed but also fewer hands to work the land. Dad's weekly blue registered envelope with the neatly folded English banknotes inside and "Dear Winnie" letter to Mom still came, as it had for as long as I could remember, except when my father was in the hospital. His letter was usually a single, lined blue sheet, written on both sides. He would ask Mom how she was doing and how we were, and how the work was coming on the land. He said little about Birmingham, his home for decades, and maybe a few words about his job at the bakery, or maybe about bumping into a neighbor from home at the pub, like one of the McIntyres from Corthoon. He might add a comment or two about the other half of the family in Birmingham, some of whom he saw more often than others. Some of the away family also helped with a few pounds and a few dollars fairly regularly. We were finally beyond want, and for the first time ever in my memory, we were free of debt. Praise the Lord!

The big event that people were waiting for, probably with mixed feelings, was the day when Shan Mohangi would go on trial for his life for the murder of Hazel Mullen. I think most people just wanted to get it over with. The collective national psyche had been numbed enough with the terrible events of 1963. There was also debate about the death penalty and whether or not it was an appropriate punishment regardless of the crime. A number of countries had already abolished it, and Britain was expected to follow soon. If Britain abolished the death penalty, it was almost certain that Ireland would too. On February 10, the trial began in Dublin. Sixteen days later, as expected, Mohangi was found guilty and sentenced to death by hanging.

As the guilty verdict was immediately appealed, there was no expectation of a final resolution for at least a year or so. Maybe by then there would be no death penalty. What we did have now that we didn't have before was a loss of innocence, the feeling that we were immune to the kind of brutal crimes that heretofore we had only read about in crime magazines from England and America. Our only consolation was that this terrible crime was committed by a foreigner, not one of our own.

Whether it was the loneliness of living his life mostly by himself down near the railway or his natural desire to propagate his own kind before passing from the earth, Coco had become an embarrassing problem. He had developed an uncanny ability to escape, and I was finding it almost impossible to keep him within the boundaries of our land. When the urge struck, fences would not hold him back. He would go over them or through them or around them until he found a weak spot to make his escape—so I was having to spend time I didn't have to go look for Coco and repair broken fences and broken gates. Once past our house, Coco had a clear run up the boreen to the Main Road, and he was gone. I might find him quickly, or it could take precious days. Sometimes a neighbor or a more distant farmer would have lassoed my ass and locked him up in a barn, waiting for me to learn by word of mouth where he was and to come by. Without fail, these farms that Coco had broken into all had one thing in common: they had a female donkey, a bess, on the land. It didn't matter a damn to Coco whether the bess was in a welcoming mood or not. He would chase her until he was cornered and roped.

He chased cattle, too, in his helpless frustration, if he wasn't having much success in wooing the bess. It was bad enough when the invaded farm was miles from home and the farmer was a complete stranger but much worse when it was a neighbor, and he showed me his broken fences and his terrified donkey and cattle worn out from running. I could only apologize and promise that it wouldn't happen again—but it did.

A fetter seemed like a sensible solution. A fetter was a length of rope secured to the bottom of one of Coco's front legs and then to the hind leg directly behind. This meant he would have difficulty walking, because the two linked legs would have to move together. The problem here was that Coco quickly got the hang of moving the two legs together and in no time was able to run—and break out again. Next I tried securing his left foreleg to his rear right leg, and this worked much better. He was still able to walk but unable to run.

Still, he wouldn't give up. Going to fetch him one day for a job, I found that he was missing. As no fences were down and it was near impossible for him to move very far with a cross-fetter, I feared he might be in one of the maren trenches. He was. It was a pitiful sight to see. Trying to jump the trench into Drennan's land, near the railway, he didn't quite make it and slid down into the muck. He was standing upright in the trench but half buried in thick, gooey muck, his forelegs stretched out over the rim, and there, poor Coco, too weak to struggle anymore, was just holding on. To free him I had to get into the trench and put my shoulder under his arse and lift and push for all I was worth until he was able to scramble out. After washing him down, I felt so sorry for him that I removed the cross-fetter from his foreleg—his frantic thrashing about had already caused it to slip off the rear leg.

That was a mistake, for Coco did not feel any similar sentiment for me. Two nights later he made his next attempt. I awoke around midnight to hear him thundering past the house at full gallop. Approaching the house, Coco knew that this was a potential ambush, and so his best chance was to charge past with a full head of steam. In less than a minute, I was on my bike and heading up the boreen in pursuit. I easily overtook him on the Main Road, and knowing that the game was up, he obediently turned around and went home in front of me. A new main gate where our boreen met the Main Road was what was needed to stop Coco in his tracks, if he got that far, meaning he'd still have to smash through three other stake and barbed-wire gates. We purchased a heavy iron gate at Joe Finan's in Charlestown, and over a couple of days, I sunk two solid posts in concrete and mounted the gate on one. When closed, a sliding metal bar secured the gate to the other post. There was no way Coco could go over this impressive barrier or crash through it without killing himself.

Incredibly, a few nights later he escaped again. In a dead sleep, I didn't hear him pass the house, although it is possible he was wearing pads on his feet—after what I discovered later I'd believe almost anything. Next morning I found the gate at the Main Road open. No one in the family had done this, nor would any neighbor. Another precious two days were spent looking for my wayward donkey, and more embarrassment. I had to find out what had happened, and there was only one way to do this. I had to lie in wait by the Main Road, out of sight but near the closed gate. Never making it easy for me, Coco didn't try for a couple of nights, but on the third night, here he came.

It was dark but not so dark that I couldn't see him clearly. He approached the gate, and after shuffling around a bit and walking back and forth from one side of the gate to the other, he hooked his heavy lower lip on the sliding bar that held the gate shut. Jerking his head to the right, he pulled the bar back, then stepped away from the gate, allowing it swing open on its own. I was in such a state of disbelief at what I had just seen that I let Coco proceed onto the Main Road and head toward Swinford. After pulling off this caper, he deserved a few minutes of freedom.

There was a hole in the sliding bar so that, if necessary, the gate could be locked closed. With a piece of wire, I was able to foil further breakouts without actually having to put a lock on the gate. Besides, I figured, if I used a lock, he'd find the key. At last Coco was contained in the prison of our farm, unable to do his propagating. It was hard not to feel sorry for him, and in a way I did. He didn't have much of a life. When he wasn't working, he was mostly alone in the long, swampy Field of the Rushes that stretched to the railway. Rarely treated with cow manure or special, the grass—along with the rushes—was plentiful but without much sweetness, and probably without much nourishment either. I think maybe Coco was looking for a better grade of food as much as female company.

In May, when spring reluctantly began to give way to summer, a busy time for Coco and me, he went missing one last time. At the south end of the farm, the gate to the Main Road was closed. At the north end, the railway gate was closed. No fences were down. Where was Coco? I reckoned he was in one of the trenches again. He was, and in almost the exact same spot where I had found him the first time—but this time Coco was dead. The trench around him was a terrible mess, showing his desperate struggle to get out. As before, he had half freed himself from the fetter, but it didn't help. He was upside down in the trench, his head mostly covered in water and muck, his four stiff legs pointing straight up. He had struggled until his strength was gone and in his last attempt fell back off the rim and upside down, doomed.

Why did I put the fetter on him when I knew he could no longer make it through the final barrier to the Main Road? I looked at my handiwork and cursed myself in despair and guilt. Coco was dead and it was my fault. I fettered him because I was afraid that he would still find a way out. I was so tired of looking for him, so often embarrassed on securing his release from some farmer, near or far. Coco was devious and clever, but also brave and full of heart. And now I realized just how desperately he wanted to escape his miserable existence. Like Eamon, who bought him at the fair, Coco, too, wanted to bail out.

I went to my friend Brian Kavanagh for help in pulling Coco out of the trench so that I could bury him. We tied ropes around his forelegs and hind legs and pulled and pulled and pulled, and slowly retrieved Coco. The next morning I returned with spade, shovel, and slean under arm to dig the largest grave I had ever dug. I brought the slean with me because I knew that just beneath the surface I would find pure bog, turf that I could cut with the slean, making this unhappy task a little less difficult. I would dig the grave like I was cutting turf. Coco's grave was about human size—about three feet wide, six feet long, and six spits deep—and out of it came the finest glossy black turf you could ever hope to see. I dragged Coco over to the edge and he toppled in.

On top of him I placed the beautifully cut sods of turf as a bricklayer would build a wall or lay a sidewalk, each sod in its place. I had some sods left over after replacing the top *scraith*. These I spread out to dry, for what was the point of letting good turf go to waste? I blamed myself for Coco's death and would always remember his great heart and willing spirit. No job was too hard for him. On this he trusted my judgment and would go for it if I asked him to. He lived a hard and lonely life—mostly, I was his only company, and in the end I let him down. While we were out of debt, we had little extra money for emergencies and, with Coco now dead and buried, we had an emergency.

A few years back, we had heard about a special government program that would help farmers with small holdings in the West of Ireland to move to the Midlands in some kind of land swap—there was still land available there more than three hundred years after Cromwell's arrival to put down a Catholic rebellion. His "To Hell or to Connaught" punishment was the banishment of vast numbers of Catholics from the more fertile parts of Ireland to the poorer, wetter areas west of the Shannon, like County Mayo. For a while there was a lot of excitement about this repopulating-the-Midlands scheme with worthy candidates who would give up their humble farms in Mayo and maybe another county or two, and relocate to larger farms in Westmeath.

It seemed like a great idea, but details were scarce and takers were few. And then, suddenly, there was no more talk about it. Maybe the big farmers of Westmeath didn't care to have new neighbors from Mayo, or maybe they let the government know that a better idea would be to help them make their own big farms bigger still. Whatever the reasons, the farmers in the West of Ireland continued to complain about their hard-scrabble lives, sometimes with humor, sometimes not.

Tom Gallagher

As for me and the matter at hand, I had to buy a new donkey and quickly—but had to wait a couple of weeks until the next Fair Day in Swinford. If God had not been with me on Coco's last days, I had no doubt that He was with me on that Wednesday morning on Bridge Street when, after selling a young heifer that we had hoped to keep, I spotted a huge donkey, as big as Coco or bigger, and lively too. It was his first trip to town, I figured, and he was not liking it. His owner, a bloke from Killasser, claimed he had yet to see his third birthday and was fully broken in, meaning used to the cart. I checked his teeth to confirm his age, pretending that I knew what I was doing – but didn't, and asked Killasser what he was asking for his ass. "Fourteen pounds and worth every penny and more," said Killasser. Less than a half an hour later, with the help of a couple of old men, there for the craic, the deal was made and I was on my way home with this fine-looking ass for the sum of twelve pounds even. It was four pounds more than Eamon paid for Coco, but that was years before, and everything had gone up. We might have been better off now—and we were—but everything cost more, too. I named our new ass Coco Too in honor of Coco. I wasted no time in trying out Coco Too.

That afternoon I put Coco's bridle on Coco Too, and it fit perfectly. I tackled him up with Coco's tacklings, collar, hames, straddle, and britch. He was not at ease at all and seemed to be very anxious about being harnessed up. Still, he was in unfamiliar surroundings, and I figured he'd soon settle down and get used to his new home. I was definitely going to take better care of Coco Too. He would not spend his life mostly by himself as Coco had—and he would be better fed. With some coaxing I managed to get my new donkey between the shafts of the cart and hooked him up. Then, without warning, he took off like a bat out of hell. In less than ten seconds, it was over: the cart was upside down, a shaft broken, and Coco Too frantically struggling to break free. Desperately, I worked to get him out from under the mess before he broke a leg and made things much worse. I removed the heavy wheels and righted the cart, but now I

264

had a broken cart. I also had an ass that had never been hitched to a cart before. Killasser had lied to me, and God, by my side in the morning, apparently had taken the afternoon off.

I borrowed Dolly and cart from the Joyces to haul my broken cart over to Tom Tunney in Hull, the same Tom Tunney who worked on the railway with Jim Horkan, but Tom was also a rough-and-ready carpenter on the side. A long week later, I had my cart back, the new shaft having a distinctly unfinished look about it, but for thirty shillings there was nothing to complain about. I bought some sandpaper at Joe Finan's and sanded down the shaft from end to end and painted it, then painted the other to match. I was back in business but a bit uncertain about my recent purchase at the fair. While the cart was being fixed, I urgently needed to get Coco Too broken in, and I had no experience at this task, but I did have an idea. He was powerful and fast and needed to be slowed down and calmed down, so I hooked him up to the heavy iron plough and tried a little ploughing in an unused patch of ground near the barns. If Coco Too wanted to take off again, it was fine with me because he was not going to break the plough. Incredibly, he pulled it. He was doing what we wouldn't let Molly do on her own.

The good news was it certainly slowed him down, and after several repeat trials, Coco Too was almost the picture of docility—and probably wishing that he was back home in Killasser. This was a good time, I thought, to jump on his back and ride him. Boy, he had me fooled! He reared and bucked and snorted and farted and tried to bite my legs, both of which were wrapped around his girth like a vice, and did everything he could to throw me. The problem for Coco Too was that I had lots of experience riding his predecessor who had, over the years, tried every trick his donkey brain could conceive to tumble me. But Coco Too came up with one that I had never seen before. Breathing heavily, he seemed to give up the fight, then suddenly laid down on his belly and tried to roll over me. I had on my hands a fast, powerful, clever and devious ass, very much like the one I buried near the railway. Cautiously, I reintroduced Coco Too to the cart and, holding a firm grip on the bridle, led him around the smaller flat field just above the barns. A few times he tried to break free and run, but in a couple of days, he was broken in to the point where I was able to get in the cart and guide him by the reins. We had made peace with each other.

CHAPTER 21

⚜

By the summer of 1964, Rusty had grown into a big mutt, or something else, larger than Rover now and not nearly as keen on working for his keep as Rover and Flower had been. He wasn't quite as lovable either—there was something different about this dog, but I couldn't put my finger on it. On the positive side, he was still wearing the shiniest coat of soft black fur you could ever rub your face into. He didn't like to help with the cattle much, and there were no more rabbits in Madogue for him to hunt—myxomatosis, the rabbit virus, had killed them off. But he did like to stalk, first some of our young calves—but they just ignored him—and then our chickens. At first, I thought it was hilarious to see Rusty sneaking up on a lone chicken or maybe a small cluster and then pouncing to no avail as the birds scattered in all directions, even taking to the air briefly in the initial panic, and loudly protesting this assault by a family member whom they had every reason to believe was there to protect them from foxes and badgers and hungry dogs and the like.

What I didn't realize was that Rusty was practicing, honing his skills, biding his time, salivating. I witnessed this game on several occasions and was a little concerned that Rusty did not seem to mind in the least that I was there watching him. On the other hand, he was still a young dog, and this may have been just a puppy game. Still, the next time he did this, I scolded him severely, and he looked very sad and a bit perplexed.

That was the end of it, I thought: no more pretend attacks on the chickens. And then one afternoon, a couple of weeks later, Anne found a badly injured chicken near the henhouse, all feathers and skin scraped off of her back. As she wouldn't survive, I had to put her out of her pain—and we had an unplanned chicken for dinner the following day, Rusty happily devouring the inedible parts. I suspected Rusty but couldn't believe that our dog, the family pet—for a pet is all he was; he was no worker—would attack one of our chickens. I had never heard of such a thing. Soon, my worst fears were realized. I caught him in the act, in broad daylight, in the middle of our little field above the barns. He was sitting on his arse, his hind legs tucked under his body, and under his big paws was a struggling chicken. That was bad enough, but what he was doing was completely unnatural.

Using his mouth, Rusty was plucking the feathers off the chicken's back, licking and plucking. I approached in disbelief, and he didn't move. "Rusty," I screamed at him, "what are you doing?" Without releasing the terrified chicken, he looked up at me with that same perplexed look I had seen earlier, as if to say, *Are you a complete fecking eejit? Can't you see what I'm doing? I'm preparing dinner.* I kicked him hard in the side, and he fell over, then quickly regained his footing and gave me a look that sent a chill right through me. It was the look of a wild animal, a wolf. Baring his teeth, he skulked away, not in fear but in anger.

The chicken was lucky, more in shock than injured, and I was just in shock. I had no choice but to tie Rusty up during the day until he outgrew this insane urge to pluck live chickens. Each day he cried and whimpered and howled and chewed on a thick rope that refused to give. At night, with the chickens safe in the henhouse, I'd untie him and let him join us for a while in the kitchen by the fire—to let him know that he was still part of the family. After a couple of weeks, I had to let him loose. It was so hard to see him in such distress. Each time one of us approached him, he'd go wild with joy, in anticipation of being freed. When it didn't happen, the crying and howling would start again. The girls pleaded with me to give him another chance—they'd watch him like a hawk, they said. And I gave in. For a week all was well, and then disaster.

It was around one in the afternoon. We were all around the kitchen table having dinner when there was a loud, angry knock on the door. We were startled at the unknown visitor's insistence. I opened the door to see our neighbor, Sean Kenny, in an absolute rage. His face was all puffed up and purple, he was stuttering bits and pieces of sentences, and in his left hand, dangling between his fingers, were two bloody chickens, alive but not for long, their backs without feathers or skin and clearly missing flesh, blood streaming down. "Your dog did this," he finally managed to say, "and there are two more half-dead chickens down in the field with me mother." He dropped the bloody evidence of an unnatural crime on our now-bloody doorstep and stormed off without another word. I looked at Mom, and she gave me that grave look that only confirmed what I already knew: I had to kill Rusty.

Mom finished off the two dying chickens and boiled water in which to steep them, to soften the skin and the feathers for plucking and clean them out so she could deliver them ready to cook to Kate Kenny, Sean's aging mother. Meanwhile I prepared to do what I had to do. Rusty was not in hiding after his crime. He was practically asleep by the gable, having eaten a portion of several live chickens. I used an old special bag, just big enough to contain Rusty's body, and with great difficulty forced him into the bag. I tied it shut and, trying to ignore his terrified howls, dragged the heavy bag to a water hole in the bogeen and pushed it in. The water wasn't deep enough, and a part of the bag remained on the surface—Rusty was able to breathe and was struggling frantically. I had to suspend all feelings of compassion and affection for a dog I must kill when there was no other alternative. Otherwise I couldn't do it. I couldn't just give him to another unsuspecting mug, like me. I jumped into the water hole and stepped on top on the bag, forcing it under water. Rusty struggled so hard that I lost my balance several times but, at long last, the movements under my feet slowed, then stopped.

I dragged the bag out of the water hole and went for a spade to dig Rusty's grave, near the water hole where he died—not the Sloe Garden. This wasn't like digging Rover's grave, but it hurt. Rusty wasn't lovable like Rover or Flower, but he was our dog and for reasons we couldn't understand, we had to kill him. Rusty, I decided, was half dog and half wolf. He was wolf enough to need to eat fresh meat on a regular basis, but dog enough to know that killing chickens was not acceptable. He tried to find the middle ground. He would try to eat the prey without killing it. Poor Rusty could not bring himself to actually kill the chicken—that was the dog in him. But he did need meat regularly—that was the wolf in him. I knew it sounded crazy, but that's what I thought. I knew we'd need to replace Rusty, but after this experience I was in no hurry.

After burying Rusty I went to my old refuge below the railway, to walk the length and breadth of our bog, to look over the barren, empty, peaceful landscape, to envelop myself in its loneliness, to seek solace and maybe forgiveness. It's one thing when you have to drown newborn puppies whose eyes are not yet open, who could not look their killer in the eye, but it was quite another to drown a large, beautiful dog who trusted you because you were his friend. I grieved over Rover, but I had no part in his death. This was different; I was Rusty's executioner. At times like this, I needed to be in the bog. Ireland's ancient bogs hold many secrets accumulated over hundreds of generations and mostly they remain silent.

Occasionally a discovery was made, often when cutting a bank of turf. It might be a five-thousand-year-old elk skull and antlers, or church treasures hidden from Viking marauders a thousand years ago, or a terrifyingly well-preserved human body, a poor soul who came upon death accidentally or by intention centuries earlier. Or it may be a supply of arms, rifles and revolvers, buried by local guerillas during the War of Independence and still in working order. Or maybe a keg of homemade country butter buried in the bog decades ago and still edible, thanks to the remarkable preservative properties of oxygen-free peat. I feel the bog knows my pain and keeps quiet about it.

Mom took the two ready-to-cook chickens to Kate Kenny, who was, according to Mom, very gracious and understanding. "Sure who could have known that a beautiful pup would grow into an evil dog, possessed by the devil himself," she said. John had buried the other two chickens—the

Kennys didn't need to make meals out of them. Kate kindly offered Mom one of the two chickens. Kate Kenny was in comfortable straits now, but like so many of our neighbors she, too, had seen hard times earlier in her life. She was born and raised in Sonnagh. Her mother was Mary Jo Henry, and as the story goes, Mary Jo was shot dead, accidentally or otherwise, by Marty Kelly, aged nineteen, in the late summer of 1922 as the Civil War was at full throttle. The Henrys were for Michael Collins, his peace treaty and his Irish Free State, while the Kellys were for Dev, his republic and his Dail walk-outs.

On that Sunday afternoon, Marty Kelly was out hunting rabbits and hares for the pot and returned empty-handed but with a still-loaded shotgun. On his way home on a little byroad, he had to pass the Henrys' place. Mary Jo came out to confront him. No one knows for sure what happened, but in fairly short order, Mary Jo Henry was dead and Marty Kelly's shotgun was empty. There was great commotion in Sonnagh and beyond. With many local supporters on each side in the ongoing war, Marty Kelly's life was in imminent danger, but also with imminent prospects of rescue. His younger brother, Colin, went to the den of the enemy and volunteered himself in place of his nowhere-to-be-found brother for whatever punishment the local Free Staters might have had in mind. It was said that the Free State boys were highly impressed with this display of manly courage and let young Colin go. His brother wound up in America, never to see Ireland again—for health reasons.

There was also another member of the Kenny household that we knew little about. His name was Barney, younger brother of Sean, who was, to us, the face of the Kenny family; he was the only one we saw regularly, working on the land or, on rare occasions, in town. There was another brother too, Joe, named after the father who was long dead. Joe and his family lived in England but would visit the home place in Culmore every few years. We knew they were in comfortable circumstances because they were always driving a nice, big car and seemed quite content to keep to themselves—no neighborly visits or even a wave of the hand. For as long as we could remember, Barney Kenny was the source of some trepidation for the young Gallaghers. He was scary because we seldom saw him, and when we did he'd be limping around the Kenny land—sneaking, we thought—and leaning heavily on a walking stick, his head bent so far to the side that it was almost resting on his right shoulder. My young sisters would have the odd nightmare about Barney Kenny coming for them in the night.

Before I left Ireland I had come to know Barney, who was indeed a recluse but not by choice. Reluctant at first to talk, over time he began to trust me and soon we were having regular conversations across the maren fence between us—and I began to learn about this gentle and intelligent man whom we had so feared in our youth. I was already interested in and fairly conversant, I thought, in world affairs, only to realize that he knew far more than I did. Like Tom Horkan, relatives abroad would send him newspapers and magazines, and on Sundays his brother, Sean, would buy him the Irish and English newspapers on sale outside the church in Charlestown. Not able to work much and mostly confined to the house, he spent much of his life reading and educating himself.

The Kennys also had one of the first radios in the village, and Barney told me that he often listened to the BBC and AFN, and would patiently work the dial trying to tune in other stations, whether in English or not. Though he was much older than me, we became sort of friends. He no longer shied away. He learned my routine and would wait for me when he knew I'd have a little time to chat. We talked about the news of the day and important things going on in the world. As with Tom Horkan, I was more the student.

I was living in California when I received a letter from Mom telling me that Barney Kenny had died. Imprisoned in a crippled body and shut off from the world around him, death came before old age but was probably welcomed. In more enlightened times, his birth defect could have been easily corrected with surgery while in infancy, but it was not to be. In Catholic Ireland—and deeply religious rural Ireland—where graveyards have a sacred purpose, to accept the body for later resurrection on the Day of Judgment, Barney Kenny had made arrangements to have his body donated to science at the National University of Ireland, School of Medicine. I was not surprised.

Uncle Pat, Aunt Jo, and their daughter Peggy returned to Ireland on holiday in July 1964. The Gallaghers of Philadelphia and the Morans from Flushing, New York, were our favorite American cousins, and it was great to have the Flushing yanks visit us again. It was also an important occasion for me. Walking with Uncle Pat through fields he had once worked on himself, I broached the subject of maybe my emigrating to America rather than England. Without a moment's hesitation, he offered to sponsor me.

"As soon as I get back to New York, I'll see what needs to be done on the legal side for me to be your sponsor. Tell me, does your mother know of your intentions?" Uncle Pat asked.

"She knows I want to join Patricia in New York, and she knows I don't want to go to England."

"And you don't want to stay here, do you?" asked Uncle Pat.

"No, there's nothing here for me."

"When would you plan to leave?" he asked.

"Next year, when I'm eighteen, probably in the fall when most of the year's work is done."

"You're the last of the boys. Your Mom will miss you a lot."

"Yeah, I know, but she won't hold me back. She told me she'd never ask me to stay when my time had come."

Uncle Pat warned me that without an education or a trade, it would not be easy for me—even in America. I already knew this, but I also knew that there were all kinds of schools that you could attend, day or night or both: trade schools, high school, and college or university. I told Uncle Pat that I intended to go to night school and eventually graduate from university. He was delighted to hear this. Over in New York his son, Bobby, was completing his doctorate in psychology. "That's the great thing about America," Uncle Pat said. "If you have the get-up-and-go,

America will give you the opportunity." There would have been opportunities in England too—but being Irish in England was not the same as being Irish in America. Since Patricia left I had my heart set on going to America and in quiet times had given that prospect a great deal of thought. I knew that I would have to work during the day and go to school at night and that I could also face the draft, being called to serve my two years in the U.S. Army. I had faith that if I was given the chance, it would all somehow work out.

Now that America was a real possibility and not just wishful thinking, I had to take care of a problem that had plagued and mortified me for much of my life: my ruddy complexion. Poor Mom had tried so many times—to absolutely no avail—to convince me that my blood-red face was clear evidence of robust health, and that all intelligent girls with an eye to the future would see the value of this outstanding feature. I didn't see it that way at all, and my focus was very definitely on the here and now. This was an impediment that required remedy, and I knew exactly what the remedy was, for I had correctly diagnosed the problem. I had too much blood. It was as simple as it was blindingly obvious. The question was, of course, what to do about it. I had briefly considered blood-letting, cutting myself, but I didn't like that idea, and besides, it would take too long to lose enough blood from a cut to make a difference, and cutting a vein or artery was too scary to even contemplate.

Looking through our local newspaper one day, purely by accident, I saw an advertisement, and in a single shining moment, like a thunderbolt, the remedy was staring me in the face. For the first time ever, as far as I knew, the Irish Red Cross bloodmobile would be coming to various towns, including Charlestown, for the purpose of collecting blood from donors for hospitals in the West of Ireland. The paper said that this would be a very noble and decent thing to do to help our fellow citizens needing blood transfusions during serious operations. The only requirement was to be in good health and be at least eighteen years of age. I ignored the second requirement. The schedule and location was provided and immediately burnt into my memory. The Old Town Hall in Charlestown it would be.

The bloodmobile was taking blood day and night: daytime for those who could stop by the Old Town Hall at their leisure—in other words, the townspeople—and nighttime for others, mostly from the country, who couldn't just drop everything in the middle of the day. As fate would have it, it was windy and raining hard when I rode my bike into Charlestown. But this, for once, served my purpose and helped make my case—my face was practically glowing in the dark when I arrived at the place of selfless sacrifice for the benefit of others. There was a doctor and two nurses running the mobile blood bank. I was warmly welcomed by one of the nurses, who asked me right away if I was eighteen and I said, "I am." It was the easiest lie I ever told—and for a doubly good cause: mine, and the unfortunates needing my excess blood.

She asked me to remove my wet coat and cap, and also my jacket. She was looking at my face, and I could tell she knew I was the perfect donor, a very ripe candidate for this most worthy contribution. I lay down on a kind of portable table/bed, and in no time at all was hooked up. It was one of the happiest moments of my life: deliverance was at hand. It was thrilling to see my blood, my unneeded blood, traveling out of my arm and up the tube and into a clear plastic container.

All too soon, the nurse reached to shut off the suction, saying that I had now given one pint of blood. I was stunned. "No, please," I begged, "get another bag. I've got a lot more blood to give, at least another couple of pints," I pleaded. The nurse, visibly moved by my generosity, explained that she could only take a pint. That was the limit for everyone. I begged for an exception to this silly rule, which didn't take into account people like me at all—surely she could see that I had far more blood than I needed. She seemed to think that this was very funny and called the doctor over, who also thought it was funny and laughed out loud. A couple of other donors who had come in joined in the merriment. My brief period of bliss turned into something decidedly less. And worse, the doctor told me that my body would replace the blood donated in about three weeks. I was devastated.

I was given three Jacob's Kerry Cream biscuits and a glass of lucozade and asked to sit on a chair and enjoy my snack before braving the wind and the rain. On leaving, the nurse told me that they would love to see me on their next visit to Charlestown. I don't recall responding to that pleasantry. I was now a living example of the age-old truism, "No good deed goes unpunished." I could only pray that over in New York, and, hopefully, working indoors rather than outdoors, I would be cured of this terrible affliction.

In August I was back at Finner Camp for my two-week summer holiday, and this time it was a little more serious—just a little—than last time because I was to be trained in the art and skills of leadership: about how to drill and train troops and about how to command respect in the most dire circumstances by staying perfectly calm and in control, even if the world around me was being rapidly converted into a large pile of shit. In battle, soldiers must have confidence in their corporals and sergeants and lieutenants and captains and maybe the occasional commandant because they were the ones yelling out the orders on the battlefield; the more senior ranks didn't have high mortality rates in battle because they were mostly not in battle. I had no trouble understanding why good leadership was important. It inspired confidence and trust, and it earned respect.

Captain Hume was the picture of calm; he had an easy, almost casual air about him, but there was also an unmistakable confidence there. His very presence commanded respect. Sergeant Tierney had a very different manner, more learned than inborn—but no less confident in command. And my good friend Sergeant Neary, though not physically large, when he spoke, whether instructing on weapons or calling out orders in training exercises, displayed an authority in that voice that did not invite challenge. If I had to choose a single word to describe all three, it would be confidence. They were completely comfortable in their professional competence and in their ability to command respect—and obedience.

Why am I talking about leadership? Because I was being promoted to corporal, the lowest of the command ranks but still a step up. I would happily replace the three stars on my sleeves for a corporal's stripes. I felt a little guilty for not telling Captain Hume of my plans to go to America, but then nothing was definite at this point anyway. And besides, the FCA rolls were being constantly reduced by these part-time soldiers bailing out—and constantly being replenished with new, mostly underage, farm lads joining up.

I eagerly returned to the dancehall where I had met lovely Eileen from Bundoran, who never danced with army lads but did dance a slow waltz with me exactly one year earlier. Alas, she was not there, but hope springs eternal, and I returned again a week later, but, again, no Eileen. I would have told her that I was about to be Corporal Gallagher, but she probably wouldn't have been impressed. Back home in Culmore, I was also going to the odd ceili, once a month or so. The ceilis were at the New Town Hall, built kind of onto the back of the Old Town Hall, which isn't used for much anymore. Ceilis weren't quite as demanding on fad and fashion as modern dances, which included rock-n-roll, jive, and the latest dance, The Twist. Modern dances were held at dancehalls like the Central Ballroom in Charlestown and Tooreen, up near Ballyhaunis, and the huge new ballroom, Pontoon, near Foxford. Providing the music for these more expensive establishments were scores of show bands that toured the country in small buses and big buses, with electric guitars and electric organs, trumpets and clarinets, and all manner of musical instruments that would be alien to a ceili band.

Patricia and Kathleen used to take ages to get dressed up for a modern dance: hair teased, back-combed, and sprayed with a foul-smelling misty vapor that would hold it in place even in gale-force winds; hi-fi makeup, eye shadow, and lipstick; dresses, skirts, and blouses that were form-fitting and elegant but modest—no plunging necklines in County Mayo, thank you; the new seamless nylons; and, holding it all up, stilettos.

Young men, too, were required to be dressed fashionably. In 1964 the rage was brown suits of good-quality material, and better still if they were custom-made by a tailor. The pant legs had be as narrow or narrower than blue jeans—for this was the latest fashion. A white shirt and red tie almost completed the picture, *almost*. The lad must have a heavy crop of hair on his head, and if he was blessed with straight hair like the Beatles, it should be combed to resemble the mop of John, Paul, George, or Ringo. Curly hair was okay as long as there was a lot of it and it fell down over your ears and forehead, making you look adorable and as innocent as a wee babby. Finally, a smart and fashionable young man would have a pair of shoes that were pointed at the toes, like a lady's high heels—"the devil's shoes," as Tom Horkan called them. Shoes with rounded toes could get you a quick turn-down from an observant lass at a dance, for this was a sure sign of one who was hopelessly old fashioned, stuck in neutral back in the 1950s. With regard to dress and appearance, I confess I did not meet all of fashion's requirements.

Remembering Kathleen's remark about having to be kind to neighbor lads and cousins, I began wisely by asking girls I knew—and knew that they wouldn't refuse—to dance. This always worked, and I was able to build up my confidence while, at the same time, becoming more comfortable talking with girls at dances. I was learning to ignore my ruddy face and, incredibly, the more I ignored it, the less it glowed in the dark. Mostly I stuck to old-time waltzes but was sometimes forced into a Siege of Ennis or Haymakers' Jig by a neighbor who expected me to return her favor. I obliged without enthusiasm, for I had no interest in linking arms and twirling around until my head was dizzy. I was always on the lookout for pretty and shapely girls. The problem was that most other lads were doing the same thing, and the most attractive girls were in the greatest demand. With notable exceptions, thank God, they were well aware of this and weren't shy about exercising the privilege of refusal that came with this unearned and sometimes misused good fortune.

Still, mustering up the courage to ask a gorgeous girl to dance was a bit daunting. You knew that there are many competing eyes on her, and if you hesitated for more than a few seconds after the music began, you could be too late. Yet, if you were the first across no-man's-land, a refusal could be brutal on a lad's confidence. If you were going to go for it, the first thing to do was to be in the best possible spot to make your move the moment the band strikes up. The best spot was always the shortest distance between you and her, to be the first there for the old rugby try, and if she said, "No, thanks," meaning, "No, thanks; I'm waiting for a better offer," you had the shortest distance back to the wall of tempestuous testosterone, into which you mercifully melted for a little wound licking and to ponder your next move.

I had my own way of approaching the challenge. I was sure other hopeful lads had their methods too, but after close observation I knew that the wobbly ones, arriving around eleven after the pubs had closed, were not capable of much strategy in the serious business of seeking romance. I admired their courage, though, as they moved with dogged determination, more or less in a straight line toward the quarry, with only two simple requirements: was it female and was it standing? If he was lucky, the kind-hearted girl obliged and tried her best to keep her toes from being flattened. If he was unlucky and accidentally or otherwise asked the wrong girl, the results could range from hilarious if she was righteously offended and wished all to know—and he was still good-natured enough to meekly accept her wrath—to downright ugly if he was a nasty drunk who called her a stuck-up bitch and a hoor and departed the scene, but not before spitting on her feet.

Choosing the right girl to ask, as least for me, means that I like her overall looks and the amount of air she displaces in the right places—and she seems approachable. Fine-looking girls who exude a stuck-up air, as though they belong in a better class of place and with a better class of people, are a bit chancy. Yet that was a game I had tried to play myself. I knew I was shy and didn't have a lot of confidence around girls, but I was improving and willing to try anything that wasn't too outrageous or stupid to distinguish myself from competitors. My strategy was to try to look aloof and pretend to be above it all, as though I didn't' give a shit. I was there to pass the time simply because I had nothing better to do at that particular moment. I gazed over the female line with only mild interest, head high, chin out, trying my best to appear to be looking down at the world around me—difficult when height wasn't one of my outstanding features.

I knew from watching American pictures at Mulligan's cinema that Americans smoked an awful lot, and that there was something sexy about the way a woman exhaled smoke, especially when she blew it through pouty lips coolly and deliberately into a man's face. I knew that women found something sexy about the way a man lit up a cigarette. So I tried my hand at this. I didn't smoke a whole lot, but I did enjoy a fag after a hard day's work, or when I needed something to do with my hands, like at a dance. It didn't work out well for me, and I gave it up after my first and only badly botched attempt at drawing female attention to myself in a very Hollywood kind of way.

My idea was to make a grand entrance, coming through the main doors at the back of the dance hall, which directly faced the bandstand at the other end. At around 9:15 p.m., more than an hour before pub closing, the male contingent on the left side of the dance hall was still fairly light. On the right side, the female contingent was practically fully present and appearing cautiously hopeful, often glancing toward the entrance to see who was coming in. The ceili band was on stage but just warming up, and the lights had not yet darkened.

This was my time to impress. I was almost properly fashionable. Most important, I had my tailor-made brown suit, made by Tommy Morrisroe, the best tailor in Charlestown—and the only one at that. This suit had cost ten pounds, almost my entire pay plus gratuity from my holiday at Finner Camp. It had trouser legs so narrow that I had to sit on the side of the bed to get into them—but they were the height of fashion. I was wearing my brown pointed-toe shoes, red socks, white shirt, and red tie. I was ready for Broadway. I smoked Players, the ten-per-box size. For my grand entrance, I needed the twenty-per-box size because you couldn't look like a man-about-town casually removing the smaller, cheaper box from your pocket. I found an empty, discarded twenty-pack cigarette box and put my remaining seven cigarettes into the larger box. I wished I could have had an elegant silver cigarette case, with my initials engraved on it, that Hollywood stars carried in their breast pockets—but at least I had the right box size. I was ready to make my entrance. I walked in through the wide open doors and paused by a pillar supporting the balcony overhead. It was still early, and I was the only one entering at that moment, as planned. All front-line female eyes were on me.

This was exactly what I had hoped for. I leaned by the pillar and slowly, casually took out the cigarette box from my right jacket pocket, making sure that the larger box size was clearly evident. Looking aloof and detached, I removed a cigarette and tapped it on the box just like they did in the pictures, maybe to tamp down the tobacco flakes inside the paper-wrapped column or maybe because it just looked good to do this. With the greatest of ease, I placed the cigarette in my mouth, carefully looking over the multi-deep line of prospects before me, as many of them were looking me over in serious interest. I loved it! I replaced the cigarette box in my pocket and removed the silver Ronson cigarette lighter from my left jacket pocket—I had found it in a lavatory at Galway City train station last November while waiting for a train back to Swinford after my fall holiday at Renmore Barracks. I lit my cigarette just like they did in the pictures: moody, looking over the quarry, disinterested, like *what am I doing here anyway?* and placed the lighter back in my pocket. So far, so good. Now, suddenly realizing that there were more female eyes on me than ever before in my life, I inhaled deeply, very deeply—and then everything went horribly wrong.

My plan was to exhale slowly, blowing the smoke out with not-so-long-practiced ease—but I could feel the cough coming on from way down and I couldn't hold it back. At this precise moment, the smoke wafted back, doing a complete about-face, and found my eyes wide open and receptive. My eyes began to water and sting, and I started an uncontrollable bout of coughing and sneezing. This catastrophe was vastly more embarrassing than my worst days in town with No-name because I was now the absolute center of the worst kind of attention at the worst possible time. The only sensible thing to do was retreat, back away, get out of there, go home, live it down, and never try this stunt again.

What went wrong? Simple: in my excitement, I inhaled too much too deeply and my windpipe rebelled. My experience at exhaling cigarette smoke did not include the practiced elegance of doing it to impress. No more pretensions of a status I didn't have and clearly couldn't fake. I was back to being me, painfully shy but still determined to overcome it—in less pretentious ways, like devouring the dictionary to increase my vocabulary. And I still liked to play the part of being aloof and disinterested, with the hope that reverse psychology would work, that by appearing detached from all around, I might appear interesting to at least some of these lovely girls across no-man's-land. I found that it did work—sometimes.

Not too long after my entrance debacle, my wounded pride healed and back at a dance, I was told by a lovely and seemingly fashion-conscious young lady while we were dancing my kind of dance that, while it was clear I had made some effort, I was in need of improvement, fashion-wise. I took it in stride, expressing disdain at the very mention of the word. I reply that I have never been one to let fashion get in the way of style and good taste. "Fashion, young lady," I said, "is as fickle as the summer wind, ever-changing, while style endures through all seasons and for all time because it comes mostly from within. Either you have it or you don't." These words didn't exactly come from within either. I had seen the sentiment somewhere and improved on it. It sounded smart and maybe had more than a ring of truth to it. Martina Ronan laughed and said that she was only joking. Still, a few days later, I took the opportunity to have a long critical look at myself in a full-length mirror and finally concluded that, if this was fashion, it was dumb and I was dumber for going along. The top half of my expensive, tailor-made suit looked quite respectable, as did the lad housed therein.

Alas, the bottom half looked downright silly, more like riding britches that a jockey would wear. My suit pants, minus cuffs but with a three-inch fashion slit at the bottom on the outside of each leg, fitted so tightly that you'd think they'd have to be peeled off. Fearing that this was what Miss Ronan was referring to brought much of my fully replenished blood supply gushing into my face. Fashion and style are most definitely not the same. In some distress I took the pants back to Tommy Morrisroe to see if there was any remedy. Mercifully, he was able to let each leg out about three inches—which, I'm happy to say, made a noticeable difference. Tommy Morrisroe did what his would-be fashion aficionados asked him to do—whether he considered it sensible or not. Fortunately for me, he deliberately left extra material in the seams in case his customer grew a brain.

In November, with most of the year's work done, I was back at Renmore Barracks near Galway City with my friend from Madogue, Martin Neary, for our two-week fall training with the FCA, and for me this time as a brand-new corporal, I was entitled to certain benefits and obligations not accorded to or required of mere privates. The most important benefit is that NCOs had their own dining quarters and we were served politely at our table—and we could eat as much as we wanted. This alone was worth all the extra hours I put in and the hardship I endured to make the grade—except that there were no extra hours and there certainly wasn't any hardship. I was recommended for promotion by Sergeant Neary and Sergeant Tierney and approved by Captain Hume. The rest was easy. And the truth is that I enjoyed the better class of dining establishment and the better food—at least it tasted better in these better surroundings—plus second and third helpings if I needed them. On the obligation side of the equation, I was expected to act like an NCO at all times while in uniform—that is to say, to look like I was in charge or capable of taking charge at a moment's notice—of squads, platoons, companies, or whole battalions. Well, maybe not whole battalions. Thank God for NATO holding back the Godless communist hordes east of the Elbe. Out of uniform I could engage in the usual acceptable devilment that is more or less normal to my nature.

One day we were out on the firing range at Oranmore refreshing our skills with various weapons, and it so happened that one of the lads quite unintentionally pocketed a 303 round, altogether understandable in the excitement of this one-way battle with a determined hillside that refused to give an inch, and the smell of gunpowder heavy in the air, practically intoxicating. The soldier's name was Seamus Connolly from Castlereagh, and back in barracks he proudly showed off his acquisition. He was an innocent lad, and when he was asked his name he always answered, "I'm Seamus Connolly from Castlereagh and Ireland." As the only NCO on the scene at the time, I thought it advisable to relieve Seamus of his misappropriated 303 bullet lest it be inadvertently discharged in a misdirected direction at some future date. Seamus Connolly from Castlereagh and Ireland didn't object and handed it over to a higher authority without fuss.

Now that I had the bullet, the question was what to do about the situation at hand. Well, I certainly did not want to report him for this minor oversight so I, with as much authority as I could command, advised Private Connolly that such oversights could not be tolerated in the FCA, but fortunately, as the bullet was now safely in my possession, I was going to let the matter rest. Sergeant Neary would later admonish me privately for this gross dereliction of duty in not subjecting Private Connolly to the majesty of military justice for theft of military property, while also complimenting me for making the right decision. I was pleased that he did not ask about the bullet, assuming, I reckoned, that it would be suitably disposed of—and, of course, that was precisely the plan.

With the able assistance of Johnny Johnston, a former schoolmate and friend, we rendered the bullet quite useless in its present form, kind of like defusing a bomb, I thought, with a momentary flush of pride. Johnny secured a pair of pliers and, together, we removed the bullet from its brass casing and poured forth the precious black powder. I readily confess that I then removed a single cigarette from my ten-pack box and, with a safety pin, very carefully plucked out the tobacco fibers from one end of the cigarette, about three quarters of an inch in and poured in the gunpowder from the bullet. Then I very carefully replaced as much tobacco as could be packed in. We now had a small explosive device.

The devilish idea was to offer the modified cigarette to Private Connolly, who loved th'oul fag as often as he could borrow one. Poor Seamus had the habit of asking, with almost pitiful reluctance, "Do you have the loan of a fag for a minute?" He just couldn't come right out and ask for a cigarette because he probably thought that was too shameful, evident that he could not afford to buy even a small box of Woodbines. So he would ask to borrow the fag—as though he were going to return it later, presumably partially smoked, or perhaps replace the smoked one with a new one, which he never did in either case. Well, next time he asked to borrow a cigarette, he would be given a loaded fag, in a manner of speaking. Who could argue that this wasn't military justice in a refreshingly appropriate, if unusual way—an unmistakable linkage of the crime to the punishment, important in the administration of military justice.

It was after our evening meal and we were all back in the barracks. Everything was in order. We were lighting up cigarettes and I was careful not to take out the one with the visibly disturbed end. Seamus Connolly, as usual, asked if he might borrow a fag from someone. My moment of truth had arrived. Shit! I couldn't do it. I gave him a good cigarette. I didn't know if the loaded fag would flash or fizzle or explode and, in the end, couldn't take the chance. Seamus happily smoked his borrowed cigarette down to a butt so tiny that the last couple of drags had to burn both lips and fingers.

Later, Johnny Johnston, cold sober and a willing volunteer, offered his services in the detonation of our wee missile. I gave him the fag and lit it for him, stepping quickly away—but only a few feet. In demonstration of our sacred bond of brotherhood and bravery, five FCA lads stood in a circle close but not too close to Private Johnston, whose only protection was a pair of rubber goggles, helpful when gathering turf in the bog on windy days—to keep the blowing turf-moul out of our eyes. We didn't have to wait long before the blast came...well, not exactly a blast. There was a small flash and a fizzle almost simultaneously—I think the flash was maybe a tenth of a second before the fizzle. We all survived without injury, though Private Johnston had a slightly blackened face below his goggles. Gunpowder, we ascertained, didn't explode in a cigarette; it just flash-burned very quickly.

While Seamus Connolly had narrowly escaped the cigarette bomb, his crime still cried out for punishment. Justice had to be done, and so it was agreed. Renmore Barracks was near a railway that terminates at the Great Southern Hotel facing Eyre Square in Galway City, about a mile away. A well-worn pathway leads from Renmore alongside the railway to the city, used mostly by FCA lads and regulars as a shortcut, getting you to the center of town faster than the bus on its roundabout route. Invariably, a group of us would head for the city in the evening after duty and dinner, provided we had at least enough money for the pictures or maybe a ceili on the weekend.

A couple of evenings after the missile fizzle, several of us were on the pathway bound for the big city—at least big compared to anything most of us had seen. Seamus Connolly was in the group, his large mop of unruly black hair Brylcreemed into slick and shiny submission. Rain clouds overhead held the promise of a shower or two, but this was no cause for concern. In fact, the plan afoot required some rain but hardly the downpour that came. About halfway to town the rain started, and in a couple of minutes, it was coming down in buckets. Suddenly Seamus Connolly's head began to mushroom into a veritable sea of foam. Before our eyes his head and shoulders were engulfed in soapy suds and the lad was in a terrible state of confusion.

Crime and punishment, justice was done—and in the pouring rain, drenched to the bone, we laughed until we couldn't stand up, Seamus Connolly, after the shock had subsided, enjoying the moment as much as the rest of us. We know this for sure because although his head, face, and upper body were now enshrouded in goo, we could easily hear his undisguised mirth escaping through a hole near his mouth. How did this mishap occur? Recognizing that Private Connolly's Brylcreem had the same color and texture of one of the lads' shampoo, we squeezed some of it into his jar of Brylcreem and, as expected, it stayed on top—and we left the rest to chemistry. We did not make it to the big city that evening—we were all too wet—so we headed back to barracks in fairly good form.

Martina Ronan was the second great love of my life, and she didn't even know it. Tall, beautiful, elegant, slim, shapely, smart, and quite unobtainable, she was a pupil at the Marist Convent in Charlestown. Our entire relationship was restricted to a few dances and serious, grown-up conversation at the occasional ceili, and the slightly more frequent furtive glances rapidly exchanged when Brian Kavanagh and I would stop by her father's pub in Charlestown on a Sunday night to play a few games of darts in back of the shop, before going on to the pictures or a ceili. Brian would have his one or two pints of beer, and I would have my one or two cidonas—this was a Sunday night ritual that continued until I left Ireland for good in my tailor-made suit, modified for a more comfortable fit in the lower regions.

At the ceili, Martina knew that I would ask her to dance—as often as I dared—and she would, I believe, happily oblige. We always talked a lot as we danced, me practically entranced to be in her company, she intrigued that I, a lad from the country, seemed smart and aloof, and using all these big words. We never went on a date—I wouldn't have known how to ask her, or what to do if I did and she said yes—but she wouldn't have said yes anyway because, at sixteen, she was too young to be allowed to date. I do know that a date in Ireland was not quite the same thing as a date in America. For one thing, all Americans, even sixteen-year-olds, seemed to have a car. At sixteen we were lucky to have a bicycle. A date American style meant big flashy cars and parties and going to the hop, and secret places for quiet, romantic moments. It was hard to find secret places for quiet romantic moments in Swinford or Charlestown.

Tom Gallagher

If the lad didn't have a car—and most didn't—and he "squared" at the ceili or at a modern dance, the best he could hope for was to find an unoccupied doorway in town. These recessed doorways, mostly entrances to shops, closed for the night, provided, in addition to shelter out of the rain, a kind of a stand-up bonding nest for couples to spend a half an hour or an hour alone together, to whisper somethings or nothings, before saying good night and heading off in different directions to different homes in different villages or towns. Here in this small, semi-darkened space, they could talk, hold hands, maybe put their arms around each other, maybe kiss, but certainly nothing more, for there was little privacy in a doorway, a foot or two in off the sidewalk in the middle of town.

I liked Martina Ronan's parents; they were nice people. My mother liked them too—she shopped there sometimes and knew about her father's earlier hard times. Still, I could tell that her father, who saw these furtive glances, was concerned that his lovely daughter might be in need of a little sorting out on the very serious matter of her future. Jim Ronan had grown up in the country. He had known hardship in his life but rose above it. He now owned a successful business in town, a grocery shop and pub, and in a shed out back were all kinds of farm tools, fencing materials, farm gates, seed, and lumber. I wanted to tell him that I planned to be successful too, but I couldn't fault him for the worried look he'd throw after the apple of his eye as she dashed back through the lounge and into the family's private quarters. I knew that if she were my daughter, I would want only the best for her too, and right now I was like so many others that Jim Ronan had grown up with: maybe nice enough, but with future prospects unknown at best, and doubtful at worst.

The high point and low point in our friendship came at the same time, handed to me by our postman, Jim McNicholas. Martina mailed me a greeting card with a very brief note inside. It said "To Tom, greetings from a fan. Martina." I spent hours in the bog trying to figure out what she meant. "Greetings from a fan"...she was a fan of mine! What did that mean? Never before in the history of the English language were four of the most ordinary words analyzed and agonized over for meaning, for intent. Did it mean that something special was beginning to blossom between us? Why else would she send me a note in the post? This was unheard of—I lived a thirty-minute bike ride from her. Or did she mean she was a fan of mine like I was a fan of the Beatles or Elvis Presley or Patsy Cline? If she was a fan only because I'd impressed her with my clever repartee, then there wasn't much to hope for. I concluded painfully that it was the latter. My beautiful Martina was not for me, nor I for her.

The pain was lessened a bit by the indisputable fact that I knew she would never follow me to America, regardless. I knew that Martina Ronan would complete her five years at the convent, then probably go on to the university and become a teacher or professor—and live a happy and fulfilling life in Ireland. Emigration was definitely not in her future. I tore up the card and buried it in the bog, the appropriate place to bury stillborn dreams, as it unsentimentally swallows up everything entrusted to it and keeps its secrets in bleak silence for ages at least.

CHAPTER 22

IN THE LONG twilight evenings of 1964, following a hard day's work, tired (but not the kind that welcomes sleep), my friends Martin Neary and Brian Kavanagh and I would meet fairly regularly, sometimes prearranged, often not. Unplanned get-togethers were common: I'd go to Brian's house or he'd come to mine. We wouldn't knock on the door because this wasn't a "Come in, sit down" visit. When you got to the house, you just whistled. If there was no response in a minute or two, a quick peek in the kitchen window revealed the usual reason: the family was still on its knees saying the rosary, and then you just had to wait until they were finished.

The Kavanagh and Joyce families were dead serious about the rosary, going down on their knees every night, while we were only half serious. We said the rosary when the worry was on us; but the worry was on us a lot, so when Mom got on her knees on the bare cement kitchen floor, we all dutifully followed suit without a word. We started with the Apostles' Creed and followed up with an Our Father and three Hail Marys, at which point we came to the heart of the rosary, the Five Decades, each one consisting of an Our Father and ten Hail Marys and ending with a Glory Be to the Father. Before we began the Five Decades, Mom announced which of the several different sets of Mysteries of the Rosary we would use to contemplate while we recited each decade. There were the Joyful Mysteries, the Glorious Mysteries, and the Sorrowful Mysteries. Mom seemed to prefer the Sorrowful Mysteries, so we got to contemplate these a lot as we went through our Hail Marys.

Mom would start with First the Agony in the Garden, and we'd have to try to imagine the agony of Jesus as he awaited his betrayal by Judas. I would recite the next Decade, Second the Scourging at the Pillar; more contemplating. Then Anne's turn, Third the Crowning with Thorns; more contemplation. Then Angela, Fourth the Carrying of the Cross, and, finally, Christina, Fifth the Crucifixion. By the third decade I was fully contemplated. Next came the Hail Holy Queen and a couple of other rosary prayers, and then we came to the optional prayers—and this is where we could get bogged down if Mom was feeling especially prayerful or worried. We'd pray for our dead relatives and for all the poor souls in Purgatory, and we'd pray for the family in England and the starving babies in Africa, and, above all, we'd pray for good weather—to save the hay, to bring the turf out of the bog, for a good crop of potatoes, for a good harvest, for an easy winter, for a life with less worry—but remembering always to thank God for our improving circumstances and our willingness to accept any fortune or misfortune that He might send our way.

With our rosaries done, Brian and I might walk over to Tom Horkan's shop to meet other neighbors and stand around sharing the craic for an hour or two, or we might head for Madogue to whistle on Martin Neary. And then, walking nowhere in particular but walking, or biking if we had more definitive plans farther away, and minds awash in righteous or unrighteous devilment, well any loony plan might take shape. Like the dummy man. We concocted this caper quite innocently while sitting around a bonfire at the intersection of the Main Road and Madogue Road. We loved to light fires at night, to keep warm, to show the authorities in Mayo and Dublin that we were unafraid of lighting a big fire on the edge of the Main Dublin-Ballina road, or just to let the heavens above know that we, a few Mayo lads, were down here on earth and alive, despite the odds. We loved the joy of sitting around an open fire having the craic like they did on cattle drives across the American prairie ages ago. Here we talked about girls, about our neighbors, and about freeing the North from John Bull. We recited poetry and sang songs and, on occasion, planned devilment.

One night when the fire was especially bright, we could see the dark, ghostly outline of the Half-Way Bush about fifty yards down the Main

Road. We could make out that long singular branch extending out over the edge of the road—and then the idea struck me. What if we were to suspend a dummy man at night, hanging by its neck from the extended limb. In less time than it takes to fart, we agreed to create a fairly lifelike dummy and hang the poor bastard from the lonely limb overhanging the Main Road and see what happened. The rest, as they say, is history—well, not quite, but certainly eventful. The construction of the dummy was dead easy: a few sticks anchoring the top and bottom of a body filled with straw and crumpled-up newspaper and stuffed into a pair of worn-out blue jeans, the upper torso filling out nicely in a leather jacket that Eamon brought from England and left to me but which was now only fit for this most unworthy purpose.

Attached to the bottom of the blue jeans by twine was an old pair of FCA boots, my worn out army boots that had never seen combat but now had the opportunity to be part of an action that, while not exactly military in nature, had some small elements that might be considered so. The head and the hands we didn't even try to fake. We simply stuffed the ends of the sleeves, already stuffed with straw, into the pockets of the jeans, kind of like in the English Teddy Boy style. Around the straw head we wrapped a hood, as in a lad keeping out the rain. It was only proper that we give our dummy a name, so we called him Mr. McGoo, a name befitting one who might be innocent enough to partake in or be the unfortunate victim in such a scheme. We were ready to go.

On the first night, we suspended Mr. McGoo on the lone branch overhanging the Main Road with darkness all around and a mindless, cloudy sky holding back a universe of sparkling brilliance. Hiding close by and with a mixture of excitement, fear and apprehension, we waited for a car to approach, and it did. Coming from Charlestown, it crested the hill between the McCarricks' farm on the left and the Durkins' farm on the right, and suddenly, the full glare of headlights was on our dangling dummy. The car went promptly off the road and into Terry Nap's ditch. The last thing this driver expected was a hanging on a lonely, rural road in the middle of nowhere. Fortunately, for him and for us, there was no major damage or injury to car or driver. The motorist quickly reversed out of the ditch and, with tires a-squealing, sped away to Swinford to report this horrific crime. We knew that the gardie would show up and certainly didn't want to have Mr. McGoo confiscated, so we took him down and hid him nearby for further use—and then we waited for the gardie.

It took the garda squad car from Swinford more than an hour to appear, probably because it took a while for them to screw up the courage to visit the crime scene. The squad car parked, not unreasonably, a safe distance from the anticipated grisly sight, and two gardie, flashlights in hand, cautiously approached the Half-Way Bush and found, no doubt to their great relief, that all was well. Clearly, the poor motorist had been hallucinating. Fairly satisfied with our first night's work, we crossed familiar fields in the darkness, home to bed. Another hard day's work on the land awaited—but so did another night! We decided, however, not to repeat the hanging. Appearing suddenly in the motorist's headlights, it was just too frightful a scene for a driver behind the wheel of a car or lorry and, while we wanted to have a bit of fun, we certainly didn't want anyone to get hurt—a bit of a fright, yes, but not get hurt.

A couple of weeks later, we took Mr. McGoo from his hiding place as darkness covered the land, and huddled to consider what we might do with him. We decided to lay the poor lad face down by the side of the Main Road, where he would be clearly visible in the headlights of an oncoming vehicle. For realism, we poured some red paint around Mr. Goo's hooded head to suggest that whatever misfortune had befallen him, whether by accident or violent assault, Mr. Goo had bled profusely from a head wound before death mercifully overtook him. Even I and my fellow highway hell-raisers were slightly sickened by the sight of our work, but we were still infused with total conviction that northeast Mayo was a very dull place at night, with the very stillness itself crying out for relief.

Answering this lonely call, we went ahead with Act Two. Unlike our hanging caper, which gave the motorist almost no time before confronting a dangling body, here on a flat stretch of road, a motorist would come upon the accident/crime scene at a more leisurely pace, allowing the mind to process the human-like shape, face down in the road. Still, the reaction was not quite what we had expected. Instead of stopping to investigate, a couple of motorists slowed down, almost stopping, then decided that, discretion being the better part of valor, the sensible thing to do on a lonely road, enveloped in blackness, was to rapidly leave the scene and, we hoped, report the incident to the law.

Finally, a neighbor coming from Charlestown stopped his car, fearlessly got out and, with flashlight in hand, investigated the accident/murder scene. In no time at all, he determined that our lad had never been alive in the first place. Avoiding the "blood," he carefully picked up Mr. McGoo and tossed him across the ditch into Paddy McGrath's field. Watching from behind the ditch on the other side of the road, we quietly commended our neighbor's bravery—of course it's possible that he had heard of the earlier hanging incident, but we gave him full credit anyway. We recovered Mr. McGoo and, once again, put him beyond the reach of the law.

As hoped, two Swinford gardie eventually arrived on the scene. We didn't know which garda barracks received the report, as the Charlestown gardie didn't have a squad car, just bicycles; so if they received the report, they'd have to call Swinford for swift and effective response. With long, powerful seven-cell flashlights at the ready—easy to use as a weapon, if necessary—the gardie, in time, found evidence of something having occurred. They conducted their investigation on the spot, smelled the sticky stuff and agreed that it was paint. Further brief discussion concluded that unless the now-missing victim bled paint, there was no crime at this location, or at least no murder.

We laid low for a month or so to let things settle down and avoid a commotion in the land. Then we brought the luckless Mr. McGoo to the Main Road for Act Three in defense of fun and war on boredom. On that memorable night, after some deliberation, we concocted a different plan for our ever-willing dummy. This time there would be no hanging, no blood, no frightened motorists, just Mr. McGoo and, of course, the Main Road. Only a few hundred yards from our earlier presentations, we laid Mr. McGoo down near a slight bend in the highway. It was about 10:00 p.m., the first Wednesday of the month, which meant it had been Fair Day in Swinford, so that cattle and pigs and horses, sheep and asses and goats, second-hand clothes from portable stalls, and all manner of other things would have changed hands, with good deals and bad deals, honest and dishonest ones, lots of spitting in hands, and the commingling of spit in handshakes to seal the bargain—and pray later that it was a bargain.

And, bargain or not, there would have been the usual celebrating in the usual way. The pubs happily catered to everyone, for this was their day too, and they eagerly looked forward to the Fair Day, which made up for the slow days in between. All of this meant that there would be more than the usual amount of traffic on all roads leading out of Swinford. In truth, it would be a lie to say that we didn't consider the effects of alcohol on motorists—indeed, some slight impairment would serve our purpose well, we agreed. Mr. McGoo did not offer an opinion, nor was he asked if he had one.

We laid him face down on the edge of the road a few yards beyond the entrance to a farm of land, fronted by an impressive iron gate and supported by two handsome concrete pillars. Most of Mr. McGoo lay on the narrow grassy margin between the road edge and the six-foot-high earthen fence separating the farm from the Main Road. To ensure that he would be seen in the glare of headlights, we allowed Mr. McGoo's legs protrude slightly onto the roadway. His dirty, well-worn blue jeans nicely covered his lower body and extended over the tops of my equally dirty and well-worn FCA boots. My stuffed black leather jacket again served as Mr. McGoo's torso. As the dummy's hands were undisguised clumps of straw, we tucked them under his body and safely out of sight. Alas, there wasn't much we could do about the lad's head, so again we just covered it in the same hood that we had used in our earlier presentations. For a little more realism, we included a blackthorn walking stick that I had cut from a bush in our Sloe Garden. We laid it near Mr. McGoo. With the aid of a flashlight, we critically inspected our presentation and, as the Bible would say, saw that it was good.

To the gardie, on first appearance, this would be an open-and-shut case of hit and run, resulting in a fatality. The unfortunate man, possibly elderly and probably a local, had been coming home from the fair in Swinford or perhaps visiting a neighbor and was hit by a vehicle, the driver of which may have been drunk—or the victim may have been drunk—or, since it was the Fair Day night, they both may have been drunk. On closer inspection of the accident scene, of course, all of these tedious deductions would prove to be without merit. With everything in order, we waited for the next oncoming car from either direction. As the headlights approached, we would jump the fence and take up our hiding positions, concealed but close enough to get the full measure of unfolding events.

First on the scene was not a motorist but a cyclist. Mary Welch, aged sixteen, worked at Cooke's Knit Shop in Swinford. She had put in a long day—for a good Fair Day was a good day for all businesses in town, though not necessarily for poor Mary, and I'm afraid we didn't improve on her evening. Mary was on her way home on her bicycle. She lived fairly close by, just off the Main Road. As she approached Mr. McGoo's lifeless corpse, cycling very close to the edge of the road for safety on this Fair Day night, the flashlight on the front of her bike lit up the body. Poor Mary practically ran over Mr. McGoo's legs and then she promptly fell off her bike, mercifully into the soft earthen fence. She did not scream out. She did not faint. She looked at the body, blessed herself twice and fervently asked for God's help, then picked up her bike, turned it back toward Swinford and pedaled off like mad. She wasn't going far, less than half a mile, to Lenihen's farm. The Lenihens' house was surrounded by a wood-full of trees where all manner of winged robbers gathered, nested, planned attacks on fields of grain, and made a commotion that could be heard a mile away.

The woman of the house was Elsie May; an aging widow, humpbacked and a bit witch-like in appearance, she might well have had the crows and blackbirds and jackdaws in her pay. When I was younger, a few of us lads would occasionally get up the nerve to visit at night to listen to her blood-curdling stories of gruesome murders committed by the likes of Jack the Ripper and other notorious serial killers, like Haigh, Heath, and Christie, all English, as Elsie May emphasized with vigor. No detail was too horrible to omit. We didn't visit often because of the nightmares that invariably followed each visit. Her bachelor brother, Billy Joe, who lived in the house, would punctuate her narrative with repeated exclamations of, "Aacht, the truth, the truth," to reinforce the matriarch's credibility. Elsie May's daughter, Kitty, also lived in the house. Kitty owned one of the few cars to be found between Swinford and Charlestown, hence Mary Welch's quick thinking to head for the Lenihens'. In no time at all, we saw the Lenihens' outside lights come on, and moments later a car turned onto the Main Road, bound for Swinford. This was a promising beginning, we thought.

Now with the pubs in Swinford and Charlestown officially closed for the night, traffic began to pick up, and almost immediately cars began to stop. The first car, coming from Swinford, passed Mr. McGoo and then suddenly braked to a stop and backed up carefully, giving the body a wide berth. The driver reversed past Mr. McGoo and parked on the margin, leaving his headlights squarely on the accident scene. We watched and waited...and waited.

"Fecking hell, what is he waiting for?" Martin whispered. "We have a man lying face down here desperately in need of medical attention, and this gobshite is just looking."

"He's probably waiting to see if the bloke will get up and walk away laughing his arse off," I offered. I was mindful of the many times when I was younger I would stand on the railway tracks between the rails and stare down the angry train engineer as he barreled toward me, horn blaring, and then jump off the track with moments to spare.

Tom Gallagher

Another car approached from Swinford and our brave lad in the first car sprang into action. Out he jumped, and in the blink of an eye, he was in the middle of the road, arms waving up and down frantically. The second car pulled in behind the first one. The driver got out and was quickly apprised of the situation by No.1, who explained that he had only just come on the scene himself and didn't want to leave his wife alone in the car, as she was quite frightened. Now they both tentatively approached Mr. McGoo.

"Holy Mary, Mother of God," said No.1. "I think he's dead."

"God have mercy on his poor unfortunate soul," said No. 2. "And what an awful way to die—hit with a car on a lonely road with hardly a sign of civilization annywhere."

"Ya think it was a car then?" said No. 1.

"No doubt about it," said No.2. "No sensible man would just lie down here in this barren place of his own accord and die. It was a car that did it all right, maybe a lad with a pint or two too manny."

Other vehicles come on the scene from both directions and were flagged down by the first arrivals. Soon there was a gathering of people—a few women but mostly men—congregating around the body. There were expressions of sympathy for the dead man's family—if he had one—and more sympathy if he hadn't, for then the poor creature had lived alone and died alone. There were angry assertions of the shameful state of Irish roads and the general lawlessness found in rural Ireland. God's great love and forgiveness, extended to all, were solemnly cited. *But no one touched the body. No one!*

Now into this sad—but clearly happy to be among the living—gathering of mostly nonlocals passing through came Elsie May Lenihen and brother, Billy Joe, with rosary beads and lantern in hand—if indeed more light was needed, for now car headlights from both directions illuminated our presentation a little more than we wanted. Elsie May viewed the body and confirmed to all present that there was indeed no earthly life left in Mr. McGoo. She assured the assemblage that help was on the way,

298

as her daughter had gone to Swinford for the gardie, a doctor, and a priest. "And while we are waiting," said Elsie May, "we should all get down on our knees and say the rosary to help this poor man's immortal soul safely find its way to the Gates of Heaven." Notably, she didn't say "through the Gates of Heaven," presumably in deference to the gatekeeper, St. Peter. And on their knees they went to say the rosary.

Only feet away, behind a solid but not-too-high earthen fence, we were speechless. We had fully expected our prank to be uncovered in short order. We would still have had our fun and a good laugh afterward. But this was turning into something else entirely. A fair number of people, mostly strangers to each other, were kneeling by the side of a country road saying the rosary for the soulless soul of a dummy. More cars were stopping, now lined up on each side of the Main Road as far as you could see—and still no gardie, no doctor, and no priest. *And still no one touched the body!* We were in disbelief. Was it because they assumed the first arrivals had already confirmed that the victim was dead, or did they all believe they were in the midst of a crime scene and must not touch anything? Hardly. They just didn't want to touch poor Mr. McGoo because he was dead.

Now we had two concerns: what if nature called and one of the mourners needed to relieve himself or herself and came across the fence, as we country people do regularly. Well, the jig would be up, and we'd have to run for it. Seemingly, the drama on the road held the call of nature in check, and our mirthfully shameless eavesdropping continued undisturbed. The other concern was more serious. With all the commotion on the road, what if some lunatic motorist, footless drunk, came on this scene at eighty miles an hour? This was seriously troubling and amid the murmuring of prayers from over the fence, in whispering tones, we considered how we might bring this episode to a close. The trick was how to do this while remaining unseen, unknown, and, more importantly, alive.

Thankfully, we didn't have to do anything. There was in a sense a combination of both divine intervention and not-so-divine intervention.

Another vehicle arrived from the direction of Charlestown and parked behind the line of cars. We heard the door slamming shut and a few minutes later the latest arrival was on scene. He politely interrupted the rosary and said, "Excuse me please; I am a priest. We got a telephone call from Swinford, and they had no priests at hand, so I am here to anoint the poor man if he is still alive."

Elsie May Lenihen assured him with authority that it was too late for Extreme Unction. Father Cryan said that he could at least say a special prayer for the dead and anoint the body postmortem with holy water. He took a small bottle of holy water from his pocket and was about to commence reciting the Prayer for the Dead while, we reasonably expected, sprinkling the holy liquid over the body. We were certain that Father Cryan would have to turn Mr. McGoo's head enough to make the sign of the cross on his forehead.

Then, at the moment of revelation, the not-so-divine intervention occurred and Father Cryan, too, was interrupted, and rudely, by the next-to-last and most momentous arrival, Matt Rooney. Matt was a neighbor who lived with his pensioned father less than a mile away, their handsome, well-maintained house on a low hill facing the Main Road, proud in appearance but not ostentatious. He had been visiting another neighbor, Terry Nap, and was walking his way home along the Main Road. Like his father in earlier times, Matt was known as a horse of a worker. Like his father, too, he was easy on the drink, maybe a pint in town once a week or so, with the odd week skipped now and then. He loved the land almost as much as the woman he worshipped, but she did not love the land and she did not love Matt—or so the story was told. His unrequited love left him heartbroken and confined to lonely bachelorhood. As the years passed, Matt became a bit simple minded. He cared for little except his work on the land, which he performed with a grim determination, occasionally getting seasonal tasks out of order with comical and sometimes serious consequences.

Apart from the land, his only pleasure was in visiting Terry Nap after a day's work. He and Terry, a long-lived bachelor himself, would play cards into the night, and when they didn't want to play anymore they'd tell each other ghost stories until Terry was almost too afraid to go to bed and Matt almost too afraid to go home. But this Fair Day night he was coming home. Matt came upon more parked cars along each side of the Main Dublin-Ballina road than he had ever seen in his life. In broad daylight it would have surely appeared to a stranger that there was one monster funeral procession about to commence. He reached the accident scene just as Father Cryan was about to begin his Prayer for the Dead over the lifeless corpse of Mr. McGoo. Without as much as an "Excuse me, please," Matt pushed his way through the huddled crowd of rosary-sayers and lookers-on to the epicenter of events. He looked for a moment at the body and then, in a tone of utter disdain he growled, "Arrah, fecking hell, ye bunch a eejits, can't ye see this is only a dummy?" And with that he stepped back and then suddenly gave Mr. McGoo a vicious kick in his side, so violent that poor Mr. McGoo rolled right over onto his back, his outstretched arms exposing the total absence of hands, his face of straw pointing to the heavens.

Finally, the moment of truth that we knew had to come was at hand, and yet my heart was pounding so hard I was terrified it might be heard in the sudden deathly quiet on the other side of the fence. Mercifully, the silence was broken by Matt Rooney, who declared with undisguised mockery, "Well, here's ye're dead man for ye. Now then, Father, can ya tell us when the funeral will be? I wouldn't want to miss this wan." As roars of laughter exploded from those capable of appreciating a good joke—even at their expense—so too were howls of righteous condemnation piled upon the lawless hooligans responsible for this outrage on a public road. Soon car engines began to start up, and as the crowd thinned out, there was one final arrival on the scene: the gardie. Sergeant Blake smartly stepped out of his squad car followed by the driver, another garda. As the situation was now well in hand, there was little for the gardie to do but gather up the evidence. Mr. McGoo's body was unceremoniously dumped into the boot of the squad car along with my blackthorn walking stick.

Responding to a question from one of the mourners who saw no humor in our presentation and wanted to know why An Garda Siochana was, in keeping with long-standing practice, the last to arrive at the scene of a crime, Sergeant Blake sharply rebuked the woman for the unwarranted and vastly exaggerated accusation. The reason for their late arrival was very simple, the sergeant explained: because only a month or so ago they had investigated two other incidents. The first one was a report of a man hanging from a tree no more than half a mile distant from this very spot—and a week or two later another report, this time a man lying in a pool of blood by the side of the road. "Sure we fairly assumed that the boys who had pulled those capers were also responsible for this wan. And being the Fair Day night in town, Missus, we were busy doing our work keeping the peace."

And then a surprising admission from the law. Sergeant Blake complimented us for our efforts in generating a bit of excitement to ease the boredom of pastoral living but then said to the few remaining motorists, "But this time they have gone too far, interrupting people's travels, causing a commotion, and creating a hazard on the highway. We'll find the culprits so we will and bring them before the law."

Their efforts at finding the culprits were modest, to say the least—not that we were complaining, mind you. The last thing we needed was a garda investigation into rural lawlessness. In the wee hours of the morning, before returning to Swinford, Sergeant Blake and his driver visited a couple of sleeping homes whose silhouettes they could make out in the distance. In waking up two families, they created their own minor commotion. This was to no avail, but at one it was a close call. When asked if she had young sons of hooligan age, Mrs. Kavanagh admitted that she did have two sons approaching that age but that they were sound asleep in bed. Not doubting her word for a moment, the sergeant politely asked if he might take a quick look for himself and then be on his way. Mrs. Kavanagh happily opened the bedroom door, and Sergeant Blake beheld the angelic faces of Michael and Patrick, all snuggled up and clearly in dreamland.

Mrs. Kavanagh did not show the sergeant another bedroom where the empty bed of Brian would have raised the most serious questions. At this point we were quite content to declare victory and retreat across the fields to our homes. As for the missing Swinford priests, we could only conclude that they were probably still in the pub—for closing time, as everyone knows, does not apply to men of the collar and certain other men of high respectability and good moral character.

We were very disappointed that our dummy man caper didn't make it into the newspapers. We were confident that the provincial newspaper, *The Western People*, would learn of the shocking events that took place at the dead of night along a half-mile stretch of the Main Dublin-Ballina Road between Swinford and Charlestown. At the very least we expected the county newspaper, *The Mayo News*, to report the tragic tale of the nameless soul who suffered multiple horrific deaths at various locations. We considered the possible reasons for this shameful concealment of a major story: a) the gardie wished to avoid embarrassment for being unable to apprehend the perpetrators; b) the gardie, understandably, did not wish to encourage copycats; c) both newspapers got the story but declined to publish it for fear of causing fear and trepidation among the people. We settled on all three reasons as being more or less equally responsible because...well, it made us feel better. While we had no published acclaim for our derring-do, we had that sublime satisfaction of riding our bicycles down Church Street in Charlestown and seeing out of the corner of the eye a curtain on an upstairs window being drawn back slowly and almost hearing the words "They're the wans; they're the wans that made the dummy man." We were, in our own minds, latter-day Wild West desperados.

CHAPTER 23

❖

————

JIMMY WEAVER LIVED in Sonnagh. He was a bachelor of about thirty-five living precariously with his elderly parents in a secluded little thatched cottage on a farm near the Main Road. The reason that I and Martin Neary and Brian Kavanagh palled around with Jimmy on occasion is that he had the mind of a much younger lad. You might say that he just couldn't bear to part with childhood—and simply didn't—but he was a big, powerful man and only a fool would challenge Jimmy Weaver to a test of strength or to a fight. He enjoyed our company and we enjoyed his. He had a nickname for practically every grown-up in Sonnagh and other villages beyond. His nicknames were strangely fitting, often hilarious, and mostly couldn't be repeated in polite company. He took his responsibility of renaming people very seriously and spared neither women nor old people. He had a special contempt for those exhibiting airs and graces and most especially for those who wished to have nothing to do with him.

Sometimes we preferred to have nothing to do with him either, like when we were doing a little salmon poaching late on a winter's night when all sensible people were asleep, except for the barger whose job it was to protect the salmon in their spawning season. Taking salmon from the river out of season had been done around here for countless generations. In lean times it was an important source of food in a long, mean winter. Respectable people and disrespectable people engaged in it without shame. Our schoolmaster, Mr. Brannigan, at Corthoon School, never refused a salmon brought by a neighbor and delivered to him in the porch just outside the classroom—and kindly neighbors also remembered a priest or two in town, and maybe even the garda sergeant who willingly accepted the odd salmon dropped on his lap, so to speak.

You never knew when the barger would be on the river, prowling for poachers. In olden times bargers—and gamekeepers on large estates—used to be armed and could legally shoot and kill—but, thankfully, we didn't face shotguns anymore, just a barger armed with a strong flashlight and a summons book to write you a summons. If he wrote you a summons, you'd have to appear in court, be found guilty of poaching, pay a fine of a couple of pounds, get your name in the newspaper, and stay away from the river for at least a fortnight after court. Fortunately, none of this had ever happened to us because we'd never been caught. We had been chased but never caught—but it was in the chase that there was great risk if Jimmy Weaver was with us. A skilled salmon poacher would have a five-cell flashlight in one hand and a gaff in the other. The flashlight beam was to be directed only in the river to spot the salmon and cause it to fixate on the light. The salmon, in the appalling innocence of nature, would be lying in shallow water, facing upstream and minding her own serious business. The gaff was a much-enlarged metal fish hook attached to the end of a three-foot broom handle. Spotting the salmon was easy; the trick was landing her on the bank. This was where the gaff came in. Continuing to dazzle the salmon—and wading into the river if necessary—with the light in your left hand and with the gaff in your right hand, you would swiftly bring the monster hook down from above and behind your head in a clean, smooth strike, going underwater to *gaff* the salmon broadside and land her.

The problem for us was that Jimmy Weaver had only the basest contempt for five- or seven-cell flashlights—which he regarded as a prime example of modern technology out of control, robbing man of the primitive thrill of an ancient hunt. Jimmy preferred the "oul way" of taking salmon from the river: the flaming torch. The flaming torch was two sods of nicely dried turf, soaked at length in paraffin oil and attached, one each, to the two prongs of a hayfork, held high in the air, so that the holder wouldn't get scorched. The beauty of this method of lifting salmon from the river was that you really did light up a fair length of river. The problem was that you also lit up a fair piece of countryside around you—which meant that you could only do this in the early morning hours when there was no one—except maybe a mean-spirited and determined barger—within miles of your very brightly lit location.

Which, of course, was our problem with Jimmy. He insisted on the torch—and for a very simple reason. If we were chased by a barger, Jimmy needed to know where we—actually *he*—must go to escape. We were mostly in the bog in these times of duress, and bogs were notorious for bog holes and swallow holes where you might quickly disappear and never be seen or heard from again. Jimmy must see the ground underfoot—and how could you do this without sufficient light to see where your substantial weight was landing with every footfall?

A most spectacular sight was to see him running, as though for his very life, being chased by a barger, with his flaming torch held high over his head. He must have the light because he couldn't see where he was going without it—and we must scatter in all directions, our only goal to get out of the large halo cast by our not-so-saintly friend. Torch or no torch, Jimmy had never been caught, most likely because bargers knew who the flame runner was and were reluctant to get too close to their dangerously armed quarry. We also easily escaped in the darkness.

One night, we three desperados—Martin, Brian, and I—cycled our way to Sonnagh to meet up with Jimmy Weaver and maybe do a little fishing. Jimmy was not at home. Old Tom Weaver, his father, said his son was in town, meaning that he was in the pub, most likely Healy's in Church Street, Jimmy's favorite drinking establishment. We had no intention of continuing into Charlestown to coax Jimmy from the pub. In this case, discretion really was the better part of valor. Jimmy would leave the pub only under one of three circumstances: a) he had run out of money; b) it was closing time; c) Jim Healy wouldn't serve him anymore for the usual reasons. So with Plan A no longer operative, we quickly cooked up Plan

B. Going home was not an option; there was too much night left. It was a cold night and, as we were all members in good standing in An Forsa Cosainta Aitual, known to all as the FCA, we were suitably attired in our heavy bull's wool FCA coats. These coats had kept many a country lad warm on wintry days and wintry nights.

Located by the side of the Main Road near the boreen that led a few hundred yards over to the Weavers' was McGowan's slate-roofed bungalow, home to Jim and Mary, long wed, and up in years but still farming their land that was split in two when the Main Road came through before they were born. Jim and Mary McGowan were Jimmy Weaver's uncle and aunt. Old Annie Weaver was Jim's sister. If this relationship had not existed, we would not have hit upon Plan B. Plan B was beautiful in its simplicity but a little dicey in execution. Helping our caper was the fact that it was a very dark night and, like most country houses, there were no outside lights to be turned on—most of us now had electricity inside the house but that was it.

The McGowans knew all three of us and would immediately recognize us under an outside light. That would not do at all because Plan B required us to be strangers in the village of Sonnagh. While Martin Neary stayed out of sight as lookout, Brian and I, with heads slightly bowed and caps pulled low on our foreheads, walked up to McGowan's front door. I knocked on it with some urgency, a quick, loud four knocks. After a few moments, Mary McGowan opened the door, and before she even had a chance to open her mouth, I asked in a ludicrously bad Northern accent if this was the McGowan home.

"It is, it is, but who are ye? What do ye want?" asked Mary McGowan, more concerned than alarmed.

"We're from Donegal," said I. "We're down here workin' on the Moy Drainage Scheme.* We were on our way to Ballina in our car when we hit a man, a big fella, down the road about a mile from here. Sure he wobbled out in front of us an' there washn't a thing I could do."

---

* A major public works project to improve the drainage area of the River Moy.

"Well, for God's Sake, do ye have the poor man with ye? Is there annything I can do?" asked Mary.

"Ah no," says I. "We're here because he's been identified by the guards as James Weaver of Sonnagh—an' that the McGowans are close relations. We were directed here to ask that you convey the unfortunate news to the parents. The guards thought it would be less of a shock on th'oul peeple coming from their own relations."

"Merciful God in Heaven," said Mary. "Where is he? Where is Jimmy now?"

"He's on his way to the hospital in Castlebar," I said. "He's not hurt too bad. He's a lucky man, he is. It would have been much worse if we had goin' faster."

To this Brian Kavanagh, who'd been standing to my left and a little behind me, responded in an equally bad Northern accent, "Aye, but then if we had been goin' faster, sure we'd have passed him before he wobbled out into the middle of the road an' we'd be in Ballina by now, wouldn't we?" A fair point: speed wasn't always a bad thing.

While I was conversing with Mary McGowan, Brian had been furiously smoking cigarettes, lighting one up, taking a few heavy drags, then throwing it down and lighting up another. While a half-dozen perfectly good cigarettes were sacrificed, it had the desired effect: Mary McGowan thought Brian was in a state of shock following the harrowing experience on the Main Road. I, in the meanwhile, had been desperately trying to suppress the urge to burst out laughing, and indeed some half-strangled gurgles did escape. Mary McGowan, thinking that I was beginning to cry, tried to comfort me.

It was definitely time to end this meeting, and in the nick of time too, for Jim McGowan—who had been milking the cows in the cow barn out behind the house—arrived on the scene. His wife told him that Jimmy Weaver had been hit with a car and that "these poor lads were driving the car and they're in a terrible state." We bade our good-byes and left, not wishing to be subjected to Jim's own interrogation.

We didn't have to wait long before Jim McGowan came out the back door of the house. With flashlight in hand he opened the gate to the boreen that led to the Weavers'. We followed along, concealed behind the earthen fence, as Jim made his way the two hundred yards to the Weavers'. Crouched by the gable of Weavers' thatched cottage, and easily within listening range, we heard Jim McGowan's knock on the door. Annie Weaver was, apparently, in bed for the night and Tom barked out from the kitchen, "Who is it? Who's out there?"

"It's me, Tom, Jim—open the door."

A little hard of hearing and not recognizing the voice, Tom said, "Who's that? Who are you?"

"It's me, Jim McGowan; open the door, Tom."

Tom Weaver opened the door and Jim McGowan got right to the point. "Tom, I have bad news for you, Tom."

"Well, get it out man, get it out," said Tom Weaver, a man long in the tooth and short on patience.

"Jimmy was hit with a car."

"Hit with a car, you say—an' where is he now?" asks Tom, thoughtfully.

"He's in Castlebar hospital."

"Well that's the right place for him—we couldn't have done annything for him here annyway. Was it bad?"

"Not too bad, from what I hear. Mary said the lads that hit him an' brought us the news were in a bad way about the accident. They're from the North an' down here working on the Moy job."

"Well, maybe if they're feeling bad enough," said Tom, "they'll get Jimmy a Job on the Moy when he comes outta the hospital. An' while he's in Castlebar, Annie an' me will have a bit more peace around here, please God."

After a few more pleasantries, mostly about the sudden peace that seemed to have descended on a small part of Sonnagh, Jim McGowan bade his brother-in-law good night and started back down the boreen. We gave him a good head start, then followed past the McGowan house to the end where the boreen meets the Main Road. We had a couple of hours to wait now—before the pubs in Charlestown closed and Jimmy Weaver headed home to Sonnagh, about a half an hour's walk. Then the real craic would begin. It was a slow two hours, but on long winters' nights we were well accustomed to passing the time while keeping ourselves company. We'd have made a fire, but that would have given the game away, so we just huddled close and speculated as to how the night might end. There was no telling.

Brian Kavanagh's wristwatch, a novelty around here, told us that the time had come to head back down the boreen toward the Weavers, and so it did. The appointed time came and we were off—at a nice leisurely pace. Tom and Annie Weaver were now fast asleep, maybe dreaming of a coming calm, of more peaceful days in the immediate future. We arrived at the earlier spot by the gable of the Weavers' house and began our final wait—with a fair degree of anticipation. Happily, the wait was short. Taking a well-worn shortcut from the Main Road, Jimmy arrived from the opposite direction whence we came. We could make out the lumbering shape in the darkness, a little unsteady on his feet, compliments of Arthur Guinness, and humming a tune known to none but himself. He turned the familiar knob on the familiar door and gave it a slight push but, bolted from the inside, it didn't budge. The reason it didn't budge was simple: the Weavers were not expecting their son home that night—and probably not for a fair number of nights with God's help.

Jimmy tried again and again, but the door stubbornly refused to give. He was known well for his intemperate and unpredictable behavior, and, true to form, he exploded in rage. His own father and mother had deliberately locked him out. He thumped on the door with his fists, abruptly ending his parents' blissful slumber.

"Jumpin' Jasus Christ, open this friggin' door, y'oul cunts," Jimmy screamed, making only a modest effort to keep his language in check.

"Whoever y'are ya better get away from here. I'm well armed an' I'll send for the guards if I have to," said Tom Weaver, showing, we thought, remarkable courage, a lying unarmed man prepared to defend life and property with or without assistance from the law—which he, most assuredly, was not in a position to summon.

"It's me, Jimmy, an for the last friggin' time, open this fecking door or I'll bring it in with me, along with the jambs, mortar an' walls, if I have to, an' lay them all on the friggin' floor in front a ye."

"But you're not Jimmy; Jimmy is in hospital in Castlebar," said Annie Weaver, now fully awake and not quite ready to give up on her holiday.

"Ye stupid fecking cunts, I'm not in Castlebar. I'm right here on the wrong side of my own fecking door. Why in feck sake would I be in Castlebar?"

"Because you were hit with a car coming out a Charlestown, that's why," said his mother, hanging on to the last thread of hope.

"Who said I was hit with a car?"

"Jim McGowan brought us the news. He said that two lads from the North came by the house an' told them that they hit you with their car because you were all over the fecking road like a drunken eejit," said the father.

For several moments Jimmy was silent—we could almost hear his brain processing the obvious: Neary, Gallagher, and Kavanagh were behind this caper. Tom and Annie Weaver, *finally*, painfully convinced that their son was not in Castlebar hospital, unbolted the door and let their unbeloved son in. Having nothing better to do, we returned to the Main Road, recovered our bicycles, and went home. In doing our postmortem on the way, Martin Neary, with just a hint of regret, said that maybe we should have ensured that Jimmy did wind up in Castlebar hospital so that old Tom and Annie could enjoy a holiday from their son. Jimmy Weaver never mentioned the incident to us, and we never mentioned it to him. It was as though it never happened. It served all concerned to let this sleeping dog lie, as Mom would say.

CHAPTER 24

❖

NINETEEN-SIXTY-FIVE BEGAN WITH Shan Mohangi's retrial. The murder conviction had been thrown out and a new trial granted. This time around Mohangi was convicted of the lesser crime of manslaughter. The defense offered a novel argument, which state pathologist Maurice Hickey was unable to effectively refute. "Vagal inhibition," the defense argued, was as much the cause of Hazel Mullen's death as Mr. Mohangi. Apparently, the vagus nerve, passing from the cranial area through the neck, is very sensitive to pressure being applied to the throat. This important nerve affects heart rhythm. In short, the defense argued that even slight pressure applied to the throat could cause the vagus nerve to stop the heart, bolstering Mohangi's story that he never intended to strangle his girlfriend. The result was a conviction of manslaughter and the addition of vagal inhibition to some medical dictionaries. The sentence was seven years in prison, of which Mohangi served four and was then deported home to South Africa. Was justice done? I don't know. Hazel Mullen's mother forgave Shan Mohangi and wished him well. If she could forgive, perhaps we could too.

January 24, 1965, is a date that will probably be forever remembered in England. We had just heard on the radio that former British Prime Minister Winston Churchill died at the age of ninety. There would be much commemorating across the pond and in Northern Ireland, but not here in the Republic of Ireland. In the darkest days of World War II when his country hung by a thread and stared defeat in the eye, the old bulldog refused to blink. He walked the bombed-out streets of London as the city burned around him, encouraging the people to take heart. His ferocious determination to win against all odds was infectious and inspirational. We knew well in Ireland that there was no love lost between Churchill and President Eamon de Valera, going back to the War of Independence and the Peace Conference of 1921, so it was unlikely that Dev would be attending Churchill's funeral.

He released a statement saying that while Churchill was a great Englishman, he was also a great adversary of Ireland. Perhaps, but in the tumultuous period of 1922–1923, many of his countrymen and country-women might have considered Dev to be an equal or greater adversary of Ireland, the country of which he fancied himself the father—Ireland's George Washington.

The treaty ending Ireland's War of Independence against Britain was bitterly debated by pro-treaty and anti-treaty forces. Dev and his anti-treaty Sinn Fein faction lost the vote to the pro-treaty TDs in Dail Eireann in January 1922. Rejecting the Dail vote, Dev and his followers walked out of the country's national parliament, a body of which he had recently been president—until he had himself appointed president of the nonexistent Irish Republic. Afterward he said that "if the treaty were accepted [by the people in the upcoming General Election], the fight for freedom would still go on," later adding the infamous prediction that "the IRA [his faction of the IRA] would have to wade through the blood of the soldiers of the Irish government, and perhaps through that of some members of the Irish gov-ernment to get their freedom." The general election that followed in June 1922 overwhelmingly approved the treaty and almost immediately Dev had his civil war—with Irishmen wading through the blood of their former comrades-in-arms as well as some government officials. So, in the end, the hopes and aspirations of the Irish people didn't matter all that much to the father of his country. Dev's Sinn Fein/IRA lost the civil war. Dev made peace with the Irish Free State and reentered the Dail in 1927 as leader of his own brand-new party, Fianna Fail. Some of his former supporters in the political and military Sinn Fein/IRA organizations could not and did not make peace. They were to remain a shadow force long into the future.

Churchill, like de Valera, was no saint, but he was, in the hour of his country's greatest peril, the indispensable man. As soon as the war was over, Britain's electorate unceremoniously booted Churchill from No. 10 Downing Street. He had shouldered a burden that none but he could bear, and then it was time for the country to move on without him. Churchill, the war leader, had little role in postwar Britain, beloved and venerated but safely removed from the levers of power. Alas, no such fate befell de Valera. Instead of being awarded a generous annual stipend befitting the father of his country and a nice IRA pension honoring his role in the Easter Rising and the War of Independence—and then sending him off to a lifelong retreat in Connemara to write a history of Ireland's epic struggle against the ancient enemy—the Irish electorate, in its collective wisdom, kept Dev at the center of political power past all understanding.

Churchill and I had something in common, though he would have had no knowledge or appreciation of it. January 24 was also my birthday. On this day in 1965, I was eighteen years old. My birthday and Churchill's deathday would forever be the same. Yet, the manner in which these two events were remembered could not possibly have been more different. Churchill, the savior of his country, would be given a state funeral and remembered forever on January 24th. Farmers, on the other hand, were not big on celebrating birthdays in rural Ireland, but on this occasion there really was something for me to celebrate. No, it wasn't the old bulldog's death—for I was in agreement with President de Valera that Churchill was indeed a great Englishman. My celebration, personal, private, and without ceremony, was that I now knew that this would be my last birthday in the land where I was born and raised. More to the point, much more, was that I would be going, not to England, but to America. Uncle Pat, true to his word, was sponsoring me. My sister, Patricia, would pay for my one-way airplane ticket. This would be my last year of work on the farm. My sponsorship papers would be sent directly to the American embassy in Dublin—which would then advise me by letter of my interview appointment date. I would visit Pat Philips in Charlestown for help with the arrangements. Pat was a travel agent, and some of the travel he arranged was one way, as it had been for my sister. Pat would help prepare me for the questions I would be asked and the papers that I would need to fill out and sign. I hoped to complete as much of the year's work on the land as I could before leaving. In the meanwhile I had about six weeks before the spring's work would begin in earnest. Winter, as always, was the time for repairing fences on the land in Culmore and Madogue. And now, rarely a day passed without my mind taking flight, not of fancy but of hope, across the ocean to the city of skyscrapers and a land of promise.

As I began the spring's work for the last time, I was confronted with a truth that had not dawned on me previously, or if it had I had not given it much thought. Perhaps I didn't want to. Now the reality of what my leaving would mean for the ones I was leaving behind hit me hard. When Dad stopped coming home from England in the spring, Eamon was there to take over, to do all that he had done and more. When Eamon bailed out, I was there, ready or not, to do all that he had done and more. Mom and my younger sisters had been there to help; working on our farm had always been a whole-family effort. But the hard physical labor of cutting a year's supply of turf in the bog, sod by sod, ploughing seochs behind a heavy Pierce iron plough, mouling a field of potatoes, ridge by ridge, with a long-handled shovel, mowing a field of oats with a scythe, and the other tasks that fell to me as they had to Eamon—how would they manage without me, for the work must still be done. The excitement of going to New York, of seeing my sister again, of beginning a new life very different from that which I'd known all my years, was now tempered with a nagging feeling of guilt that would linger long.

I know well that this was the story of Ireland, especially the West of Ireland, the unending saga of emigration, large families getting smaller and smaller, maybe dwindling to one—maybe a son who inherited the land and took care of the parents in their old age, who may well remain unmarried, either by choice or by unhappy circumstance. Sons and daughters, brothers and sisters, scattered to the winds in cities with all-too-familiar names like Manchester and Liverpool; Birmingham and London; Glasgow; New York and Boston and Philadelphia; Chicago and San Francisco; Toronto and Montreal; Sydney and Melbourne—and for the few lucky ones, Dublin, only a bus ride from home.

New branches of dismembered families would sprout in many cities far from home, the bonds of blood and memory and tales of hardship, told and retold for a generation or two, and then for the descendants of the transplanted, Ireland slips into the mists of history. The bonds of blood and memory do not last forever. This last son, this youngest brother, would not be staying to inherit the land, and his mother would not ask him to stay even though he was needed. I was bound for New York before the year was out.

The spring's work went on and the much-anticipated letter arrived from the American embassy on March 24. My interview was scheduled for Thursday, April 8. I visited with Pat Philips, who had been expecting me. He booked me a room at a small hotel on Talbot Street and assured me that while it was inexpensive by Dublin standards—but not Mayo's—it was quite respectable and in the City Center area. He called the establishment, by way of the local post office operator, and booked me in for two nights, April 7 and 8. Little preparation was needed for my interview as Pat felt I was capable of handling the situation, but then he dropped a minor bombshell right in my lap. It was a good thing I was sitting down. "You'll have to get a clearance letter from Sergeant Blake in Swinford—as you live in Swinford parish."

The American embassy required this, Pat told me, because they must be assured that I came from a respectable family and had no record of criminal activity on file with An Garda Siochana. Pat immediately noticed my reaction and grinned the width of his face. "No, Tommy, getting stopped by a guard coming into town at night for not having a light on your bike is not a crime—it's a ten bob fine, but not a crime, all right!" That wasn't my concern at all. In truth, I had never been stopped by a guard for this fairly common but minor offense, and not because I always had a light on my bike. Often I didn't, but when I didn't, I wasn't dumb enough to ride my bike down Church Street. I'd hide it about a half a mile from town and swagger in on foot like a man-about-town. The gardie, of course, knew that these swaggers walking into town at night had hidden their lightless bicycles out there in the darkness somewhere but would rarely venture out to look for them. Even if they were lucky enough to find a hidden bicycle, they would then have to wait maybe hours for the owner to return. The lads in black had better things to do than stand a lonely vigil on a dark road.

"What if I was suspected of a crime?" I asked Pat.

His eyes narrowed a bit, and he looked at me very seriously, no grin now. "What are you saying Tommy? Are you suspected of a crime? Was your name taken down?"

"No, no," I said, a bit too quickly, "my name wasn't taken down; they didn't even come to our house—they came to other houses but not ours."

Pat relaxed a little and a slight hint of a smile softened his face. "Would you like to tell me about this, by any chance?" he asked. And I began to tell him about Mr. McGoo and our caper on the Fair Day night. I say began because I didn't get beyond the words "fake body" when Pat Philips slapped his knee with considerable enthusiasm and let out an unholy yell.

"You were involved with that!"

"I was," I said, trying to sound remorseful.

"By God," said Pat, "ye pulled off a good one that night. Father Cryan told a few of us in the pub a while back of how he came to almost anoint a mortally injured man made of sticks and straw."

"Aye," said I, my spirits picking up by the second.

The long and the short of it was that Pat Philips did not think my juvenile display of hooliganism would cause a problem. It didn't. I informed Sergeant Blake in Swinford that Jimmy Groarke, one of the most respected men in town—publican, shopkeeper, government dole officer, uncle of Pairig Carney, and proud member of the Old IRA—was both my uncle and my godfather. In short order I had my garda clearance letter, signed by the sergeant, stating that I hailed from a respectable family with near-heroic lineage and was a law-abiding member of the community.

On the morning of April 7, with a small suitcase in hand, I caught the bus to Dublin. It was a five-and-a-half-hour journey to travel the 150 miles from the wilds of Mayo to Ireland's capital city. The bus made many, many stops on the way, picking up and letting off passengers, lingering for a short while in towns along the way and a little longer in the larger towns, like Longford, where a thirsty man could disembark and down a quick pint of Guinness at a conveniently close-by pub before climbing back aboard, refreshed or not. Traveling through the large, well-to-do farms of the midlands where a single roadside field might stretch the length of our farm, it was impossible not to imagine the difference between my own life and the lives of the owners of these beautifully flat manicured farms and big houses with abundant sheds and barns nearby, happy well-fed cattle that were the picture of contentment, and abundant machinery to make life easier on the hands and back and legs.

Life looked comfortable here. I didn't think that the "curse of emigration" affected these parts. More or less on schedule, we arrived at the bus station in Dublin around 3:00 p.m., and I made my way on foot to my fairly humble but clean accommodations on Talbot Street, just a short walk from Europe's widest thoroughfare, O'Connell Street, asking only once for directions. Dublin, I found, was a fairly easy city to get around in, even on foot, which was mostly my mode of travel while there.

As dinnertime had passed and tea time had not arrived, I decided to do a little exploring before I ate. I headed for O'Connell Street and turned right—and in a few minutes I was outside the Gresham Hotel. It looked like a very fancy place, and I'd heard the name many times on Radio Eireann—and the Shelbourne Hotel too. For no particular reason except that I had time on my hands, I walked into the large lobby of the Gresham and literally bumped into the first Negro that I'd ever seen up close and in the flesh in my life. Startled by the unexpected encounter, I mumbled an awkward apology. The stranger laughed and said, "It's all right; no apology needed," and I detected a foreign accent.

As he was still looking at me and still smiling, I felt compelled to say something, maybe even something intelligent—and I blurted out, "You're not from Dublin, are you?"

"No," he said. "I'm from South Africa; I am studying here in Dublin." South Africa, studying here—my expression told him that I have made the connection. "Ah, Mr. Mohangi," he said. "He committed a terrible crime—that poor, poor girl. He has made it difficult for the rest of us here."

My brand-new acquaintance told me that he was also a medical student at the Royal College of Surgeons and knew Mohangi, but clearly wanted me to know that they were never friends. I told him that I was in Dublin to apply for my American visa and was just walking around doing a little sightseeing. "Ah, then you need a map," he said. "Excuse me for a moment." He walked over to a very elegant-looking desk behind which an equally elegant-looking uniformed gentleman was sitting. In a few moments, he returned and handed me a city map of Dublin, which had all of the monuments and important buildings clearly marked. I thanked him sincerely for his kindness—this was exactly what I needed, given my limited time in Dublin. The friend he was waiting for arrived, and I turned to leave. "Good luck in the United States," he said. "It's a great country," then added with a grin, "especially if you're white. Enjoy your walkabout."

I was going to mention the Civil Rights Act signed by President Johnson the year before and maybe, with a bit of luck, a Voting Rights Bill that would be signed later this year—but I didn't, because the simple truth was that if I were a Negro, I wouldn't want to go to America. I was keeping myself well informed on events across the Atlantic and knew about the march on Washington in 1963 and the bloody struggle for civil rights and indeed *human rights* in the American South. I knew about the kidnapping and cold-blooded execution of three civil rights workers the previous year in Mississippi by members of the Ku Klux Klan—which included police officers. Life was a little easier for Negroes in the North, but I knew that equality in law was one thing; equality in hearts and minds and in practice was quite another.

Speaking on racial discrimination in June, 1963, shortly before his visit to Ireland, President Kennedy said, "We are confronted primarily with a moral issue. It is as old as the Scriptures and as clear as the American Constitution." JFK's heart was in the right place, but his hopes for a Civil Rights Bill ended on that terrible day in Dallas. President Johnson took up the task and, against bitter opposition in the US Congress, forced a landmark Civil Rights Bill through. In 1964 the American South was as solidly Democrat as it was solidly racist, and President Johnson, a Southern Democrat, knew the cost of this victory to his party and himself. The Democrats lost the South, and LBJ lost many friendships a lifetime in the making.

With my map in hand, I headed for the General Post Office, a short walk down O'Connell Street. The GPO is at the very heart of Irish independence. For an Irish Catholic not to know the heroic story of the GPO is like a Texan not knowing about the Alamo. It is only forgivable if you fell hard on your head when you were a baby. This was where Patrick Pearse and James Connelly, commanding the Irish Volunteers and Irish Citizen Army, began the Easter Rising on Easter Monday, 1916. It was here that Pearse read out the Proclamation of the Irish Republic: "Irishmen and Irishwomen: In the name of God and of the dead generations from which she receives her old tradition of nationhood, Ireland, through us, summons her children to her flag and strikes for her freedom."

Following the reading of the proclamation, Pearse and Connelly and their comrades-in-arms occupied the building and took up their battle positions of defense. Against vastly superior forces and firepower, they held out for a week, and surrendered when the GPO was in flames around them and near collapse. Pearse's order to lay down arms also extended to other locations in the city being defended by the volunteers, including

Boland's Mill, under the command of Eamon de Valera. When the fighting ended, much of central Dublin was in ruins and a great many British soldiers, Irish rebels, and civilians were dead. Sixteen of the leaders, including Pearse and Connelly, were court-martialed and shot. Although initially sentenced to death, de Valera's life was spared, possibly because of his American birth and citizenship. The failed rising led directly to the largely successful War of Independence a few years later.

Looking up at this impressive, rebuilt, multicolumned edifice, instantly familiar to me from seeing so many pictures of it, I felt a mixture of pride and sadness—and humility. It was easy for me in 1965 to look back on history and, with full benefit of hindsight, question motives or ask what some down in Mayo ask: what was it all for? The joke in the West of Ireland was as it had been for generations: our only certainties are death and emigration—in olden times both waking events. Emigration, Ireland's perennial safety valve, kept discontent and despair from rupturing the delicate fabric of social order and ensured that privileged government officials would not want for a good night's sleep. Since independence, Irish governments, mostly led by Dev and his dominant Fianna Fail party, had done little to alleviate "the curse of emigration."

But as I stood on the broad sidewalk, a few feet from where Pearse stood on that Monday morning in 1916, I wondered what if, by divine intervention, Pearse could meet his friend and fellow volunteer, Eamon de Valera, today over in the president's mansion in Phoenix Park? Would he compliment Dev for his stewardship of the country that was bequeathed to him? Pearse and Connelly and the others must surely have known that their small band of rebels could not hold out for long. They must also have surely known that if they survived the battle, they would face certain execution. That was enough to humble me to my knees. I had the luxury of hindsight but *I wasn't there.* I saluted the GPO and the ghosts of 1916, and continued on to the Custom House, another Dublin landmark and an unwilling participant in the War of Independence, situated on the north bank of the Liffey. It, too, was partially destroyed and rebuilt.

Heading back toward O'Connell Bridge, I stopped by the O'Connell Monument, which anchors Lower O'Connell Street. The monument is a massive bronze statue of Daniel O'Connell, one of Ireland's most revered heroes. A brilliant constitutional lawyer, O'Connell was elected to the British parliament in 1828, representing a district in County Clare. To take his seat in parliament required him to take an oath that was contrary to his Catholic faith. He refused to take the oath and was denied his seat. This caused such an uproar in Ireland that the government in London pushed through the Catholic Emancipation Act the following year, and the offensive oath was dropped. After his emancipation victory, O'Connell devoted most of the rest of his life in an epic struggle to repeal the Act of Union, which in 1800 had abolished the Irish parliament in Dublin and transferred all power to London, creating the political entity of the United Kingdom of Great Britain and Ireland.

O'Connell was an apostle of nonviolence, but his dream would not be realized—though even then not fully—until 1922, seventy-five years after his death—and it would be achieved largely by force of arms. He was called "the Liberator" by some historians and the "Great Emancipator" by many, but to his millions of adoring followers, he was their uncrowned king. To his foes—and his opponents in the British parliament—he was "Swaggering Dan" and "Blathering Dan" and, by God, Dan O'Connell could swagger and blather like no other man!

Going back up O'Connell Street, I passed Clery's famous department store, and then there I was in front of Nelson's Pillar. Admiral Lord Horatio Nelson, England's greatest naval hero, defeated a combined French-Spanish fleet in the Battle of Trafalgar off the southwest Spanish coast in 1805. For the United Kingdom of Great Britain and Ireland, it was a spectacular and decisive victory...at least for the Great Britain part. The battle was won but at the cost of Admiral Nelson's life. In Georgian Dublin, second city of the empire, loyal citizens of means provided funding for the erection of a fitting memorial to a fallen hero. The memorial consisted of a 121-foot-high granite column, upon which sat a 13-foot statue of Nelson looking out over the city. It remained a dominant Dublin landmark and a popular meeting place: "I'll meet you at the Pillar."[†]

After a café meal, I walked over to the Dublin Cinerama Theatre on Talbot Street, near my hotel, and saw *The Wonderful World of the Brothers Grimm*, on the widest screen I'd ever seen. It curved around toward the audience on each side. I enjoyed the picture immensely.

Next morning I headed over to Ballsbridge for my 9:00 a.m. appointment. I employed the luxury of a taxi to ensure that I would be there on time. The American embassy on Elgin Road was brand new, impressive, and memorable. The only multistoried office buildings that I had seen were boxlike squares or rectangles—walls mostly concrete, windows an after-thought, as though they were concealing secrets or just keeping daylight to a minimum so that workers inside wouldn't be distracted by the existence of life outside. The American embassy was completely round—five stories of roundness, three above ground, two below and, incredibly, mostly glass, huge angular windows all the way around, and just enough concrete and steel to hold the structure upright. What style! The building was inviting you to come inside and see the world from a different perspective—and, while you're there, we'll give you a visa. What a place! After about a thirty-minute wait, I was ushered into a spacious interview room. I was a little anxious, but not worried. The interviewer was Irish-American, about thirty-five, I'd say. The interview was more of a friendly chat between new pals. I was telling him about growing up in Mayo, and he was telling me about his father from Kerry and his mother from Galway and how much he loved Dublin.

I felt like I could tell him that I killed a couple of people and buried them in the bog and he'd have said, "No problem; I'm sure they deserved it." I signed several documents, including one that said if called upon to serve in the armed forces of the United States, I would honor the call to serve. Pat Philips had told me about this one, so it was no surprise.

[†] Nelson's pillar was blown up by the IRA in 1966. There were no casualties, save for Lord Nelson.

As our meeting was coming to an end less than an hour later, he asked me if I had any obligations of a legal sort that might create a problem in issuing a visa. More pleased with myself than a pig in muck, I assured him that I had none. And then he asked, "Have you ever served in the Irish military?"

Without thinking I said, "No," and then corrected myself. "Well, I've served in the FCA, but that's only…like the reserves, you know, like a part-time army."

"No problem," he said, "but you have your discharge papers, right?"

As innocent as a newborn babe, I laughed out loud and said, "No, no, no one is ever discharged from the FCA; when you're ready to bail out you just bail out—make sure you've turned in your rifle and that's it." In the blink of an Irish-American eye my pal was no longer my pal.

"Well then, I'm afraid we've got a bit of a problem," he said. "As you are a member of the Irish military, you are automatically ineligible for a permanent visa to emigrate to the United States."

I was in total shock. How stupid of me to mention the FCA. "What can I do?" I asked, feeling sick in my belly.

"Well, we can't proceed with your visa application until you have your military discharge in hand to present to us," said my former friend. Then, a wisp of hope: "Wait a minute," he said, more to himself than to me. "I remember a situation like this about a year ago—happened with a colleague of mine. Excuse me; I'll be right back."

He left the room, and I stared out a huge angular window. I did, indeed, see the world from a very different perspective, a truly depressing one. In five minutes he was back—and with hopeful news. He told me that the embassy was willing to call Irish army headquarters at the Curragh and see if they would be able to help. He needed my FCA serial number, battalion number, and company. With measured relief I provided the information requested: serial number 737807, Eighteenth Battalion, C Company, Swinford. I even offered to give him the serial number of my rifle, but he said that he didn't think that was necessary.

I was asked to wait outside in the waiting room while the embassy called the Curragh to see if anything could be done in an extremely expeditious manner. An hour later the interviewing officer came out to give me an update. They had called the Curragh and were waiting to hear back from them. It was now approaching dinnertime down in Culmore or lunchtime here in Dublin, which meant that nothing would happen between noon and 2:00 p.m. My embassy pal—who was my friend again—told me to go get something to eat. I left, but only to walk around the embassy. I had no appetite. I returned at 1:30 p.m. and took up my wait in the waiting room.

At 2:00 p.m. my friend returned and greeted me. "Corporal Gallagher," he said, army headquarters contacted your Eighteenth battalion in Castlebar and confirmed your honorable standing in the FCA and that your rifle was turned in to C Company headquarters in Swinford. They will authorize Collins Barracks over in the Arbour Hill area, near the river, to issue you a discharge."

I was so relieved I was about to piss in my pants. "Take a taxi," my friend advised. "We can't wrap this up today, but if you can get your discharge before end of day today, I will make some time for you tomorrow morning. Good luck."

Another taxi ride, this time to Collins Barracks, and another long wait, but by 4:00 p.m. I had my official discharge in hand. I had sort of expected a simple hand-written note saying that I, Thomas J. Gallagher, a member of the FCA, was hereby honorably discharged, signed by a commandant or colonel. Instead, it was an official printed discharge with all of the blank spaces filled in with pen and ink. I had served in the FCA for three years, one hundred and forty eight days.

On Friday, April 9, I returned to the American embassy, completed the visa application process, received my visa and bade farewell to my good, if temporary friend. I now had the rest of the day to squander on frivolous things. I visited Trinity College, established in 1592 during the reign of Queen Elizabeth I. Its purpose was to educate the Protestant classes in Ireland and ensure their undying loyalty to the English crown, and to never, ever succumb to papist impulses or impurities. In fairness, it must be said that after a brief period of some two hundred years, it was decided to allow Catholics to attend. Still, from what I learned, there weren't many Catholics wandering the hallowed halls and quadrangles of Trinity even in 1965. Again, in fairness, that may be because an Irish Catholic must receive permission from his or her diocesan bishop to attend Trinity College. The risk of contamination to the faith went both ways, and the Catholic scholar's ability to withstand such contamination had to be evaluated. As for myself, in such a test, I had no doubt that the Most Reverend Bishop Fergus of Achonry, whose ring I had kissed, would find me somewhat wanting.

I enjoyed my walkabout among the centuries-old buildings and spacious grounds but regretted not having a few books to carry in the crook of my arm so that I could have passed myself off as a Trinity scholar rather than a culchie from "Mayo, God Help Us." I had hoped to see the world-famous Book of Kells, on display sometimes in the great library, but not when I visited. This illuminated manuscript containing the four Gospels in Latin, written by Irish monks, was more than a thousand years old. It's probably Ireland's greatest national treasure, safely housed at Queen Elizabeth's Trinity College for more than three hundred years. I would have to see it another time.

After absorbing into my brain as much of the rarefied collegial atmosphere of Trinity College as I possibly could in an hour, I headed over to Grafton Street and to another famous establishment, Bewley's Café, for tea and sandwiches. Then I was off to see Leinster House, seat of Dail Eireann, the Irish parliament. On the way I passed another Dublin landmark, the Shelbourne Hotel, still bearing visible scars of its involuntary role in the Easter Rising. During the night of Easter Monday, 1916, a contingent of British troops sneaked into the hotel by way of Kildare Street and at dawn began firing on a rebel outpost across the street in St. Stephen's Green. The rebels returned fire and, sufficient to say, the hotel was a bigger target than the concealed British soldiers. I just did a walk-about around Dail Eireann. No point in venturing in, I thought—even if I could. In my mind I was still feeling the stimulating afterglow of my visit to Trinity, and in my belly the warm and pleasant sensation of tea and sandwiches in happy union. Why bollocks it up by entering that out-wardly impressive but inwardly unholy place? I headed back to O'Connell Street and turned north to the Parnell Monument, which anchors Upper O'Connell Street at its junction with Parnell Street.

Charles Stewart Parnell was another of my limited list of heroes in the struggle for Irish independence. Parnell was a bit of an oddball, a bitterly anti-English Irish Englishman and a landlord to boot. Like many wealthy pedigreed Anglo-Irishmen, Parnell was also a member of parliament in London, and leader of the Irish Parliamentary Party. Remarkably, he became a driving force behind the Land Reform movement, which, if suc-cessful, would break the power of the landlord class in Ireland. He found an ally in William Gladstone, British prime minister and leader of the Liberal Party. Together, these two men were instrumental in forcing pas-sage of the watershed Land Act of 1881. This act did not end landlordism in Ireland—and more Land Acts would follow—but it did make it a very bad business to be in. Between 1885 and the Easter Rising in 1916, a large majority of Irish farmers became owners of the land on which they and their forbears had been impoverished tenants for centuries. This marked one of the greatest transfers of wealth from the privileged to the dispos-sessed in history—and it was done without bloodshed. It also marked the beginning of the end of British rule in most of Ireland. The monument was a tall, triangular obelisk with Parnell positioned at the bottom rather than the top. His right arm was outstretched as though emphasizing a point to his long-dead followers. Behind him, inscribed in golden letters on the obelisk was his point: "No man has a right to fix the boundary to the march of a nation. No man has a right to say to his country thus far thou shalt go and no further…"

CHAPTER 25

LATE IN THE afternoon, I took the train out to Dun Laoghaire harbor on the coast and later boarded the night boat for the sixty-seven-mile trip across the Irish Sea to Holyhead in Wales. On arrival, four hours later, I was out of Ireland and in Britain for the first time in my life. I was here to see the larger part of our family, now in England: my father; brother Jimmy and his family; brother Eamon; sisters Maureen, Kathleen, and Eveline. This would be both a short reunion and a long farewell for, in truth, I didn't know when we would all meet again. At Holyhead the trains were waiting for the Irish travelers, diesel engines already running, impatiently, I thought. I took a train that would complete the first leg of my journey, changing at Crewe and continuing on to New Street Station in Birmingham. It was early Saturday morning, and Dad was waiting for me on the platform. I had not seen him in several years, but I recognized him immediately. He was dressed as he was always dressed when going out in public: blue suit, white shirt, colorful bow tie, polished tan shoes, and a gray hat tilted a little sideways, giving him an elegant, if slightly jaunty look. Again I thought of Jeff Chandler in my long-ago toffee transfers of film stars and beautiful cars.

We met in an awkward handshake. He was taller than me and, at this point I suspected, always would be. He was my father and I was his youngest son, but our bond was one of blood and kinship, not love and affection. We were almost strangers.

Dad suggested that we have breakfast at the train station because he didn't think there would be any restaurants open at this early hour on a weekend morning. We found a small café where the food was edible but hardly anything to write home about. I filled him in on my trip to Dublin, and he seemed to enjoy the story, especially my mishap at the American embassy. Then, suddenly, he said, "Tommy, you know what's happening over there in Vietnam, don't you?"

"I do," I said. "I had to sign a consent form in Dublin agreeing to be drafted if called up."

"Why, in God's name, did you do that?" he asked, visibly upset.

I told him that I'd had no choice: no signed form, no visa. He looked out the window and said nothing. To break the silence, I asked him about his time in America. He just said that it was a long time ago and that America was a very different country now.

After breakfast we took one bus, and then another, that would take us to within a short walk of Dad's flat at No. 11 Haughton Road in Perry Barr, a district of Birmingham. On the outside it looked like many other buildings on Haughton Road, all multistoried, all looking like places where flats or rooms were rented out. Dad didn't have a flat, just a single room with the bed in one corner. I was struck by how small and cold it was. There was an electric heater, masquerading as a fireplace, into which Dad put some coins, which turned on the heat. In another corner there was a stove for boiling water on top and underneath an oven. Outside and down the hallway was a shared toilet and bath. There was little furniture. I felt a sudden sadness coming over me.

This was where my father lived. He dressed like a Hollywood film star and lived in a little place where you had to drop coins into a little slot in a little heater in a small, cold room to keep yourself warm. I didn't feel so much a stranger now. I felt a compassion for him at this moment that I had never felt before. The distance between us was always more than land and sea. Despite my earlier awe of his swanky dress and appearance – and my bitter-sweet memories of his annual visits home, I had long felt anger toward him—for staying in England all those years and leaving Mom behind to raise our large family, for evading a responsibility that she could not evade, a responsibility that I often feared would drive her mad, or worse.

Dad said that when the shops opened he'd take me to the Bullring. He took off his jacket and bow tie and sat in a well-worn armchair and was soon drifting off to sleep. I told him that I was going to take a walk, and he said, "Don't go too far, Tommy; this is Birmingham, not Culmore."

"I know, Dad, I know."

A walk was what I needed now, to sort out mixed feelings, mixed emotions. In happy times, like after a field of hay was saved and secured in the hay garden in the nick of time before the rain came, or at the end of a hard day's work in the bog, sitting on a heathered turf-bank with bluebells waltzing in the breeze, Mom would light up a Sweet Afton and talk about the early years with Dad. She was young and happy then. Life was hard from the beginning, but they were together and worked in the fields and the bog, side by side. I would notice sometimes maybe halfway through a reminiscence she would look off into the distance, and I could see the tears wetting her face. Whatever happened in the later years, it was plain to see that she loved Dad during the brief period when he was in her life full time. All too soon it would end. As money was scarce, Dad went to England where work was plentiful, with many jobs to fill as young British men were drafted into the military services to fight Nazi Germany. The visits home were brief, and as time passed they became more brief and, eventually, more infrequent. And in those visits home, most of us were conceived.

I also remember Mom reminding us often that many dads left wife and family and never returned—and never sent that blue, reinforced, registered envelope that, for many years, kept want from our door, especially in the long, hard winter months. I also knew from the tales told in whispers and with a nudge and a wink of so-and-so who's over in Birmingham, wife and children above Swinford or below Charlestown, abandoned—while he had taken for himself a common-law wife and lived openly in England, without shame.

My father, the flute player, who played such beautiful music that I could still hear it in my brain; my father, who searched Birmingham looking for a pair of Gaelic football boots and a Gaelic football uniform for me; my father, who never started a fight but who could finish one quickly and without fuss; my father, the reluctant farmer whose skills I learned from my brother, who learned from him; my father, the handsome, distant husband who lived a life apart from my mother and who never took another woman into his life; my father, who kept his faith private and personal—and went to Mass every Sunday without fail; my father, who lived a life large on two continents, or so it had seemed to me, now lived in a small room. I could understand now why he visited the pub weekly and why, for better or worse, he had an abiding friendship with Arthur Guinness and John Jameson. I headed on back to No. 11 Haughton Road. Dad was out on the sidewalk waiting for me. "Tommy, for Christ's sake, where have you been? I was worried sick."

"I'm sorry, Dad; I lost all sense of time." It was the truth.

We took the bus to the Bullring, a large enclosed shopping center. Dad asked repeatedly if there was anything I needed, and I kept on telling him no, not because there weren't some things I needed but because I'd seen the little place he called home. After our visit to the Bullring, he took me out to Jimmy's flat in the Birmingham district of Handsworth, not far from Dad's place in Perry Barr. I greeted Jimmy, the first time I'd seen him in years, and met Kay, his wife, and said hello to their two young children, Bobby and Susan. Kay was very pregnant with their third child. I liked her immediately. She was from Donegal and was gorgeous and kind. For dinner we had roast lamb and roast potatoes and carrots and peas and gravy, and it was all delicious, as good as Mom's rare treats. After dinner we watched television for a while, then listened to music on the radiogram. I heard the beautiful song, just released by Lucille Starr, the "French Song"—which made me wish I could speak French, and made me wish I could sing. At around ten, Jim drove Dad home, and I bedded down for the night on the sofa in Jimmy and Kay's living room.

On Sunday afternoon, after Mass, the family met at Jimmy's home: Dad, Maureen, Eamon, Eveline—and Kathleen, who took the train down from Stoke-on-Trent. At this moment, including me, more than half of our large family was gathered in one place in Birmingham. We were gathered for a reunion and a farewell. To celebrate both, we all headed out to a local tavern for a pub meal and liquid refreshments to wash it down, and then washed it down some more. It was a happy occasion. On parting, some good-byes were said and good lucks tendered—without sadness, I am happy to say.

Later in the evening, Jimmy, Eamon, and I went to the Shamrock, an Irish club on Hurst Street, near the city center. There was music and dancing for those inclined to listen or take to the floor. For most there was that joyful union of drinking and the craic. I felt at home immediately at the Shamrock, and we soon met up with some friends of my brothers, who teased me about going to America instead of coming over to joining my brothers in one of Britain's most Irish cities. Early the next morning, Jimmy dropped me off at New Street station on his way to work. I was on my way home to Mayo, where I had to make up for lost time on the land.

April quickly passed to May, and the summer months of June, July, and August came and went at the speed of light. As I was no longer in the FCA, there was no Finner Camp for me this summer, and no time to go anyway. The little jobs that could normally wait until winter could not wait and must be squeezed in. This was my last summer at home; my life as a farmer was coming to an end. The work had gone on as in summers past and years past—my mother, my sisters, and me working like mad when the weather was good and praying at night that it would last until the work was done or at least until the task at hand was finished. I had told myself a thousand times that I would not miss my life on the land. After years of hard work, I had little to show for it, save for a skinny, muscled frame, a ruddy face, and a pair of calloused hands that had aged but not well. I had longed to be free of this endless dependence on the weather, year in, year out. I had fantasized about seeing the heavens open and a deluge drench the earth—and experience the sheer joy of not giving a fiddler's damn. I would look to the Heavens and scream out, "Come on, come on down, rain. Show me what you can really do. I don't care. I don't give a shit."

I had long had a feeling that I didn't quite belong here, that I was just marking time in the land of my birth, waiting for the inevitable summons to the boat or the plane, to follow the well-worn path. And yet, here on these twenty acres of God's earth, I had also felt the pride and satisfaction—and usually immense relief—as each year's work came to a close and I could look back at what had been accomplished by our diminishing family. And it was accomplished with remarkable harmony, not always present in the absence of urgent purpose. I would miss it. I was already missing it. I would miss my family and the friends of a lifetime. But I had my plane ticket now. I would be leaving Ireland on September 17 on Aer Lingus—Irish International Airlines, EI Flight 105 out of Shannon Airport and bound for New York, only weeks away.

The last major task to be completed before the dreaded goodbyes was to bring the year's supply of turf from its temporary location just above the railway to its permanent location at the side of our house. To do this with Coco Too and cart, even in good weather, was a two-week job, and then to reek the many, many thousands of turf sods, another week. Coco Too got a break—there wasn't enough time to haul the turf by cart. We hired Mick Burns and his tractor and trailer rig to do the job in a single day. Mick brought along his brother, and I asked Brian Kavanagh to help out. Four of us, each with a long-handled turf fork, working hard and fast, could quickly fill a trailer, which can held five ass-cart-loads of turf. It was a long, hard day, with only a brief break to eat a meal of bacon and cabbage and potatoes. At day's end the job was done but, with no time to stack or shape the rapidly emptied loads, there was much to be done before there would be a beautifully shaped and fried reek of turf that would withstand rain and wind. The turf-moul track on which the reek stands was well defined, having been there long before I was born.

Frying a reek of turf is like building a brick wall all around the reek—but a wall made of individual sods, each one selected to fit snugly in place to make the best seal possible. The sod wall is built around the outside edge of the track, down both long sides and around the back end. Inside the protective walls is the rest of the precious fuel that must last at least a year. The front of the reek, closest to and facing the house, is left open, unsealed—from which the daily requirements to keep the kitchen fire burning will be taken. As the reek takes shape, the walls slope inward to a width of less than two feet at the top. When completed, our reek is about thirty yards long, eight feet wide at the bottom and about eight feet high. The long, narrow top gets a coating of two to three inches of turf-moul, which, we pray, will absorb and hold the inevitable downpour until God, in His mercy, calls it off and the moul can dry out to await the next liquid bounty. A well-fried, well-shaped reek of turf is a thing of beauty. Compliments of my brother, Eamon, I have learned to do it well. When I was passing sods of turf to him, the "master bricklayer," he would often throw a sod back at me because it wasn't the perfect fit. With my sisters' help, we completed the job with two days to spare. It was September 15.

Emigrating-to-America farewell parties were now going out of style, in part thanks to Boeing's 707, which could fly you 3,000 miles to New York in a fraction of the time it would take to get 380 miles to Birmingham. There will be no going-away doo for me—as there was none for Patricia. I spent much of the next day, September 16, visiting neighbors and lifelong friends like Martin Neary, and my cousins in Swinford, with lots of hand-shakes and well wishes but no embraces, Heaven forbid, no hugs in rural Ireland. It just wasn't the manly thing to do and, in this time-splitting moment, with emotions close to the surface, I was grateful for this.

On my last evening at home, Brian Kavanagh and I walked over to Tom Horkan's shop to have the craic with Tom and whoever else was there. Pairig Convey and Josie McDermott, both from Cloonaghboy, the village next to Culmore on the way to Swinford, were there. The big news of the day was the lorry, full of mattresses, that caught fire on the Main Road at the foot of Cossu, close to where Pairig and Josie lived.

Tara's Halls

The driver brought the lorry to a halt and bailed out just moments before the entire vehicle was engulfed. There were no shortage of adjectives to describe the spectacular fire that captivated Cloonaghboy until well after the burned-out hulk had cooled to touching temperature. The lorry was burned down to its steel chassis and tireless wheels, a complete write-off, including its cargo, which was incinerated at such blinding speed that it would make one think twice about bedding down on a mattress, especially if you enjoyed a fag before drifting off to sleep.

Again, good-byes and good lucks. Holding my hand in a true farmer's grip, Tom Horkan seized his last opportunity to give me one final lecture about making something of myself in America. Tom's advice, like Mom's: Go to school; get an education; don't get too fond of the drink; choose your friends carefully. When I got home, the girls were in bed, and Mom was sitting by the fire, a cup of tea resting on the hob. She turned away quickly when I came in, but I saw the redness around her eyes. I made myself a cup of tea and joined her, taking up my usual place on the other side of the hearth. There were no words, no need for words, hearts too full. We looked into the fire, still happily crackling with fresh new turf, the bond between us never stronger than at this moment. Memories flooded my brain, shared memories of shared hardship and shared pain and shared laughs, the small and big victories when defying the gods and beating the rain in its own merciless race to win. And for Mom, her treat after the win, a cigarette, the sweetest Sweet Afton.

Sleep did not visit this last night. I felt I was straddling a giant chasm, being dragged in two directions with no happy compromise possible. It had to be all of one or all of the other. The only in-between was the middle of the Atlantic, and that's how I felt. In quiet reflection I had my own fears of going to America, never conquering my optimism but lurking there in the back of my mind, waiting for the right moment to rise up, like this last night in my own bed in what we still called Grandma's room. Everyone knew that there was great opportunity in the United States, and for the Irish there was no longer the old stigma that still lingered in

England. America was all about the individual. Uncle Pat had told me that in America when someone asked you your name, unlike Ireland, they weren't asking for your surname; they didn't give a damn about your family name—America didn't care about surnames. People wanted to know who you were yourself. I knew that success or failure would largely depend on me, and once in a while, I had my doubts. My leaving meant that my mother, now forty-seven, and my sisters Ann, fifteen, Angela, fourteen, and Christina, nine, would have to make up for my loss, hiring help for the hardest jobs, like cutting turf. I knew I was needed at home as much as I knew I had to leave.

The next morning we left for Shannon Airport in Martin Horkan's hackney car, all of us squeezed in: Mom, me, Ann, Angela, Christina, and our close neighbor and my long-time friend Brian Kavanagh. I was properly dressed for the occasion, in my only suit, specially tailored for me and paid for with summer camp FCA pay. It was highly fashionable by Mayo standards, but I was leaving Mayo standards behind, and I was doubtful that I would be wearing this suit much longer. The drive to Shannon was a repeat of the trip with Patricia and Mary Joyce in January 1963—long silences and occasional small talk to break the long silences. I checked in at the Aer Lingus counter that said in an overhead sign "EI 105, New York." With more than two hours to wait before 105 departed, we headed for the restaurant-cafeteria, all a replay of January 1963, except this time it was me, not Patricia.

After tea and sandwiches, we walked around to kill time. There wasn't much to see. It would have been great to go into the Duty Free area, where Mom could see the huge selection of top-quality Irish goods that we'd never see at home: Waterford crystal, the best of Irish linens and tweeds, fancy foodstuffs, and loads of whiskey—all at big discounts, but available only to those leaving the country. I would pass through Duty Free on my way to the plane. It was a long two hours.

There were disconnected sentiments on unrelated things but nothing about why we were here. Mom was quiet. Time passed slowly. I was acutely aware at this moment that my life, as I had known it, my intimate connection to all that was before, was ending. The lifelong bond was not breaking, but it was changing form, being pulled and stretched across a great divide.

Across the table I felt the distance growing by the minute, as if I'd already left but my body was still here. I was almost relieved when it was time to board. Now the tears, held in check all morning, gave way. I shook hands with Brian Kavanagh, who, with his usual grin, wished me good luck. I embraced my sisters in turn—Christina, Angela, Anne—heartfelt affection winning out over age-old norms. For the first time in my life that I can remember, my mother and I embraced. She kissed me on each cheek like the Italians do whenever they meet, even for lunch or a cappuccino. She didn't say good-bye, just "God bless you, Tommy. Come home to see us as soon as you can."

Walking up the stairs to board the plane, I was trying to dry my face and eyes with my hands so that I wouldn't look like a brand-new emigrant leaving home for the first time, but there were knowing looks that told me I was not successful. I had an aisle seat and was seated with a very well-dressed, elegant-looking couple. I hadn't fooled them for a second. The lady in the middle seat said, "You look like you've just said good-bye to someone very dear to you."

"I have," I said. "My family."

Pearl and Bill Watkins from Point Loma, San Diego, introduced themselves. They had been in England for a couple of weeks, touring around and visiting Bill's English cousins before leaving their eighteen-year-old daughter at Oxford University, where she would complete her university education. They then flew over to Dublin for a few additional days to visit his wife's side of the family before boarding EI 105 at Dublin Airport, where it originated. Shannon was an intermediate stop to pick up additional passengers, including at least one emigrant.

The Watkins were lovely people. Mrs. Watkins asked her husband to let me have the window seat so that I could have one last look at Ireland before we flew out over the Shannon estuary to climb high above the Atlantic. Bill Watkins gave me his business card. He was a senior executive at an electronics firm in San Diego. He asked for my New York address, and I gave him my sister's address in the Bronx, 298 East Kingsbridge Road, Apt. 4G. They asked about my plans in America and if I had a job waiting for me. I told them that I would find a job and that I planned to go to high school at night, and then to college. The Watkins assured me that this was exactly the right thing to do.

Then Bill Watkins made a remarkable offer. He asked if I had any letters of reference, which, he said, would be helpful in finding a job in New York. I told him I didn't—and joked about the letter I received from the garda sergeant in Swinford that said I was from a good family and was not wanted by the law for any crimes or misdemeanors. He said that that was good but a little more would help. He would write me a letter of reference. I was astonished at this gesture of kindness from a total stranger. I asked the obvious question: "How can you do this? You only met me a couple of hours ago?"

"Don't worry about that," Bill Watkins said. "I'll say that I've known the family for years."

We arrived at Kennedy Airport at 5:00 p.m., New York time. I bid farewell to the Watkins, who must go through customs and then wait for a connecting flight to San Diego.

I got in the line for new immigrants, my passport, visa, and chest X-ray in hand. The immigration officer removed the X-ray from the large yellow envelope and viewed it on a screen against a lighted background—and, happily for me, confirmed that I was free of tuberculosis. I proceeded to baggage claim, picked up my suitcase, and went through the big non-see-through glass doors, where Patricia was waiting for me. More tears, a big, long hug. I am home—my new home, my new life.

Two weeks later, and just in time, I received Bill Watkins's "To Whom It May Concern" letter, typewritten on his company letterhead with his name printed on top, "William A. Watkins, Executive Vice

President." It was a wonderful letter about a young man whom I didn't quite recognize—and it certainly did help in securing me my first job, not as a grocery bagger at the A & P—where a well-meaning relative suggested I start out—but as a bookkeeping clerk for Thomas Cook Bankers, Ltd., the travelers cheque and foreign exchange component of the famous British travel and banking firm. Its US headquarters were on Fifth Avenue, between Forty-Seventh and Forty-Eight Streets, in the heart of Manhattan. I was on my way.

Epilogue

I DID COMPLETE high school and college, as planned. Attending school after work, four and five nights a week, three hours a night, it would take more than ten years—with a two-year break in between. Well, not exactly a break. Two weeks after graduating from Washington Irving High School in Manhattan in August 1967, I received a letter from President Johnson. It was a form letter, and it began pleasantly enough: "Greetings from the president." And then got right to the point: "You have been chosen to serve in the armed forces of the United States." I was drafted. I really didn't need to read the letter to know what it said. Underneath a short strip of Scotch tape in the upper-right-hand corner was a single New York City subway train fare token. A month earlier I had received another form letter from my local Draft Board in the Bronx—with two subway tokens underneath the Scotch tape. This earlier letter told me to report for a medical examination—a requirement prior to being drafted—and it was round-trip. The second letter was the real McCoy, one token, one way.

First stop was Fort Jackson, South Carolina, for two days of various kinds of testing to determine what I was best suited for—my MOS, or Military Occupation Specialty. My test scores qualified me for Officer Candidate School, Warrant Officer/Helicopter Pilot School, NCO School, and various other noncombat specialties. After each round of testing, a Master Sergeant would read from the automatic disqualifier list. I only needed to hear the first disqualifier: "All non-citizens of the United States take one step to the rear." For two days I took one step to the rear. I asked the Lieutenant Colonel in charge of the testing facility why I could be drafted but denied access to many opportunities—some of which would have helped me greatly when I returned to civilian life. His reply was humorous but not helpful: "You're not a citizen, son, and that means we don't quite trust you—so you're going straight-leg infantry, up to the front so we can keep an eye on you." Later these ludicrous restrictions would be lifted but not in time for me.

Next stop was Fort Gordon, Georgia. As to where my overseas tour of duty with the US Army would be, all doubt was removed on completing my eight weeks of Basic Training at Fort Gordon. My orders were to report immediately for an additional nine weeks of Advanced Infantry Training (AIT), a couple of miles away on the same post. The sign over the entrance to my new sleeping quarters said: "If you have been assigned to this barracks you are bound for Vietnam." Payment for the visa granted at the US embassy in Dublin was coming due.

The final training session before graduation from AIT took place at Army Theatre No. 2. Its purpose was to introduce the Vietnam-bound infantrymen to the starlight scope, a brand-new, top-secret, high-tech infrared device, to be mounted on a rifle, allowing the shooter to see, aim, and fire at night at targets up to several hundred yards distant. All soldiers but one were admitted to Army Theatre No. 2 for this important how-to training exercise. As a non-citizen, I was considered a national security risk and stayed outside the theatre for the one-hour lesson. Unhappily, this gap in my combat preparation did not prevent me from shipping out to Vietnam, though not quite a fully trained infantryman. Happily, I found that my commanding officer, a lieutenant, maybe a year or two older than me, was not in the least concerned about my alien origins and welcomed me to his small combat unit, First Lighthorse Assault, a heavy mortar platoon whose mission was to provide close-in fire support to four light infantry companies, operating in the much-fought-over Iron Triangle north of Saigon.

As a private first class, I arrived in Vietnam on February 1, 1968, just hours after the largest enemy offensive of the entire war exploded across the length and breadth of the country. If ever there was a truly bad time to arrive in-country, this was surely it. Grim evidence of the massive Tet Offensive was everywhere, ground given and taken back, but at a high cost. As we quickly disembarked our in-bound flight, we saw body bags close by, containing the bodies of young GIs, some of whom had arrived in Vietnam only days before, and were now going home to shattered families to whom they had bid a brave farewell less than a week earlier. After receiving my orders for Vietnam, I was forced to confront the unthinkable, but it wasn't until this moment that I was forced to accept it—that I may not see my adopted country again, or the country so deeply imbedded in my DNA.

Vietnam was America's first teenage war. The average age of the GI was just nineteen. For all who served there, and especially for the one-third of us who experienced the war up close and personal, the memories will never be erased. Like most US soldiers who went to Vietnam, I survived. Sadly, more than fifty-eight thousand didn't. One year later, now a sergeant, and having completed my overseas tour, I boarded a "freedom bird," which took me "back to the world."

Our first landfall in the United States was at Travis Air Force Base near Sacramento, California. In a hanger in the early morning hours, we were addressed by an air force captain who welcomed us home on behalf of a grateful nation. He thanked us for our service in Vietnam and concluded his brief remarks with a word of advice—that those of us who still had civilian clothes should change before leaving the base. The idea, he said, was not to draw attention to ourselves. We knew that antiwar demonstrations were now widespread across the United States and that protesters sometimes vented their rage on uniformed soldiers who happened to be in the wrong place at the wrong time. No welcome-home parade for us down Main Street, USA. Instead, we were more or less advised to sneak home quietly from Vietnam, like thieves in the night.

I finished up my military service as a training NCO at Fort Benning's now-famous infantry school and was discharged from the army in August 1969.

Tom Gallagher

I rejoined Thomas Cook Bankers, Ltd. in midtown Manhattan—which had given me a leave of absence in order to complete my military service. Four months later my boss, who had been a British army colonel in World War II, transferred me to Los Angeles to open a West Coast office and try my hand at business development. The business of Thomas Cook Bankers, Ltd. was the issuance of travelers cheques in multiple currencies and trading in foreign exchange. It was the opportunity of a lifetime, and I took full advantage of it. Without a rulebook I had almost complete freedom to develop virgin markets wherever I believed they existed. I expanded our company's agent network into commercial banks, savings and loan associations, credit unions, and large international corporations[‡] whose executives were global travelers and whose treasurers welcomed the opportunity to keep a ready supply of travelers cheques and foreign exchange on hand in their own facilities. In time, I managed a sales force in an area that stretched from the West Coast to the Mississippi River and westward to Hawaii.

During my years in Southern California, I attended college and university at night, graduating from Long Beach City College and California State University with degrees in Criminology and Political Science/ Public Administration.

In 1979 I received a telephone call from Visa International, the global banking and financial services giant in San Francisco. Visa had decided to develop a new product, the Visa Travelers Cheque, to offer its twenty-thousand-plus member banks worldwide. The offer was too good to refuse, and I headed north to San Francisco. Here I joined a core group of product development people, including several who had been competitors of mine, hired by Visa from Citicorp and Bank of America, and who, like me, knew the business inside out. It was an exciting time. On entering the $50 billion global travelers cheque business, Visa was a disruptive

---

[‡] Note: This was a time when credit cards were still young and debit cards not yet born.

force and became a major player in an industry that had changed little in the better part of a century.

I would spend the rest of my professional career with this company and play a direct role in seeing the paper-based travelers cheque transition to its electronic successor, the Visa TravelMoney product. With Visa I saw much of the world in my frequent travels. Often, on a business trip to Dublin or London or the continent, I was able to stop off at home and visit with my mother for a few days or a week—even doing a little farm work, for the hands as well as the mind have memories, and a task, once learned, is never forgotten.

While I achieved a measure of success in my professional life, I did not find the balance I wished for—and needed—between school and work and home. Two marriages ended in divorce, each one leaving in its wake two children—who would grow up knowing their father as I knew mine, a periodic presence in their lives. A price was paid for this failing. I am grateful that it was not too much to bear, and that the bonds with those dear to me remain unbroken.

Tom Gallagher is retired and lives with his wife, Jun, in Las Vegas—halfway between most of his family in Arizona and Southern California, whom he sees often. He visits Ireland regularly.

October 2015.

Tom Gallagher, October 2015

Definitions

Word/Term	Meaning
Amadan	Someone who's a bit simple minded, an eejit
Anny	Any
Around	When an animal comes into heat, in estrus
Boreen	A small road, path, or lane
Bob	An Irish or British shilling
Craic	An all-around term for having a good time, enjoying a laugh or happy conversation between friends
Culchie	A not-so-complimentary name for someone from the country—and especially for country people from the West of Ireland
Eejit	An idiot
Farthing	One quarter of an Irish or British penny
Gardie	The police force of the Republic of Ireland
Groigin	A collection of four or five sods of partially dried turf, standing upright but leaning together with a final sod or two on top to anchor the groigin

John Bull	England
Main Road	The major highways leading out from Dublin to the provinces and counties were called Main Roads—as opposed secondary roads or byroads
Manny	Many
Maren Fence	The boundary between neighbors' farms, sometimes an earthen or stone wall, or a trench five to six feet deep
Mayo God Help Us	A lament possibly related to the Great Famine, which affected Mayo more than most counties; this became a common and mostly unwelcome expression
Moul	Soil broken and loosened by the plough in the space between potato ridges—to be shoveled by hand onto the ridge tops
MPSI	Member of the Pharmaceutical Society of Ireland
Ould Sod	An affectionate—but not always—term for Ireland
Pull	Having connections, knowing someone in government, local or national, who can pull strings for you, get you what you want

Scraith	The top sod, usually covered with heather or rough grass, which must be removed with a spade in order to cut turf
Seochs	The space between potato ridges that must be ploughed to make moul for the ridges
Slean	The four- to five-foot-long hand tool used for cutting turf
Squared	Usually means meeting a girl at a dance and taking her home if you had a car—and just going for a walk and a chat if you didn't—and maybe hoping to see her again, and maybe not
Stibhin	The three- to four-foot-long hand tool for making holes on top of the ridges, into which potato seed is planted
Tanner	Six pence; half a shilling
The Troubles	Turbulent periods in Irish history, originally referring to the War of Independence, 1919–1921, but more broadly covering the period from the Easter Rising through the Civil War, 1916–1923, and, more recently to include the Troubles in Northern Ireland, 1969–1998

Made in the USA
San Bernardino, CA
22 December 2015